The Pilot's Air Traffic Control Handbook

Third Edition

Paul E. Illman

McGraw-Hill

New York San Francisco Washington, D.C. Auckland Bogotá
Caracas Lisbon London Madrid Mexico City Milan
Montreal New Delhi San Juan Singapore
Sydney Tokyo Toronto

Library of Congress Cataloging-in-Publication Data

Illman, Paul E.
The pilot's air traffic control handbook / Paul E. Illman.—3rd ed.
p. cm.—(Practical flying series)
Includes index.
ISBN 0-07-031834-4 (alk. paper)
1. Air traffic control—United States—Handbooks, manuals, etc.
2. Airplanes—Piloting—Handbooks, manuals, etc. I. Title.
II. Series.
TL725.3.T7135 1999
629.136'6—dc21 98-47726
CIP

McGraw-Hill

A Division of The ***McGraw-Hill*** *Companies*

Copyright © 1999 by The McGraw-Hill Companies, Inc. All rights reserved. Printed in the United States of America. Except as permitted under the United States Copyright Act of 1976, no part of this publication may be reproduced or distributed in any form or by any means, or stored in a data base or retrieval system, without the prior written permission of the publisher

1 2 3 4 5 6 7 8 9 0 AGM/AGM 9 0 3 2 1 0 9 8

ISBN 0-07-031834-4

The sponsoring editor for this book was Shelley Carr, the editing supervisor was Scott Amerman, and the production supervisor was Clare Stanley. It was set in Times by McGraw-Hill's Professional Book Group composition unit, in Hightstown, N.J.

Printed and bound by Quebecor Martinsburg.

McGraw-Hill books are available at special quantity discounts to use as premiums and sales promotions, or for use in corporate training programs. For more information, please write to the Director of Special Sales, McGraw-Hill, 11 West 19th Street, New York, NY 10011. Or contact your local bookstore.

This book is printed on recycled, acid-free paper containing a minimum of 50 percent recycled, de-inked fiber.

Information contained in this work has been obtained by The McGraw-Hill Companies, Inc. ("McGraw-Hill") from sources believed to be reliable. However, neither McGraw-Hill nor its authors guarantees the accuracy or completeness of any information published herein and neither McGraw-Hill nor its authors shall be responsible for any errors, omissions, or damages arising out of use of this information. This work is published with the understanding that McGraw-Hill and its authors are supplying information but are not attempting to render engineering or other professional services. If such services are required, the assistance of an appropriate professional should be sought.

PFS

The Pilot's Air Traffic Control Handbook

Other Books in the Practical Flying Series

The Pilot's Radio Communications Handbook, 5th Edition
Paul E. Illman

Light Airplane Navigation Essentials
Paul A. Craig

Handling In-Flight Emergencies
Jerry A. Eichenberger

Cockpit Resource Management: *The Private Pilot's Guide,* 2nd Edition
Thomas P. Turner

Cross-Country Flying
Jerry A. Eichenberger

Advanced Aircraft Systems
David Lombardo

Aviator's Guide to Navigation, 3rd Edition
Donald J. Clausing

Learning to Fly Helicopters
R. Randall Padfield

ABC's of Safe Flying, 4th Edition
David Frazier

Better Takeoffs & Landings
Michael Charles Love

The Art of Instrument Flying, 3rd Edition
J.R. Williams

Aviator's Guide to GPS, 3rd Edition
Bill Clarke

Contents

Acknowledgments

In preparing the second edition of this book in 1993, I tried to give proper credit to the many people, primarily from the FAA, who contributed to that effort. Although this current edition, the third, inevitably reflects much of their input, many have moved on or retired from the FAA. Consequently, still needing authoritative advice and updating, I sought the counsel of others in the FAA as well as experts in field of general aviation.

From the FAA ranks, one person who, in 1993, helped me prepare the book's second edition is J.D. Green, Support Specialist in the Kansas City International Airport tower and Approach Control Facility. Both on the phone and in person, J.D. graciously answered by questions, brought me up to date on new equipment and procedures, and gave me a thorough tour from the first-floor offices up to the Approach/Departure Control room and finally the tower cab itself. His help was invaluable, and I am most grateful for both the time and the information J.D. shared with me.

At the Columbia, Missouri, Flight Service Station, Operations Supervisor Joe Korb spent much time with me on the phone as well as at the facility, the latter including an in-person "briefing" on the changes in the FSS since 1993. As he did a few months ago when I was preparing the fifth edition of *The Pilot's Radio Communictions Handbook,* Joe willingly answered questions, clarified procedures, and did his best to ensure that what I was trying to convey about pilot use of Flight Service Stations was accurate. Including an updating tour of the Columbia facility, Joe was the principal contributor to the FSS chapter, and for that I thank him most sincerely.

Still soliciting assistance from the FAA, I wanted a close review of the Air Route Traffic Control Center chapter I had revised and rewritten from the second edition. Accordingly, I turned to a neighbor, Chris Followell, a former Approach controller at Wichita and Honolulu and now an FPL (full-performance level) controller at the Olathe, Kansas, Center. Having helped me in the recent edition of *The Pilot's Radio Communcations Handbook,* Chris was a logical source to tap for updates on Center equipment and procedures. In reviewing my drafted manuscript on the Centers, Chris wielded an active blue pencil as he noted little and sometimes not so little things that warranted rewording or correcting. For the time he took and for the depth of this critique, I am both grateful and thankful. As usual, he performed with excellence.

The chapter on special-use airspace (SUA) required review by an authority on the subject, so I solicited the help of Rogert Wingert, Military Specialist, at the Kansas City Center. As Roger was a great help back in 1988, when I put together the first edition of this book, and again in 1993 for its second edition, he was the logical one to call on for a review of the slightly revised SUA chapter in the third. Typically, Roger thoughtfully answered my questions, raised new points that warranted inclusion in the manuscript, and then escorted me on a brief refresher tour of the Air Route Traffic Control Center. As in the past, I am indebted to Roger and thank him most sincerely for his many courtesies and the time he gave me.

I must also express my appreciation to the representatives of various Kansas City FAA offices, such as the Central Region Airspace Section, the Flight Standards Division Office (FSDO), and the Information Management Service Center. And in Washington, D.C., the same expressions of appreciation are due to members of the *FAA Aviation News* staff and the Air Traffic Graphics and Media office. Those with whom I talked in these offices couldn't have been more helpful.

Finally, of the major reviewers and critics, I must thank Col. John R. Schmidt (Ret.) of Kansas City, Kansas, and Leavenworth. A former Air Force pilot and Vietnam veteran, John holds an air transport pilot rating and is a gold seal instrument flight instructor, a safety counselor for the FAA, a currently active instructor, and a recognized GPS (Global Positioning System) authority. I asked John to review several chapters with a critical eye and a sharp editing pencil, which he did with his usual thoroughness. In addition, he spent several hours with me on the phone and in person answering questions and explaining his various editing changes. I am most grateful to John, also a contributor to *The Pilot's Radio Communications Handbook*, for his many efforts to help make this, the third edition of *The Pilot's Air Traffic Control Handbook*, as accurate a review of the air traffic control system as possible.

In that regard, I say to John and all who assisted me that if there are inaccuracies or errors of fact, the fault is mine. Those who edited my efforts or otherwise tried to help me did their part, so should any flaws emerge in the final product, I bear the blame.

Paul E. (Pete) Illman

Introduction

As one millennium ends and another begins, writing a book on the national airspace and air traffic control systems can be a risky project—risky simply because what is true today may very well be out of date tomorrow. Considering aviation in the overall, change is a way of life. Not only has change been a frequent visitor ever since Wilbur and Orville left the ground back in 1903, but also it seems to be coming at a much faster pace, almost to the point of inundation, in these days of technical, mechanical, and electronic advancements.

Similarly, as primarily an offspring of these advancements, change is continually upon us in the important but less dramatic areas of related rules, regulations, procedures, requirements, freedoms, limitations, and so on. These are those written edicts that either affect now or will affect everyone who flies, from the fledgling recreational pilot to the 40,000-hour veteran with an air transport rating. Despite the possibility that something we talk about today may be gone tomorrow, three reasons compelled me to put together the third edition of this book and to accept the risks born of change.

First, well into the dim future there will probably be at least a semblance of what today we know as controlled and uncontrolled airspaces. Changes might alter their structures, but the principles of operating in either type of airspace are likely to remain reasonably consistent with today's practices. If that's a fair assumption, it seemed that pilot understanding of how the air traffic facilities are structured, how they work, and some of the basic rules for utilizing their services would be important—important in matters of safety as well as operating economies.

Second, another constant—the human element—is now, and perhaps for the next century will continue to be, part of the scenery of flight. Although automation of one sort or another is certain to become even more prevalent, it's difficult to visualize that far-off time when everything related to flight will be totally automated from engine start-up to shutdown, without any human intervention anywhere in the formula. Yes, we're close to developing robotic military aircraft, but no replacement has yet been found for the human mind, human judgment, or human intelligence. Down the road? Well, maybe, but as far as the eye can see today, people in at least nonmilitary aviation will still be piloting planes, and people in the various ground functions will be directing, communicating, and controlling those whose well-being they are serving.

Such being the case, the chapters that follow focus primarily on the human element in the airspace environment. From the pilot's point of view, particularly the general aviation VFR pilot, what should he or she know about the functions and responsibilities of those who staff the airport control towers, the Flight Service Stations, the Air Route Traffic Control Centers, and the other facilities that make up the nation's air traffic system? And, of even greater importance, what responsibilities do pilots have when operating in controlled as well as uncontrolled airspaces? What do those staffing the various air traffic facilities expect of the pilots?

Within the broad framework of those questions, the following are just a few of the areas the book discusses:

- Synopses of 10 in-flight accidents or incidents and their relationship to rule violations or lack of personal self-discipline and self-control
- The information that should be given to a Flight Service Station briefer for a weather briefing and/or to file a flight plan
- The actions that are initiated if you file a flight plan and fail to close it after you have landed
- The aircraft equipment and pilot requirements necessary to enter a Class C airspace
- The various classes and structures of the five types of airspace
- VFR pilot regulations relative to entering and operating in a Class B airspace
- Why, how, and to what facility to make periodic position reports on a VFR cross-country flight
- The Mode C veil: what it is and how it can affect VFR opertions in Class B airspaces
- The locations and responsibilities of Approach/Departure Control
- How a Center functions, its organization, and its basic responsibilities
- Some of the things pilots do or don't do, say or don't say, that bug controllers or creat potentially dangerous situations
- What to do if you have a radio failure or an emergency in flight and how a ground facility can help you
- Operating in Class D, E, and G airport environments

These are random samples of the issues I try to address, abetted, where possible, by quotes and suggestions from personnel in the various air traffic facilities. At the same time, behind-the-scenes summaries of the physical organization and functions of those facilities are included to help give the reader a little better mental image of the environment in which those folks on the ground are working.

There's more, of course, and, yes, some of the current hardware is briefly discussed or described, but this is not a technical treatise on radar, GPS, or the state-of-the-art automation. That privilege is reserved for others far more qualified than I. Similarly, illustrations of the correct radio communications are kept somewhat to a minimum. The reason for that is not that the subject is unimportant, but that proper radio use is covered in depth in the fifth edition of *The Pilot's Radio Communications Handbook,* also published by McGraw-Hill and which I updated in 1998. Extensive duplication of material was thus intentionally avoided.

Finally, the third reason for undertaking this project was to produce a single source to which pilots could refer for basic airspace and air traffic control information. Simply put, I wanted a nontechnical publication that would address most of the VFR pilot's more common questions while, as the same time, contributing to a better understanding of what takes place behind the scenes in the various facilities. Hopefully those objectives were attained.

Because accuracy, not necessarily detailed thoroughness, is essential in an effort like this, every chapter, except Chapters 2 and 3, has been discussed with or reviewed by at least one authority on the subject. As I said in the Acknowledgments, though, if there is an error of fact in any subject discussed, direct your arrows of criticism at me. I tried to ensure accuracy and correctness throughout the book, but I encountered several instances in which even FAA authorities were not sure of what was current and correct or why certain apparent incongruencies existed. Such is often an offspring of change, and if discrepancies should appear, I can only apologize.

The Pilot's Air Traffic Control Handbook

1
The early days

THE INTENTION OF THIS BOOK IS TO LOOK AT OUR NATIONAL AIR-space system as it is today, not to trace its chronological development over the past 60 or 70 years. Others have done that in infinite and precise detail. How the airspace system evolved is indeed a fascinating story of experimentation, trials, successes, failures, delays, government bickering, politicking, philosophical differences, and economic inadequacies. As far as the matter of regulation was concerned, aviation developed faster than the bureaucracy would or could react.

From all the delays and the debating, however, the airspace system has become what it is today. Understanding the system does not demand a historical recitation. That is admitted. But a look back at the process of evolution does seem compatible with what I'm trying to accomplish in the balance of this book.

Any historical review requires the availability of sources and resources. In this case, perhaps the most valuable resource was the 1978 FAA publication *Bonfires to Beacons,* by Nick A. Komons. In minute detail, Komons has traced the evolution of the airspace system and civil aviation policy from 1926 to 1938. Without his in-depth research, reconstructing that period of aviation in this country would have been an infinitely more difficult task.

A couple of other publications were also valuable. One, *International Air Traffic Control* (Pergamon Press, 1985) by Arnold Field, provided past and current insight into worldwide air traffic control (ATC) practices. The second was Glen A. Gilbert's *Air Traffic Control—The Uncrowded Sky* (Smithsonian Institution, 1973). Gilbert was one of the first traffic controllers, and his book knowingly recounts the maturing of ATC from the early days up to the 1970s.

With these resources, as well as business and trade publication articles that appeared in the 1930s, it was possible to capsule some of the principal events that contributed to today's airspace system.

FLYING FREEDOM

In certain respects, flying around in the truly uncrowded skies back in the early 1920s must have been quite an experience. With only a few minor requirements, freedom of the air was just that—freedom. Rules and restrictions were practically nonexistent. Go where you want to go; fly where you want to fly; do as you please. Great, for those with the derring-do to trust the wood-and-wire crates powered by untrustworthy power plants.

In those days, anyone could start up a flying school, "train" and send forth an eager, would-be airman without tests or requirements to meet any standards. A wartime licensing regulation was canceled in 1919. If you wanted to build your own aircraft, you went ahead. If it flew, fine; if it didn't, it was your neck. Aircraft manufacturing standards were as nonexistent as those for pilots.

Those same freedoms, however, were fraught with negatives. Airports were primitive grass or gravel strips, lighting for night operations was still in the future, aids to navigating between two points were unheard of, and radio was little more than an experiment. Aviation was for the daredevils and the barnstormers who hoped to make a few bucks by thrilling a gawking, ground-bound populace.

This is not to say that attempts to establish some modicum of regulation were never made. They were, but for the most part opponents were more vociferous and more successful than the proponents. In the process of debate between the pros and the cons, the United States trailed the European countries in trying to bring reasonable order to a fledgling industry—if aviation could be called an industry in those start-up years.

THE AIRSPACE—WHO OWNS IT?

One of the most disputed questions in the early days of aviation, and in the development of air law, was, Who owns the airspace above privately held property? The cities? The states? The nations?

The ancient Roman maxim *cujus est solum, ejus usque ad coelum* (who owns the land, owns it up to the sky) is generally considered the first air law. Accepting that as fact, the law and its enforcers went to work in the earliest days of flying and attempted to limit free access to the airspace.

Probably the first enforcement effort was in April 1784 when a French police lieutenant issued an ordinance banning balloon flights over Paris without a special permit. This was in reaction to such a flight several months before.

Particularly in Europe, this was a question of concern and debate. The size and number of countries abutting one another made the space above their boundaries—and whether the space was indeed theirs—a matter of security as well as national sovereignty. At the start of the 20th century, three divergent concepts prevailed:

- The skies, like the high seas, were free and the common property of mankind.
- The skies above the nations were an integral part of each and of their territory.
- There was a combination of freedom of the air, while recognizing that each nation had certain rights to its own airspace.

Resolution of this issue was crucially important to the future of aviation in Europe and in the United States. A beginning was made following the end of World War I.

1919 INTERNATIONAL COMMISSION FOR AIR NAVIGATION

The war in Europe was over, and the airplane had clearly demonstrated its destructive capabilities while giving hints of its potential as a vehicle of commerce and peace. Legal and philosophical questions had to be resolved, however, as well as rules and regulations that would govern aviation—particularly international aviation.

In 1919, the International Convention on Air Navigation met in Paris to attack the key issues. Emerging from the convention was the International Commission for Air Navigation (ICAN). The convention recognized the sovereignty of the airspace above each state, but it also provided for the freedom of passage of civil aircraft over state territories. ICAN, then, was created to enforce the legislative, administrative, and judicial functions established by the convention. Further, ICAN had the power to require member states to develop local regulations that would conform to those of the convention. It also adopted the "General Rules for Air Traffic," which would be applicable to the various states.

The United States, although an original member of ICAN, did not ratify the agreements reached by the convention. As a consequence, the absence of uniformity here continued. ICAN made sense where small countries abutted one another. Flights between them demanded uniform regulation, but international traffic in those days was hardly a matter of concern to the United States. Consequently, federal inaction persisted.

Such was not the case, however, in several states. Along the eastern seaboard some of the states, as well as local municipalities, wrote their own rules—rules that only created confusion and did little to advance aviation during the early postwar days.

Failure to adopt even ICAN's simple regulations had other adverse effects as well. Without any semblance of federal control over pilot licensing, aircraft production, maintenance standards, or operating rules, capital investment in the industry was hard to come by. Investors with money to spend were more than reluctant to put spare funds into an industry that had no laws to govern it.

By the same token, insurance was difficult or impossible to obtain. The absence of control encouraged irresponsibility on the ground and in the air. With high underwriter losses and undefined legal principles relative to liability claims, insurance was as elusive as investment capital. Only some degree of order would salvage the infant industry from the chaos that was choking it.

There were those, however, who wanted no part of regulation. To quote a few examples that Nick Komons cites:

- A flier from Cincinnati: "What we want is progress—not red tape!"
- A fixed-base operator: "I think regulation will put the average commercial aviator out of business."
- A Philadelphia pilot: "As sure as the sun rises and sets, strict government regulations will retard commercial aviation 10 to 15 years, if not kill it entirely."
- And the reaction of a typical commercial operator: "It seems somewhat absurd to have all this hullabaloo and endeavor to set the massive and ponderous machinery of the law on a measly 120 [commercial] airplanes."

THE BEGINNINGS OF A U.S. AIRSPACE SYSTEM

If any single impetus forced the development of an airspace system in the United States, it was the advent of airmail. Using Army aircraft and pilots, the Post Office Department began flying the mail in 1918. A few months after the start of service, the department hired its own pilots, bought its own aircraft, and took over the operation that initially provided service between Washington, D.C., and New York. The service was then expanded in 1919 from New York to Cleveland and Chicago, and a year later from Chicago to San Francisco.

The saga of flying day and night over nonexistent airways in all sorts of weather and in open-cockpit aircraft has been well documented. Only with help of a few bonfires thoughtfully ignited by concerned citizens was any sort of an "airway" visible to the pilots. It was primitive at its best. That, however, was the airmail pilot's lot.

Yes, the Post Office Department was part of the government, but that didn't mean that aviation was under government control. During the first half of the 1920s, there was much activity, but agreements relative to federal regulations were elusive goals. The matter of states' rights was one issue, as was intrastate versus interstate commerce. Then came legal questions, not the least of which, again, was, Who owns the airspace? Progress was slow but it was coming.

The Air Mail Act of 1925 allowed the Post Office Department to let contracts to private operators for the transportation of mail by air. This was followed in 1926 by the Air Commerce Act, which was the first organized attempt to regulate the growing industry. Emerging from the act was the Aeronautics Branch as part of the Department of Commerce. It was the branch's responsibility to license pilots and planes; develop rules, regulations, and operating standards; establish airways; enforce air traffic rules; conduct aeronautical research; and, in general, ensure the safety of aviation through federal regulation. The ancestor of today's Federal Aviation Administration had been born.

THE BEACON SYSTEM

To backtrack momentarily to the early 1920s, relying on occasional bonfires while plowing through the skies at night was hardly a sophisticated means of navigating. By the same token, those bonfires, plus hefty doses of good luck, were anything but conducive to the development of an economic, dependable airmail service.

One solution, obvious to only a few, was the ability to navigate and fly safely at night. That was hardly an easy solution because it meant that aircraft landing, navigation, and instrument lighting systems had to be engineered almost from scratch. This would require extensive testing and experimentation to develop the most efficient lights for each purpose, followed by determining the best location of the lights on the aircraft for maximum effect. Another step was the need to identify the airport perimeters with a system of boundary lights, illuminate the wind sock or tee, and develop a rotating beacon or searchlight that would guide pilots to the field from many miles away. Plus, a beacon system had to be developed to provide a lighted "highway" for navigation.

An article titled "Out of the Darkness..." by Colonel Eldon W. Downs and Colonel Albert P. Sights, Jr., in the Autumn 1969 issue of *Aerospace Historian,* detailed the difficulty of the task. It was one obscure Army lieutenant, Donald L. Bruner, who, against all odds, took up the challenge. Not only was the necessary hardware nonexistent, but in 1919 and 1920, most people, including Army pilots, thought night flying too dangerous or unnecessary or both. When the sun went down, airplanes should be in their hangars. Bruner thought otherwise.

Eventually overcoming resistance from even his own commanding officer, to say nothing of that of his fellow pilots, Bruner led a small task force assigned to him through the testing and experimental stages. And it was Bruner who, in 1923, spearheaded the first lighted airway—a 72-mile stretch from McCook Field in Dayton, Ohio (where he was stationed), to Norton Field in Columbus. Between July 2 and August 13, 1923, pilots, flying one DeHaviland DH-4B, completed 25 of 29 scheduled flights. Bruner flew about one-third of those himself.

Simply described, the system, as it grew, consisted of a series of towers erected on concrete slabs. Each tower had a flashing rotating beacon and two course lights, one pointing forward to the next beacon ahead, the other backward to the previous one. Each course light flashed alternatively, providing coded signals of the particular beacon, thus identifying its position along the airway (Fig. 1-1). The site number was also painted on the beacon's shed. Spaced approximately 15 to 25 miles apart, the beacons were of such candlepower that they could be seen up to 40 miles away in clear weather.

In addition to the lights, auxiliary or emergency landing fields were constructed along the airways. Hardly "airports" in the accepted sense, they were mere strips of gravel or sod set on leveled land leased from local farmers or municipalities. At the sites where a field existed, the beacon lights were green; at all others, they were red.

Based on Bruner's work, the Post Office Department began lighting the Chicago-Cheyenne airway segment in 1923. By 1926, the entire airway from New York to San Francisco was beacon-equipped.

Fig. 1.1 *This typical airway beacon, with its site number painted on the shed, was just one of the 1500 that spanned the country.* National Air and Space Museum, Smithsonian Institution

The eventual feat of lighting 18,000 miles of airway with some 1500 beacon towers was a herculean accomplishment, especially considering the plains, mountains, and swamps that had to be conquered in the process. The goal was achieved by 1933, along with the construction of 263 lighted landing fields that offered welcome havens for pilots encountering bad weather or the all-too-frequent mechanical failures.

While the beacon system was indeed a step forward, it was obviously of little or no value in instrument conditions. Of course, in one respect, that wasn't of much concern because instrument flight—planned instrument flight, that is—was nonexistent in those days. Also, if the pilot was not flying an airway, there were no aids to guide or direct him other than city lights and dead reckoning. The system, however, was not designed for the casual pilot or the barnstormer; it was constructed for those flying the mail over routes designed by the Post Office Department, and eventually for commercial aviation. But even with its limitations, it was an important start.

RADIO COMMUNICATION IN ITS INFANCY

Almost concurrent with the development of the beacon system were the experiments with radio communication. In 1926 and 1927, successful two-way, air-to-ground communication was conducted, and the first transmitter/receiver went into production in 1928.

About the same time, teletype circuits came into being. These made it possible to transmit local weather conditions over leased landlines between stations. How the system worked was basically simple. Weather conditions, as collected by the U.S. Weather Bureau, were transmitted to airway communication stations. Then, over a given route and at prescribed times, Station A would teletype its local weather to all stations on the circuit. When the transmission was completed, the operator would ring a bell, signaling the next station in sequence that the circuit was clear. Station B would then report its weather, and so on down the line until all stations had the most current reports along the route. Before takeoff, the pilot would receive a list of all weather along a route. Changing conditions were communicated to the aircraft in flight at designated times.

But weather reporting wasn't the only benefit that radio and teletype produced. The ability to keep track of airborne aircraft was a major plus. When a flight plan was filed and an aircraft departed from Station A, that information was teletyped to all stations on the flight plan route. Then, when the pilot passed over Station B, that position was communicated by radio. If there was no transmitter, the pilot would gun the engine a couple of times or blink the navigation lights to signal the position to ground personnel, and so on, to the destination.

With weather information available and radio contact with the ground possible, those flying the airways in the late 1920s and early 1930s were not completely alone in space or darkness. Aviation was still a child but had emerged from infancy.

RADIO RANGES AND THE FIRST INVISIBLE AIRWAYS

Despite sporadic experiments with radio navigation in the 1920s, it took the low-frequency four-course radio range to move aviation from strictly contact to instrument flight. It was the radio range that permitted pilots to fly in or above the overcast and to navigate by aural signals coming through their headsets.

Without getting into the technicalities, the range consisted of four towers, erected to form a square. Two of the towers transmitted the Morse code letter A (dot-dash). The other two towers transmitted the letter N (dash-dot) (Fig. 1-2). When the two signals overlapped, the A and N codes meshed, and the pilot heard a steady humlike signal, letting the pilot know that the aircraft was on one of the four *beams* leading to or from the range station.

Flying to or from the station was determined by the change in volume or intensity of the signal. If the pilot was flying inbound, the volume steadily increased until the aircraft was over the station. At that point, all sounds ceased—the aircraft was in the *cone of silence.* The cone fanned outward from the ground up, and at low altitudes, say 800 or 1000 feet, the silence was very brief. The pilot could be in and out of the cone in only a couple of seconds or could even miss it entirely—if not smack dab on the beam—which was also extremely narrow at that point, sometimes little more than the wingspan of the aircraft. On the other hand, at 8000 feet, 10,000 feet, or higher, the silence would last several seconds, thus providing a very imprecise position fix. The installation of radio marker beacons identifying the cone did, however, reduce the imprecision.

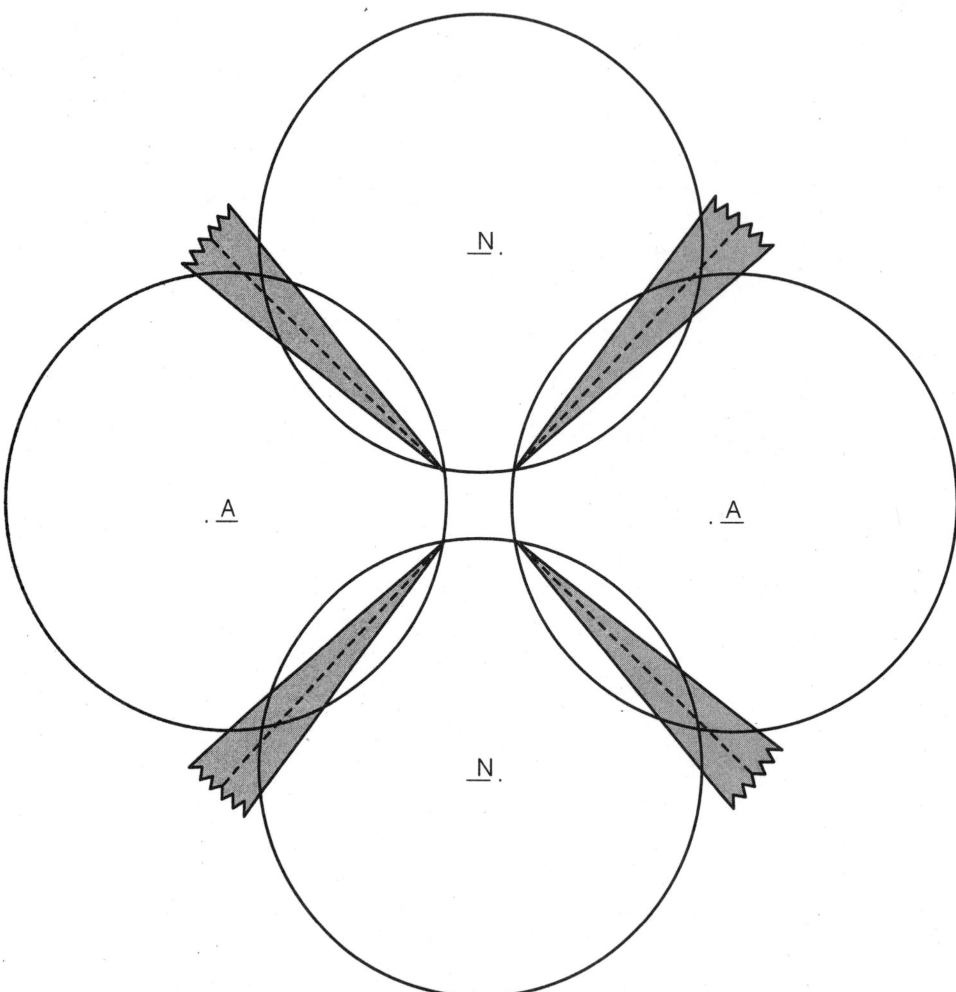

Fig. 1-2 *The four-course radio range, formed by the overlapping A and N signals, permitted the first aerial navigation without reference to the ground.*

If the pilot tuned to the range frequency and heard only a clear A or a clear N, he would know that the aircraft was in one of the A or N quadrants. If he was unsure of the aircraft position and wanted to get on the beam, then he followed a set of prescribed orientation procedures that could be time- and fuel-consuming.

Once on the beam, the practice was to fly the right side, or *feathered edge,* when inbound or outbound. The primary signal, then, would be the on-course hum, with a faint A or N in the background, depending upon which quadrant was on the pilot's right side.

The beam could be received from approximately 100 miles, and stations were spaced approximately 200 miles apart. Somewhat akin to VOR tracking today, when flying outbound from one station and the on-course signal became fainter and fainter, the pilot tuned to the next station ahead, probably picking up an equally faint hum that gradually increased in volume as the airplane approached the station.

As valuable an addition as the ranges were to navigation and instrument flight, they had deficiencies. Generated by low-frequency transmitters, the beams could be bent or thrown off their published compass heading by mountains, mineral deposits, changing weather conditions, static, railroad tracks, and even the rising and setting of the sun. As Komons indicates, and from personal experience as well, the ranges' inherent undependability was particularly hazardous in mountainous terrain or when weather factors demanded reliability. Plus, the beams were anything but precise as aids for instrument approaches and landings.

Nevertheless, the range was a most important aid to navigation, and by 1933, some 90 stations had been established, producing 18,000 miles of aural airways. Overcoming the inherent low-frequency range deficiencies, however, was several years down the road.

THE START OF AIR TRAFFIC CONTROL

As of the late 1920s and early 1930s, "congestion" at some of the larger airports demanded at least a modicum of traffic control on the ground. At some airports, this became the role of a gentleman who waved red and green flags to advise pilots to stop or proceed. According to John Knoell, an early pioneer who helped establish the St. Louis Airway Traffic Control Station, one of the first flag-wavers was a gentleman named Archie W. League. Archie would sit at the end of a runway at St. Louis, under a sun-protecting umbrella, and "control" traffic by these visual signals.

Obviously, such a communications medium was useless at night and of almost no help to aircraft in the pattern or on final approach. Becoming more sophisticated, the flags were soon replaced by a red and green light system; but this, too, was useless beyond a certain visual range.

The first control tower

The next and most logical step was radio. The first radio-equipped control tower was constructed in Cleveland in 1930 (Fig. 1-3). Its range was limited to about 15 miles, and the controller tracked the progress of inbound aircraft on a position map, based on periodic reports from the pilot. To call the controller a *controller,* however, is not quite accurate. In those days, the controller could clear an aircraft to land or take off, but the pilot was under no obligation to follow the instructions. The controller really was little more than an adviser or traffic reporter, and it would take later federal regulations to make him a true controller (Fig. 1-4).

The experiment at Cleveland did demonstrate the value of a form of tower control at and in the vicinity of busier airports. Consequently, about 20 additional structures were erected between 1930 and 1935.

"Controlling" the airways

During this period, when the airlines were growing in size and number, and instrument flight was increasing, traffic control along the airways and into the airport vicinities was

Fig. 1-3 *The first control tower was erected in Cleveland, Ohio. The partially visible device atop the tower is the wind tee.* National Air and Space Museum, Smithsonian Institution

primarily a matter of coordination among the airlines. Glen Gilbert recounts the beginning of a control system in his book *Air Traffic Control—The Uncrowded Sky.* Gilbert, then with American Airlines, initiated a program of tracking American's flights into Chicago from about 100 miles out via pilot radio reports.

Following Gilbert's initiative, the other major carriers serving Chicago soon formed an informal group, doing the same for their own carriers and keeping one another alerted if an arrival conflict seemed likely. The airlines involved would then mutually coordinate the approach and arrival of their aircraft, and would do the same with the control tower by telephone. Radio contact along the airways in those days was primarily between the pilot and the company radio operator/dispatcher (Fig. 1-5). Not until the pilot was within the vicinity of the airport did the tower enter the picture and take over visual control of the aircraft.

Based on the Chicago experiment, in 1935 the airlines operating into Chicago and Newark (then the primary airport serving New York) agreed to set up a system to control the flights at both locations. Called an *airway traffic control station,* the first station was established at Newark (Figs. 1-6 and 1-7), followed in 1936 by stations in Cleveland and Chicago. Once again, misnomers enter the picture. These were not literally *airway* control stations

Fig. 1-4 *Archie League eventually put down his flags and went inside to staff the radio at the St. Louis tower.* Federal Aviation Administration

because each station controlled airline activity within only about a 50-mile radius of its airport. Furthermore, the control was through the various airline radio operator/dispatchers and their ultimate coordination with the tower personnel.

The fact that the facilities were staffed and operated by airline employees for their airlines was an obvious deterrent to uniform traffic control because one airline had no authority to regulate the operations of another. And, to muddle the airways further, neither private nor military pilots had any requirement to take orders from a commercial operator.

Quite understandably, government and airline apprehension over the increasing potential of ground and midair collisions was mounting. Both parties were vociferous in their agreement: Federal control of the airways was essential. Finally, on July 6, 1937, after overcoming budgetary problems and a lot of confusing internal problems, the Bureau of Air Commerce took over the Newark, Cleveland, and Chicago stations. The airways, current and future, were now under federal control. Regulation compliance at last had the bite of law behind it.

Fig. 1-5 *An early Braniff radio operator maintains contact with one of the company pilots.*

National Air and Space Museum, Smithsonian Institution

Fig. 1-6 *Earl Ward, the first supervisor of Airway Traffic Control for the federal government, is at the aircraft plotting position and map table at the Newark, New Jersey, Airway Traffic Control Station.* National Air and Space Museum, Smithsonian Institution

Back to the control towers

The airways came under federal control in 1937, but one facility did not—the tower. Each tower was still the responsibility of the municipality in which the airport was located.

Depending upon the individual airport and the whims of the city leaders, control tower personnel could have a variety of duties, ranging from communicating with dispatchers and pilots to acting as airport switchboard operators. In some cases, Akron for one, they also sold airline tickets and assisted with passenger baggage as late as 1939. To compound matters, no uniform employment, training, or licensing standards existed. With such informality, standardized airport operations across the system were difficult, if not impossible.

Despite concerns and valid arguments to the contrary, Congress took no action to extend federal control to the towers until, as Komons put it, "...forced to do so by the exigencies of war." It wasn't until November 1941 that the federal government (under its newly established Civil Aviation Administration) assumed control of both airway and tower operations.

Amidst these spotty endeavors, and something that might ring a bell today, was the rising criticism of private flying and its interference with commercial aviation. As Komons summarized it, near-collisions, "miscellaneous flyers" getting in the way of airliners, private pilots landing at congested airports, small planes plying the airways in instrument

Fig. 1-7 *Another view of the Newark "Center" in the early 1930s shows the chalkboard method of posting flight information. The lantern and flashlight were used because of frequent power failure in the station.* National Air and Space Museum, Smithsonian Institution

conditions without flight plans—these and similar concerns were raised in growing volume. With talk of banning private planes without two-way radios at the large terminals "like Newark, Chicago, or Kansas City" increasing, Eugene L. Vidal, then head of the Bureau of Air Commerce, forecast in 1936 that privately owned aircraft would be prevented from landing at congested airports under any condition. His point: Itinerant flyers should not operate in or out of airports used by air carriers. Sound familiar?

During this period (the latter half of the 1930s), the airlines were facing economic as well as operational crises. In February 1934, the Roosevelt administration canceled all airmail contracts and turned the responsibility for carrying the mail back to the Army. The cancellation was an almost-fatal blow to the airlines because those mail contracts were practically their only source of revenue. The Army, however, was ill prepared for the responsibility foisted on it, and its accident record over the first few weeks of service aroused public ire as well as deep concern within government circles.

Recognizing its mistake and misjudgment, the government, in April 1934, opened bidding to the airlines for new routes and mail contracts for what was supposed to be a temporary 90-day period. Some carriers, wanting to retain the routes they had pioneered and had been serving, bid so low—perhaps 17 cents per aircraft mile versus the Post Office Department's limit of 45 cents—that operating at a profit was just about impossible. Had they known the so-called temporary routes and rates would later be made permanent by Congress, the bidding for both routes and rates might have taken on a different character.

The passing of time brought little relief. By 1937, the airlines were still afflicted with economic problems, and their safety record was a matter of serious concern. In that year alone, there were five fatal accidents in one 28-day period. Coupled with unreliable navigation facilities, air commerce was in deep trouble. The industry was crying for federal regulation. No one, not even those in the government, argued the point, but they could not agree on the solution. Self-interests, politicking, and departmental chauvinism ran rampant through the halls of the nation's capitol.

Finally, after months of government bickering, President Roosevelt signed the Civil Aeronautics Act into law in June 1938. The law created the Civil Aeronautics Authority and gave the authority the power to issue air carrier routes and regulate airline fares. In 1940, Roosevelt split the authority into two agencies: Civil Aeronautics Board (CAB) and Civil Aeronautics Administration (CAA). The CAB, an independent agency, was responsible for economic and safety rule making and accident investigation. The CAA, lodged in the Department of Commerce, was charged with air traffic control, airman and aircraft certification, safety enforcement, and airway development.

This organization existed until 1958, when the Federal Aviation Act was passed, creating the Federal Aviation Agency (FAA), and, in the process, transferred the CAA's functions to this new independent body. The action also took safety rule making from the CAB and entrusted it to the FAA. Of even greater significance, the FAA was given the sole responsibility for developing and maintaining a common civil-military system of air navigation and air traffic control, a responsibility the CAA had previously shared with others.

In 1967, the Department of Transportation (DOT) was established, absorbing the FAA and other transportation agencies. The FAA was then renamed the Federal Aviation Administration. This is today's FAA, although it has assumed several other responsibilities not originally envisioned in the Federal Aviation Act. Among the responsibilities are prescribing aircraft noise standards, establishing minimum airport safety standards, and improving the ATC radar- and computer-based system. In 1981, the FAA revealed its National Airspace System Plan, which was a blueprint for a state-of-the-art air traffic control and navigation system to accommodate the projected growth in air travel up to the turn of the century. (As of today—late 1998—much of the airspace plan, for a variety of reasons, is either dormant or on hold. Full realization of the many plans and projects now seems to be 15 years down the road.)

LANDING BLIND IN THE 1930s

As noted earlier, the radio range had a number of inherent weaknesses, many of which were not corrected until the 1940s. One weakness that defied correction was the imprecision for instrument landings.

In a certain sense, if a beam was aligned with a runway, which was sometimes not the case, it was very broadly akin to a localizer; it did provide guidance to the airport. At an airport very close to a station, however, the cone of silence was so small and the beam so narrow that only a perfect on-course approach—heading, altitude, timing, and rate of descent—would get you to the runway. Conversely, when the airport was some distance away, say, 10 or 12 miles, the width of the beam was such that the on-course signal might lead you to the airport, but being lined up with the runway was more a matter of good fortune. It, too, required stopwatch timing, maintaining the published feet-per-minute descent and airspeed, and flying exactly on the outbound course radial.

Something better was essential for military and commercial operations. Two techniques emerged: the *ground control approach* and the *instrument landing system.*

Ground Control approach (GCA)

The development of *radar* (an acronym for *r*adio *d*etection *a*nd *r*anging) fostered GCA. Used primarily by the military or at very large airline airports, the GCA system consisted of two 6-inch-diameter cathode-ray tubes (CRTs) and support equipment in mobile tractor-trailers (Fig. 1-8). One CRT scanned the immediate airport vicinity for aircraft, and its operator, via radio communications, directed each aircraft in sequence into position for the initial landing approach. The second CRT, staffed by the talk-down controller, determined the aircraft's position in relation to the proper heading and approach angle. The controller then literally talked the pilot down to the runway by verbally communicating course direction and descent instructions.

Housed inside the darkened trailer, the controllers had no visual contact with the outside world (Fig. 1-9). Their "windows" were the CRTs in front of them. Suffice it to say that it was an interesting experience to be a pilot locked in the soup with your immediate future in the hands of a small tube and the verbal instructions from a voice you just had to trust. Despite the fact that many civil pilots didn't like the system because they didn't feel in control of their own destiny, those who manned these units did a fantastic job, and many a pilot owed his well-being to their expertise.

One advantage of the GCA was its mobility. Being motorized, the entire facility could be shifted from one runway to another so that landings were generally into the wind. The risks of touching down in a strong crosswind were thus minimized. The units could also be moved from one field to another, if military circumstances dictated.

With later technical advances, the system was transferred to the tower. Mobility was lost, but precision enhanced. It became known as *precision approach radar* (PAR) and is even now being used extensively, particularly by the military. Because of its maintenance and operational costs, no civilian airport in the United States has PAR today.

Instrument landing system (ILS)

ILS is often perceived as a fairly recent development in aviation technology. Not so. One ILS form or another has been off the drawing board since the late 1920s. Experimenting with a system developed by U.S. Army Captain Hegenberger, Jimmy Doolittle made the first completely blind flight and landing in 1929, and the Army used that system for several years thereafter. The Bureau of Air Commerce announced in 1934

Fig. 1-8 *The early GCA units had the advantage of mobility and could be moved to the most appropriate runway for instrument approaches.* National Air and Space Museum, Smithsonian Institution

that it would adopt the system as its standard and that installation of the ground equipment would begin immediately at 36 commercial airports. The airlines, however, claimed the system to be "unflyable" in their aircraft for technical as well as safety reasons. That ended that.

One version that did survive was started in 1928 by a group of engineers in the Bureau of Standards. That version became operational in 1931. After the all-too-typical government delays of that era—both bureaucratic and economic—the system was finally refined and made adaptable for commercial use in 1938. *Air track* emerged.

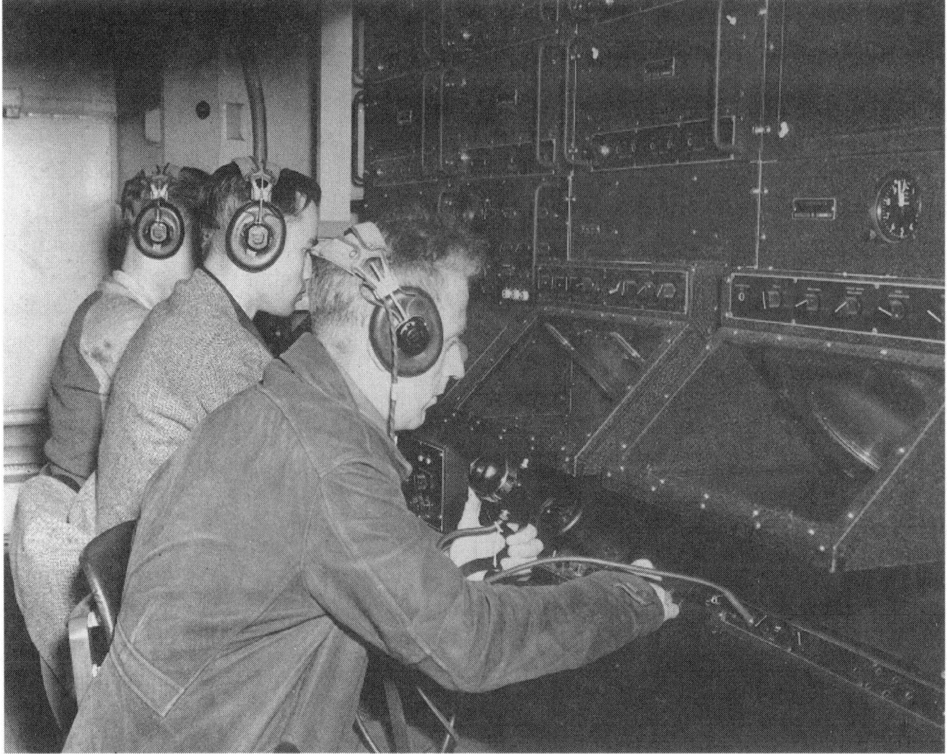

Fig. 1-9 *Not unlike today, GCA controllers relied on their CRTs and radios to lead pilots to safe instrument-condition landings.* National Air and Space Museum, Smithsonian Institution

In many respects, the elements of air track were the same as those of today's ILS: a localizer, a glide path, and two marker beacons, outer and boundary. The cockpit instrumentation also closely resembled the localizer/glide path needles in modern-day indicators.

One difference was that the glide path was a curved beam rather than the straight-line approach. The curve was formed by an infinitude of transmitted signals—rising to about 1500 feet above the airport—that resembled giant teardops. The pilot picked up the glide slope signal and then flew the underside of the teardrop that best suited the airspeed and descent rate of that particular aircraft. This was done in the usual way by keeping the glide path needle generally centered.

Although about half a dozen other systems existed at the time, air track has a special place in history. As related in the June 1938 issue of *Fortune* magazine, a Pennsylvania–Central Airlines (PCA) Boeing 247-D took off on January 26, 1938, from Washington, D.C., for Pittsburgh. Approaching Pittsburgh in a swirling snowstorm, the pilot, strictly on instruments, tuned to the Pittsburgh ILS frequency, centered the localizer, and "played" with the glide slope as the aircraft flew down the curved beam. About 50 feet above the ground, the shrill beep of the boundary marker was heard. Although the ground was in sight, the pilot forced himself not to look out, while the copilot sat ready to take over in case anything went wrong. Seconds later, with the pilot still glued to the instrument panel, the wheels touched the ground.

It was a blind landing but not that unusual. Thousands had been made before in actual as well as simulated conditions. What made it historic was that it was the first blind landing of a U.S. airliner on a scheduled flight with passengers on board. It also marked the start of the first formal blind-landing training program by a U.S. airline. (In those days the term *blind* was used rather than instrument flight or instrument landing.)

Conflict still persisted, however, over what ILS the Bureau of Air Commerce would ultimately adopt. The military had its own, and the airlines wanted something else. Two or more different systems, of course, wouldn't do. Commonality was essential for the safety of all types of operations and operators.

Despite the airline, military, and bureau debates, and despite the pressures and divergent points of view in the decision-making process, a 1938 *Fortune* article concludes with this prognostication:

> With all of the negative factors at work, we can neither say in what final form blind landing will come nor fix a date for its arrival. But you can be sure that it *will* arrive. Or as sure, at any rate, as you can be that air safety is a good thing, and that the airline operators want to make money, and that men will continue to fly.

The promise would come true, but completely blind landings wouldn't be realized until well into the postwar years.

Meanwhile, agreement on an ILS system was reached. A unit created to meet the rigid safety specifications of the CAA had been installed at the Indianapolis Municipal Airport in 1939 and tested extensively in all sorts of instrument weather. Its reliability established, the system was approved and accepted by the military in early 1940. A February 3, 1940, *Science News Letter* reported:

> A committee of the National Academy of Sciences, headed by Dr. Vannevar Bush, President of Carnegie Institution of Washington, recommended to President Roosevelt that the Indianapolis CAA system be extended to other airports in the nation, military and commercial, as the best blind-landing system now developed.

In 1945, the Army introduced its own ILS version by using very high-frequency (VHF) transmitters that eliminated the effects of static on the operation of the glide path. Also, VHF beams were straighter and less inclined to fade, swing, or form false courses than the conventional low-frequency radio beams. The Army called this unit the *Army Air Forces Instrument Approach System* or, more tersely, SCS-51 (Signal Corps Set 51). The initial Technical Order, published January 15, 1945, introducing the system, contained explanations and approach procedures that would be very familiar today. Only references to the initial orientation by using the radio range make it seem a little archaic.

VHF transmission was nothing new, but the old radio ranges were still using the low-frequency transmitters that were responsible for the range unreliability. It wasn't until 1945 that the CAA acted to modernize that vital navigation equipment.

In early 1946, a fogbound American Airlines plane crashed into a California mountain, killing 27 people. It was the worst commercial air disaster up to that time. *Time* magazine, in its March 18, 1946, issue, observed:

> This accident would perhaps never have happened had all the warborn safety devices been in general use....But as far as U.S. commercial airlines are concerned, there has been no basic change in air traffic control, airway marking, or instrument landing equipment in 15 years—a period that has seen an enormous increase in scheduled flights and the advent of 300-mile-an-hour-transports.

The wheels of government do indeed spin slowly. In 1949, the International Civil Aviation Organization (ICAO) adopted ILS as the standard international approach and landing aid; however, it was not until the 1960s that equipment had been sufficiently developed to make full automatic blind landings (called *Category III*) operationally feasible.

Is ILS the final answer? No. Somewhat like the old radio range, it, too, has its frailties. Problems with ILS include its susceptibility to interference from structures in the airport vicinity and the terrain itself, and the fact that it's locked into a single approach path to the runway. As Arnold Field puts it in his book *International Air Traffic Control,* "...There have been virtually no advances in performance since the introduction of the first Category III compatible equipment in the late 1960s."

The next step appears to be GPS (Global Positioning System), either as a stand-alone system or in conjunction with existing navigational and instrument landing systems.

INTERNATIONAL STANDARDIZATION

An excerpt from the International Civil Aviation Organization's brochure *Facts About ICAO* sums up ICAO's reason for being.

> In an afternoon's flight, an airliner can cross the territories of several nations, nations in which different languages are spoken, in which different legal codes are used. In all of these operations, safety must be paramount, there must be no unfamiliarity or misunderstanding. In other words, there must be international standardization, agreement between nations in all technical and economic and legal fields so that the air can be the high road to carry man and his goods anywhere and everywhere without fetter and without halt.

With the end of World War II in sight and the potential of international civil aviation obvious, representatives from 52 countries met in Chicago in 1944. Their purpose was to lay the groundwork for worldwide standardization of civil aviation policies and practices. From that meeting, a treaty was signed in December 1944, creating ICAO. Today, 159 states comprise its membership. Headquarters are in Montreal, Canada, and regional offices are in Bangkok, Cairo, Dakar, Lima, Mexico City, Nairobi, and Paris.

ICAO's purpose and functions

As implied in the preceding quote, standardization, with safety the paramount issue, was and is ICAO's principal charge. This means that international commonality of operating rules, navigating procedures, language, and phraseology must prevail. National self-interests or favored ways of doing things cannot be allowed to interfere with the common good. The fact that ICAO has been so successful in achieving standardization speaks volumes for what nations can do when they're willing to work together, negotiate, and then come to agreements that have universal application.

The agreements reached are not just international in scope. Each member state must abide by them within its own boundaries and see that they are enforced. In the United States, that is the responsibility of the FAA. There might be minor local variations, but any that do exist are indeed minor and do not violate the ICAO's intent.

In addition to standardization and safety, ICAO's interests reach across the whole gamut of civil aviation. It has been the front-runner of working for the removal of unnecessary customs and immigration formalities, improvement of international airport passenger facilities, automation of air traffic services, aircraft noise control, unlawful interference with civil aviation, and aviation and the human environment. It is also involved in international legal matters concerning ground damage to aircraft and crimes committed on aircraft. And it has been active in providing technical and economic assistance for aviation development in third world nations.

Accomplishing all this takes coordination and cooperation. In 1947, ICAO became a specialized agency of the United Nations, and it works closely with other UN organizations, including the World Meteorological Organization, International Telecommunications Union, the Universal Postal Union, and the World Health Organization. The same working relationship exists between ICAO and non-UN agencies such as the International Air Transport Association (IATA), the International Federation of Airline Pilots Association (IFAPA), and the International Council of Aircraft Owners and Pilots Associations.

The ICAO organizational structure

Very sketchily, the ICAO organizational structure includes the following departments.

Assembly. Composed of all member states, this is the sovereign body. It meets every 3 years to review the work done and to set policy for the coming years.

Council. Selected by the assembly for a 3-year term and made up of representatives from 33 states. The states chosen are based on three criteria: (1) the importance of the states in air transport; (2) the states that make the largest contribution to providing air navigation facilities; and (3) states that will ensure that all areas of the world are represented. The council is the governing body of ICAO and adopts recommended practices and standards.

Secretariat. Headed by the secretary general, this has five divisions: air navigation, air transport, technical assistance, administration and services, and legal. Members of these divisions are highly qualified in their fields and are recruited from all over the globe to ensure, as *Facts About ICAO* states, "a truly international approach."

One example of standardization

To a measurable degree, universal standardization of civil aviation demands standardization and simplicity of language. It would hardly do to have a Saudi pilot who spoke no English milling around over New York while attempting to communicate with a U.S. controller who spoke no Arabic, or the reverse situation of someone from the United States trying to land at Riyadh. Language commonality and standard terminology and phraseology are essential in international operations.

Addressing the problem, ICAO members agreed that English was the most universal language, or at least the language most frequently used in international trade and commerce. It was thus logically adopted as the international aviation language.

Then came the task of simplifying words and expressions so that they could be mastered by those for whom English was not the mother tongue. The phonetic alphabet is one example. For years, the United States had its own aviation and military alphabet that was fine for people from the United States but apparently caused non-English speakers certain pronunciation problems. Without going through it from A to Z, the U.S. phonetic alphabet was Able, Baker, Charlie, Dog, Easy, Fox, George, How, Item, and so on. The ICAO revision gave us Alpha, Bravo, Charlie, Delta, Echo, Foxtrot, Golf, Hotel, India, and so on to Zulu versus the old Zebra (or sometimes Zed, the French pronunciation of the letter Z).

Phraseologies and terms were also standardized: *Roger, Affirmative, Acknowledge, Say again, How do you read? Stand by, Hold short, Taxi into position and hold.*

The same standard phraseology between controller and pilot exists in all phases of flight operations—from initial aircraft movement to landing and parking on the ramp. VFR or IFR, many terms, and expressions are those of ICAO, and thus of international usage.

To quote again a portion of the *Facts About ICAO* brochure:

> ICAO provides the machinery for the achievement of international cooperation in the air; successful results depend on the willingness of the nations of the world to make concessions, to work together to reach agreement. The success which international civil aviation has achieved in the past four decades is abundant proof that nations can work together effectively to achieve the common good.

There can be little argument about that.

FULL CIRCLE

And so, in one respect, this brings us full circle: ICAN to ICAO. The first effort to establish rules of the air was the initiative of ICAN in 1919. ICAO closed the loop by internationalizing the rules through the agreement of participating member states. What ICAO has accomplished on a global level took us, in the United States, almost 20 years to achieve; however, through it all the United States was the leader in technical and commercial development, partly (and perhaps primarily) because of the size of the country and early U.S. recognition of the importance of aviation as a tool of commerce.

Whatever the case, whatever the cause, pilots and the flying public are enjoying today the technical and electronic fruits of preceding pioneers. The skies are more crowded and safer than ever. However, safety has many fathers, including a well-maintained aircraft, pilot knowledge and skill, and a constant awareness that "it could happen to me."

In addition, safety is the product of understanding our national airspace and the air traffic control system that makes it work. That's the theme of the chapters that follow, so let's get on with it—with the hope that those chapters will contribute to your understanding and thus your confidence in using the system as it is intended to be used.

2
Air traffic control: It awaits your use

Building on what the pioneers who preceded us struggled to create, we have in North America today what could be called the finest air traffic control system in the world. True, some of the electronics are out of date and radar outages, usually brief though they may be, do occur. And also true, the National Air Space Plan (NASP), developed in 1981 to take us into the 21st century, has pretty well faded from the scene as an integrated, active equipment modernization plan.

Regardless of some hardware shortcomings, it's still an outstanding system that is staffed by trained and dedicated people. It's also a system that, up to now, you and I have paid for with our various state and federal taxes. It's thus there to be used or not used, largely to whatever extent we, as pilots, choose.

Watch out for the immediate future, though. There are those, from the White House down, who would scrap much of our organizational structure and replace it with a performance-based organization (PBO) that would be separate from the FAA and responsible for air traffic control. Its financial support would come from a *user-fee* system.

Now this book is not the vehicle to debate the good or bad aspects of the proposals (there's little good), but perhaps it *is* a vehicle which can ask pilots, would-be pilots, and all who are interested in general aviation to pay close attention to the related debates and doings in Washington. Putting it mildly, if the pro-PBOers get their way and user fees, on top of current taxes, become law, the future health, perhaps the very survival, of general aviation as we know it today can be questioned.

So we have a sound system, as of now. Such being the case—and assuming for the moment that many who are reading this book may be new, or relatively new, to aviation—there are some general questions related to their use of the system that should be asked and answered, beginning with…

WHERE AND WHEN *MUST* VFR PILOTS CONTACT ATC?

There's no single, pat answer to this question. "It all depends." (I don't like that way to start an explanation. At the least, it sounds wishy-washy, indecisive, but in response to the question, it really "does depend…") Before I touch on those situations, however, a comment: If you're not familiar with the airspace system, portions of this chapter might be a little confusing. Do not be concerned, though, because the balance of the book is designed to shed light on the various control and advisory facilities as well as the nomenclature associated with the system as a whole. The purpose here is merely to establish a broad foundation for what follows—not the details—and to touch on a few of the barriers that cause even some experienced pilots to find it hard to contact various of the ATC facilities and to benefit from what those facilities have to offer.

But back to the situations in which communication with ATC is mandatory:

1. If you're operating into or out of a controlled airport—that is, one with an operating control tower—you *must* contact Ground Control for permission to move your aircraft on any taxiway. The Ground controller is physically located in the tower structure where he or she can see the movement and location of aircraft and motorized vehicles, on the surface of the airport.
2. You *must* contact the air traffic controller (*local controller* is the usual term) in the tower for permission to take off or land at any controlled airport.
3. You *must* contact Approach or Departure Control before entering or leaving a Class B (Bravo) airspace—the airspace that extends approximately 30 miles out from the nation's 35 busiest air carrier airports, or a Class C (Charlie) airspace, which extends 10 miles out from the 122 relatively medium-active airports. There is no Approach Control at the typical Class D airports, so it is the tower controller who authorizes entrance into the surrounding Class D airspace.

[If you're wondering, there is a Class A airspace, but it extends from 18,000 feet mean sea level (MSL) to 60,000 feet and is for IFR operations only. It's thus usually not a matter of relevance to the typical general aviation pilot or to those who hold only VFR ratings.]

There are a couple of other situations that require ATC radio contacts, such as Clearance Delivery at the busier airports or operating into and out of what are called *TRSAs,* or terminal radar service areas. I'll also cover how those come into play in later chapters.

Barring these three airport-related airspaces, a general aviation VFR pilot needs to have no radio contact with any air traffic controlling facility. Whether avoiding such contact is wise is another matter and one I'll discuss through the next chapters.

NEXT QUESTION: WHERE AND WHEN IS CONTACT WITH ATC OPTIONAL?

This question is a logical follow-on to the one just addressed. We have the "musts" out of the way, so what are the "optionals"?

One occurs when you're on a VFR cross-country trip and would like someone down there to know who you are, where you are, and where you're going—plus, keep you advised of other traffic that might be in your line of flight. What you would be asking for is called *flight following,* and the ATC facility that provides this service is one of the Air Route Traffic Control Centers (Centers, for short). As a VFR pilot, the choice is yours to contact or not contact a controller for this service.

Another optional situation occurs when a Class B airspace is in your line of flight on a cross-country trip. You want to continue your flight on the other side of the airspace and would like to go through the area rather than detour several miles around it, thus wasting time and fuel. So you call the Approach controller and request clearance through the airspace. Whether he or she approves the request is another matter, but the option to initiate the contact is yours. Without the controller's expressed approval, however, you cannot enter any Class B airspace. In the example cited, without that approval, your only choice is to circumvent the whole airspace. And to a lesser degree, this same scenario applies to entering or circumventing a Class C airspace. The rules are a little different, and the size of the airspace makes a detour around it less time-consuming, but the basic principle of radio contact with an Approach controller still prevails.

To summarize, then, you can fly just about everywhere, except around controlled airports (Classes B, C, and D), and never have to say a word to any controller. Again, whether that's wise is another question. In addition, there are times when *not* to talk with a controller would be very foolish—an observation that raises the following issue.

THE SAFETY AND ECONOMIES ATC OFFERS

Even though other than in the immediate controlled airport environment you rarely have to initiate radio contacts, ATC doesn't make silence on your part necessarily a wise decision. Take the safety factor alone. You leave from either a controlled or an uncontrolled airport and set out on a cross-country trip. You call the appropriate Center and request flight following. The controller accepts your request. From now on, one controller or another will be tracking your progress on his or her radar scope and is equipped to alert you to other traffic ahead of you, behind you, or potentially crossing your flight path—traffic you should know about and be watching for. It's like having another pair of eyes on guard for your aerial well-being.

That doesn't mean that the controller is sitting there focusing his or her full attention only on your aircraft. The service isn't *that* exclusive. A Center exists primarily for IFR operations, regardless of what the weather conditions may be, but it will still help VFR aircraft and provide the flight-following service...when its workload permits. None of this would have occurred, however, had you not made the first call.

There are other reasons to ask for flight following: Perhaps you've had your head in the cockpit too long and haven't been paying enough attention to your navigating. Whatever the case, you suddenly realize that nothing on the ground looks familiar. Checkpoints you had plotted on the sectional chart in your preflight planning just aren't showing up, your aircraft doesn't have the latest positioning equipment, your electronic navigation instruments (as your VOR—very high-frequency omnidirectional range station) readings don't seem right, and your fuel is getting low. You come to the uneasy conclusion that you don't know where you are. Solution: If you have asked for flight following, confess your dilemma to the controller. He or she will quickly be able to tell you where you are and will help you reorient yourself.

Or take another scenario: You've suddenly got a real emergency—engine failure, fire, personal illness—and need to land *now.* Again, if you have been in contact with him, the controller can help guide you to the nearest airport and get you on the ground as rapidly as possible.

As to the economies associated with these ATC contacts, go back to the Class B airspace and the detour it could present on a cross-country flight. As opposed to a direct 60-nautical-mile flight through the heart of a Class B airspace, going around the airspace might add 30 or 50 miles to your trip, depending on the route you took and the extent to which you avoided the outer boundaries of the airspace. Certainly not a major detour, but still it added flight time and fuel burn that were potentially avoidable. One call to Approach Control might have been all that was necessary to save time and money.

With all this discussion, however, I say again that the primary responsibility of the various ATC facilities is to IFR flight operations and that ATC will provide service to VFR aircraft on a "workload permitting" basis. By way of summary, though, in these situations, contacts with ATC are mandatory or optional:

Mandatory—and the Facility to Contact

- Ground Control at Class B, C, and D airports for clearance to taxi on any taxiway prior to taking off and after landing.
- The control tower for clearance to take off or land at Class B, C, and D airports.
- Approach or Departure Control to enter the Class B or C airspaces for landing or taking off at a Class B or C airport. Approach Control will almost always approve such a VFR request, assuming, of course, that the weather meets at least the minimum visual meteorological conditions (VMC).

Optional—and the Facility to Contact

- Approach or Departure Control to transit any portion of a Class B or C airspace with no intention of landing at the Class B or C airport in the airspace. It is the pilot's option to initiate the contact, but ATC can approve or reject the VFR request, depending on traffic and the controller's workload.

- Air Route Traffic Control Center for en route flight following. The controller can accept or reject the request, depending on the workload. In those cases when ATC rejects a VFR request for flight following or to transit an airspace, the rejection is final and not subject to appeal. VFR pilots should remember that and should neither argue nor try to change the controller's decision. The Centers exist primarily to serve IFR operations.

VFR PILOTS: WHY THE RELUCTANCE TO USE THE OPTIONAL ATC SERVICES?

To utilize the services ATC offers requires selecting the right radio frequency, picking up a microphone, and communicating your request to the controller who will respond to your call. All this is obvious and, on the surface, not a terribly difficult task. Why, then, do so many pilots find it so difficult to get on the air and spread their voices across the airwaves?

The basic answer, as you've probably already assumed, is plain and simple fear—fear of making mistakes; fear of not understanding what the controller may tell you or ask you to do; fear of sounding ignorant, silly, or incompetent; fear of not expressing yourself well or stating your message clearly.

Let's face it: When you radio anyone in the ATC system or one of the Flight Service Station (FSS) facilities (I haven't mentioned FSSs yet because they are not an air traffic controlling facility), every pilot within range is listening and perhaps evaluating what you're saying. Chances are, there's a fair-sized invisible audience out there, and unless you happen to be one of those garrulous, extroverted individuals, to realize that your voice and your words are reaching that audience can be a bit intimidating.

These fears, however, of sounding silly, incompetent, or whatever are real fears. They're as logical and natural as can be because one's self-esteem is involved. Obviously enough, though, the cause is primarily a lack of knowledge of the subject and/or lack of skill in applying that knowledge.

Expertise in any trade, profession, sport, or what-have-you starts, of course, by mastering the basic knowledge associated with that trade or profession. Next, or perhaps in concert with the acquisition of knowledge, comes the development of the skills necessary to put that knowledge to work. If we're talking about the air traffic control system, ground school classes, instructor explanations and demonstrations, books, magazines, or articles on the subject will provide the required knowledge. From then on, though, the development of the necessary skills to utilize that knowledge falls on the shoulders of the pilot him- or herself. Fear and apprehension disappear only when I know what to do, when to do it, why I should do it, where I should do it, and finally the skill factor—*how* to do it.

Here is where individual practice enters the picture. It's a little unrealistic, though, to rely solely on actual in-flight situations as the primary skill development vehicle. Obviously, the more you do get on the air, the more adept you should become, but there are better ways to sharpen your communications skills before trying them out in the cockpit.

For example, one of the first things I'd do is to invest in a relatively inexpensive receiver/scanner, if I were learning to fly or to begin operating in the more complex airspace environments. These small receive-only radios will let you listen in on communications between pilots and ground facilities such as the tower, Approach Control, Clearance Delivery, Military Operations Areas (MOAs) activity, and a host of other radio transmissions.

Just eavesdropping on these exchanges or transmissions is a learning experience in itself. You soon begin to get the feel of what should be said, the sequence and wording of pilot requests, position reports, responses to controller questions, and so on. You'll also begin to develop a listening ear which gives you general ideas of what you are likely to hear when a controller radios an instruction to you or responds to something you've said or asked. Once you have a feel for the probable sequence and basic contents of the various directives or responses, you'll find it much easier to understand what the controllers are saying.

A good receiver/scanner, such as Sporty's JD-100, with hundreds of civilian and military frequencies to monitor, will cost you something in the vicinity of $150 plus batteries and optional accessories. That's a small investment for a learning tool—especially a learning tool that's entertaining as well.

As you begin to grasp how the various radio communiques are structured and worded, that's the time to start practicing what *you* would say in the various situations you'll inevitably find yourself—situations such as a pretaxi call to Ground Control, a call to the tower requesting takeoff approval, calls to Departure or Approach Control prior to penetrating a Class B or Class C airspace, requests to a Center for flight following, and so on. If need be, write out what you would say in your own shorthand abbreviations, and then set up imaginary role-playing situations in which you are both the pilot and the controller. Base your dialogues on what you heard or may have taped. Even tape your own simulated calls to learn from miswordings, hesitations, mistakes, lack of logical information continuity, the clarity and volume of your voice, and how you would probably sound in a real-life situation.

These learning steps that will lead more rapidly to radio communicating proficiency are steps you can take on your own. In fact, you almost have to do it on your own because you're developing a very personal skill that is mastered primarily through practice. You don't become a good public speaker just by being told how to speak before groups of people. You learn the basics and then practice, practice, and practice some more. You don't learn how to land an airplane by reading a book or having an instructor sit in his or her office and tell you how to do it. No, first you learn the basics so that you mentally know what you should do. Then you go out and get the feel of the approach, the flare, the position of the nose, the crosswind corrections, the actual touchdown. You may porpoise down the runway a few times during those early landing attempts, but you'll soon begin to acquire that unteachable sense or feel of what to do, when to do it, and, subconsciously, how to do it.

I don't want to make more out of this radio communications issue than is warranted, but I can only say from personal knowledge that becoming an effective radio communicator is, for the vast majority of pilots, one of the most difficult aspects of learning to fly. Even among too many experienced pilots, the examples of radio misuse, nonuse, or overuse are myriad. The seriousness of the situation arises when pilots don't contact an ATC facility when they should—or when they don't make their intentions clear to ATC—or when they don't understand what a controller wants them to do—or when they take up precious air time rambling on about what they want—or when they pick up the microphone and start talking without listening first, to be sure the controller is not already talking with another pilot. When they do any of these things, and more, they are endangering their own safety and the safety of others.

Consequently, the primary reason for stressing the subject early in this book is that the air traffic control system demands the use of the radio. Without the radio, there would be no system—at least there would be no system as long as human beings have to pilot airplanes and human beings are responsible for tracking, advising, alerting, correcting, separating, sequencing, and generally serving their airborne customers. If for no other reason, the wise use of the radio by all pilots is essential.

So the comments here are intended to be sort of a foundation layer for the book. At the same time, I've attempted to imply that the air traffic control system is not a complicated maze of FAA-contrived regulations. Oh, there are a couple of areas where I think the FAA, by adhering to some of ICAO's international practices or terminologies, has needlessly confused things, but those are not very serious exceptions. Indeed, the system is rather straightforward and easily learned.

Despite that fact, however, there are still too many general aviation accidents and incidents that reflect pilot ignorance or disregard of the airspaces as well as of the published operating regulations. Either those pilots don't know the system and its rules, or, for whatever personal reasons, they willfully violate them. To illustrate the point, and perhaps to learn from it, brief synopses of 10 accidents or incidents are given in the next chapter. So, if you're interested, read on and perhaps gather a few ideas of what *not* to do from the experiences (often fatal) of others.

3
NTSB accident synopses: What went wrong and why?

As you could logically gather from its title, the heart of this book focuses on the word and meaning of *control,* especially the control exercised by the various FAA agencies and how it affects both IFR and VFR pilots. In this context, the word typically implies the involvement of the various air traffic controlling facilities, meaning the control tower, Ground Control, Approach Control, the Air Route Traffic Control Center, and the like. Through radar and radio, these facilities sequence, separate, direct, help, and advise airborne aircraft as well as those on the ground requiring taxiing assistance. The second and less common interpretation of *control* relates to the written FAA rules, regulations, and procedures with which pilots are expected to comply. Combined, and in the broadest sense, the two constitute the "external" air traffic control system, with the first being based on oral communications and the second on the written word.

At the same time, I think there is another element of control that should be surfaced for pilot consideration. That is the matter of pilot *self*-control and his or her acceptance of that external authority. Consequently, I offer a few preliminary words about the role of self-control in this "business" of flying.

SELF-CONTROL AND REGULATIONS AND PROCEDURES

These, again, are the rules, regulations, procedures, the dos and don'ts established by the FAA and its published Federal Aviation Regulations (FARs). The FARs are sort of the industry's bible, which, along with many other facets of aviation, govern airmen qualifications and certification, the airspaces, air traffic procedures, general operating rules, VFR and IFR operations, aircraft maintenance, air carrier operations, and so on. The FARs are thus the externally imposed rules and regulations that comprise many of the subjects on pilot written and oral examinations and by which all pilots must abide.

The existence of rules, however, whether in schools, businesses, the military, or society in general, always raises the issue of *self*-control and the extent to which I willingly conform to the applicable regulations some "authority" has imposed on me. When a positive self-control exists, it's really an internalized, perhaps subconscious, form of discipline that rejects any temptation to violate an externally imposed requirement, a few examples of which include never flying over a congested area below 1000 feet above ground level (AGL), not performing acrobatic maneuvers at altitudes lower than 1500 feet AGL, not obeying the VFR regulation to cruise at odd or even altitudes, based on compass direction, plus 500 feet, when flying above 3000 feet AGL, or not maintaining the cloud separation minimums of 500 feet below a cloud, 1000 feet above, 2000 feet vertically, and so on.

This refusal to violate is the standard of behavior, the self-control, the self-discipline, that *must* be part of a pilot's makeup. Except for a bona fide in-flight emergency situation where just about anything goes, lacking the self-control to follow the rules and do things right is, at the very least, inviting sanctions and disciplinary action by the FAA. At the extreme, the pilot can count on the reasonable possibility of an early funeral.

SELF-CONTROL AND PERSONAL HEALTH

This area of self-control obviously has a highly personal orientation. It's a matter of having the strength, the willpower to ensure one's day-to-day physical well-being, including careful control of alcohol and nonprescribed drugs. For pilots, avoidance of such substances is not just a matter of what the feds will do if you're found guilty of a substance abuse; it's the destructive effect of drugs or alcohol in a normal environment, to say nothing of what happens when they are mixed with altitude and lowered oxygen levels. When under the influence, if you haven't already done something crazy, the reduced level of oxygen (because of the lowered barometric pressure with altitude) will gradually produce a potentially dangerous devil-may-care euphoria. In a state of bravado with dulled senses of care and caution, who knows what you might try to do? Regardless of your physical condition, though, if you are exposed long enough to reduced oxygen at altitudes much above 12,000 feet MSL, hypoxia and mental confusion will develop. The worst-case scenario is hypoxia, followed by unconsciousness, and then death.

As a pilot, if you're aware of the effects that alcohol and prescribed or over-the-counter drugs can have on the system, do you have the self-control to avoid them entirely or, at the very least, for many hours or even days before you climb into a cockpit? Do you have the self-discipline to say no to yourself or to some "friend" who's urging you to have one more for the road before you head for the airport? If you don't have that level of self-control, please stay out of the air—if not for your own good, then for the good of all those who might be sharing the same airspace with you. Just as when you're behind the wheel of a car on an interstate or a city street, you're a menace to society.

AN INTRODUCTION TO THE CASE STUDIES

Having thus preached the self-control sermon, a word about the NTSB cases that follow is in order. As you'll see, almost every case reflects a lack of pilot self-discipline or self-control as far as adherence to the published FARs is concerned. In some instances, a marked absence of good judgment is an added ingredient in the accident-producing recipe.

Keep in mind that since these are only synopses of actual cases, more detailed background data were not always available. When they were, however, I incorporated in the case or in comments whatever information was pertinent about the pilot, the airport involved (if one was), weather conditions at the time, and the like.

The probable causes that follow each synopsis are those listed in the NTSB report, while the comments after the causes are basically, but not exclusively, my additions or opinions about what happened and why—the purpose being to raise issues that might not have been apparent in the synopsis or the statement of causes.

As you read these (most are relatively short), you might think about them in terms of your own personal experiences and of what lessons, if any, a given case illustrates. In other words, if you had been the pilot in the case, what would you have done? Or what would you have done to prevent this situation from developing in the first place? Or what mistakes did the pilot make that good judgment would have avoided?

But, should these cases not raise meaningful issues for you (and that's always a possibility), bring up NTSB on the internet (http://www.ntsb.gov), click on Aviation, then Accident Synopses, and finally "Select from monthly list of accidents." A month-by-month calendar from 1983 to the present will then appear. Once you start opening the many files, you'll find enough learning examples to keep you busy for many a TV-less evening.

THE CASE STUDIES: SYNOPSIS, CAUSES, COMMENTS

Case 1

Location: California
Date: 05/22/87
Aircraft: Cessna 206; T-38
Aircraft Damage: Both destroyed
Fatalities: 4

A U.S. Air Force T-38 aircraft and a Cessna 206 collided in midair during visual flight operations in a military operations area (MOA). Radar data indicated that the overtaking T-38 collided with the Cessna from the right. The Cessna was on a local government contract terrain photographic mission and had almost completed a left 360° turn. The T-38 was transiting the MOA in connection with a military mission. Both aircraft were operating under VFR and were not in contact with the MOA controllers. Neither pilot was required to establish or maintain positive radio or radar contact with the air traffic control facility responsible for the area. However, the *Aeronautical Information Manual* (*AIM*) states, "Pilots operating under VFR should exercise extreme caution while flying within a MOA…prior to entering an active MOA, pilots should contact the controlling agency for traffic advisories." Radar and radio assistance was available to either pilot. The T-38 was using a transponder with Mode C readout. The collision occurred at about 8700 feet MSL.

Probable cause(s)

Visual lookout inadequate—both pilots; procedures or directives not followed; communications not used; radar assistance to VFR aircraft not used.

Comments

Said another way, both pilots must have had their heads in the cockpit and not scanning the skies around them. Neither was in contact with a traffic controlling facility in a frequently busy military airspace. This was apparently a simple but tragic example of inattention in flight, lack of radio communications, and failure to establish contact with the responsible ATC facility.

Case 2

Date: 08/31/86
Location: Cerritos, California, Los Angeles International Airport
Aircraft: Piper PA-28; McDonnell-Douglas DC-9
Aircraft Damage: Both destroyed
Fatalities: 82 **Injuries:** 8

At 1140 PDT, a Piper PA-28 departed Torrance, California, on a VFR trip to Big Bear, California. After takeoff, the pilot turned east toward the Paradise VORTAC with his transponder squawking 1200. At that time, Aeromexico Flight 498 was on arrival, receiving northbound vectors from LAX Approach Control for an ILS approach to the LAX International Airport. At 1151:04, the controller asked Flight 498 to reduce speed to 190 knots and to descend from 7000 to 6000 feet. During this time, the controller was handling other traffic and providing radar advisories but didn't see a display for the PA-28 on his scope. At 1152:09, the Piper and Flight 498 converged and collided at approximately 6560 feet, then fell to the ground. An investigation revealed the PA-28 had inadvertently entered the LAX Terminal Control Area (a Class B airspace, but called a *TCA* in those days) and wasn't in radio contact with ATC. And LAX TRACON (Terminal Radar Approach Control) wasn't equipped with an automatic conflict alert system, and the analog beacon responder from the Piper's transponder wasn't displayed due to equipment configuration. The Piper's position was displayed by an alphanumeric triangle, but the primary target wasn't displayed due to atmospheric inversion.

Probable cause(s)

The principal causes included inadequate visual lookout, both pilots; no identification of aircraft on radar; procedures or directives not followed by the PA-28 pilot; inadequate FAA procedures.

Comments

Several factors contributed to this accident, but the one that started it all was the PA-28's violation of the LAX Class B airspace (TCA), later compounded by lack of radio contact with LAX Approach Control, followed by transponder equipment difficulties, and finally the fact that neither pilot saw the other aircraft—or at least not in time to take evasive action. This was a tragic and unnecessary accident that gave birth to stricter equipment and operating requirements relative to the then-TCAs and today's Class B airspaces. Think about it, though: Could it have all been avoided if those in both cockpits had been more alert to what was going on in the immediate world outside them?

Case 3

Location: Grand Canyon, Arizona
Date: 10/05/96
Aircraft: Cessna 172RG
Aircraft Damage: Destroyed
Fatalities: 4

The recently certified private pilot (he had logged 141 hours) ordered the aircraft to be fueled to capacity, which resulted in its being about 90 pounds over its maximum certificated gross takeoff weight. The Grand Canyon airport elevation is 6606 feet above sea level, but at his departure time, the density altitude was 8100 feet. The aircraft took off from the mountain airport and climbed toward gradually rising terrain. In response to a concerned call from the tower, the pilot stated that he was unable to climb and might have to land on a road. The pilot of another aircraft observed the Cessna flying approximately 5 miles at treetop level with the wings rocking and that it was in a nose-high attitude before impacting treetops and crashing. The aircraft had climbed approximately 400 feet from the runway to the accident site. No evidence of a mechanical discrepancy was found.

Probable cause(s)

Inadequate preflight preparation, resulting in inability to outclimb rising and wooded terrain; failure of the pilot to ensure that the aircraft's gross takeoff weight was not exceeded; high-density altitude takeoff conditions; the pilot's lack of experience in high-density altitude operations.

Comments

Watch out for hot days at any airport, but especially when taking off or landing at airports in mountainous areas where the air is naturally thinner than at sea level or lower altitudes.

Then add heat to the mixture, and you increase even more the thinness of the air, resulting in decreased engine and propeller efficiency and lift. Under such conditions, exceeding the maximum gross takeoff weight produces a most dangerous operating formula.

Case 4

Location: Oregon
Date: 05/24/97
Aircraft: Piper PA-32-301T
Aircraft Damage: Destroyed
Fatalities: 2

The last radio communications from the pilot indicated that they were in instrument meteorological conditions (IMC), experiencing updrafts and picking up ice on the structure. Widely scattered thunderstorms and rain were reported in the area. Light to occasional moderate rime ice and mixed icing in the precipitation were reported from the freezing level to 12,000 feet. Moderate turbulence was reported for the entire state. Witnesses reported that a "pretty nasty-looking cloud" with the sounds of thunder was in the area when they heard a sound similar to a sonic boom. After this sound, the aircraft's engine was no longer heard. Evidence at the accident site indicated that the aircraft broke up in flight. The left wing separated at the root, the right wing separated about 109 inches from the root. Both the horizontal stabilizer and the vertical stabilizer separated from the empennage. Metallurgical examination of the fractured components was typical of overstressed separations. Both the wings and the horizontal stabilizer failed in a downward loading condition.

Probable cause(s)

Overload of the airframe structure. Thunderstorm and turbulence were factors.

Comments

On the surface, this is a difficult accident to explain, in part because both the pilot and her passenger held private pilot certificates for single-engine-land aircraft and both were instrument-rated. The pilot-in-command had accumulated about 660 hours in "all make and model" of aircraft and approximately 220 hours in the accident aircraft, while her pilot-rated passenger had 892 hours and 220 hours in the same accident aircraft. The results of all postmortem medical and pathological examinations proved negative. Although the weather was not good throughout the area, the reported meteorological information cited in the NTSB summary did not indicate the likelihood of the severe weather that the aircraft encountered in the area. The pilot had filed an instrument flight plan, however, for her cross-country flight to Redmond, Oregon, and first initiated contact with Seattle Center at 1106. Between 1133 and 1218, nine dialogues took place in efforts to assist the pilot in response to her requests for various altitude and heading changes. After 1219, there was no further word from the pilot. The plane crashed at approximately 1220 Pacific daylight time. From the written materials available, it would appear that the Center personnel did everything possible to accommodate the pilot and help guide her to a safe landing.

With the given weather conditions, this would appear to be one of those situations in which qualified pilots found themselves and from which escape was impossible. Fighting the combination of icing and turbulence, the pilot may have become disoriented and lost control of the aircraft; or the turbulence could have reached the level of severity that caused the aircraft to break up in the air. Wreckage and impact information leaves no question about a breakup, as one wing was found about 800 feet from the fuselage, other parts 300 to 500 feet from the crash site, and wreckage scattered over an area of 1400 feet by 800 feet. Furthermore, metallurgist reports stated that the various fractures were typical of overstress separations.

With their combined experience, it isn't logical that the pilots would have intentionally flown into weather as extreme as what they encountered. Something to remember, though: Embedded thunderstorms are not always easy to spot, and venturing into one of these storms could be an experience full of unpleasant surprises. Also, hail, turbulence, and strong winds are not necessarily confined just to the immediate area of a thunderstorm itself, but can be experienced 20 or 30 miles from the storm. The moral, then, is to keep lots of distance between you and any of those black and threatening creatures of nature. Go around, go back, but don't go through. You'll never regret the few extra miles or minutes that storm-avoidance deviations might cost you!

Case 5

Date: 08/31/86
Location: New Jersey
Aircraft: Cessna 152
Aircraft Damage: Destroyed
Fatalities: 1

The student pilot, on a supervised solo cross-country trip, diverted from his planned route and was observed flying low over a residential area, performing maneuvers at or below treetop levels. The pilot apparently lost control of the aircraft. The aircraft impacted the ground in a nose-down attitude. The pilot received fatal injuries.

Probable causes

Intentional buzzing, violations of Federal Aviation Regulations (FARs), disregard of written and/or verbal instructions, loss of control of aircraft.

Comments

All causes listed in the NTSB findings relate directly to things the pilot in command did or didn't do. This is unfortunately a not-uncommon example of what too many beginning pilots tend to do after they have soloed or have a few hours in their logbooks. They can't resist the tendency to buzz the old neighborhood or the girl friend's house to show off their newly acquired piloting "skills." Dumb as that is, doing so also violates FARs about flights over populated areas and minimum altitudes for so-called aerobatics. Even if this type of pilot survives the buzzing experience, he or she may well face the disciplinary action of the FAA. Smart pilots don't do dumb things—and buzzing can be *very* dumb.

Case 6

Date: 02/03/97
Location: Oklahoma
Aircraft: Piper PA-28-200
Aircraft Damage: Destroyed
Fatalities: 3

The pilot met his two passengers at an airport where he purchased 10 gallons of fuel. The airport attendant estimated that there was about 1 inch of fuel in each wing tank before he added 5 gallons to each tank. The pilot commented to the attendant, "Let me see if I can't scare the guys to death." Witnesses observed the airplane flying over a lodge area. They said the plane was "tilting at 90° angle on its wings." Also they reported the airplane went "inverted" and then nosed down and disappeared from view. It then crashed in a lake and was destroyed by impact. One witness stated that "the motor was making a noise, as if it was getting gas and then not getting gas." Another witness observed the airplane earlier that day doing "tricks and stunts." The airplane was restricted from inverted flight and was not approved for aerobatic maneuvers. During examination of the wreckage, flight control continuity was established, and no anomalies were found that would have resulted in a loss of power. Toxicology tests of the pilot's blood showed 0.008 microgram per milliliter (μg/mL) tetrahydrocannabinol (marijuana), 0.014 μg/mL tetrahydrocannabinol carboxylic acid (metabolite of marijuana), and 0.052 μg/mL alprazolam (similar to Valium, a minor tranquilizer). Tests of his urine showed 0.695 μg/mL tetrahydrocannabinol carboxylic acid (metabolite of marijuana), 0.071 μg/mL dihydrocodeine (derivative of codeine), 0.155 μg/mL hydrocodone (derivative of codeine), 0.338 μg/mL hydromorphone (derivative of morphine), 4.8 μg/mL acetaminophen (Tylenol), and an undetermined amount of alprazolam and alpha-hydroxalprazolam (tranquilizers). According to the FAA's southwest regional flight surgeon, "the combined effects of these drugs could have caused impairment in the cockpit."

Probable cause(s)

The pilot's impairment of judgment and performance due to drugs, his resultant improper planning and decision, and his failure to maintain sufficient altitude (clearance above a lake) while performing acrobatic flight. Factors relating to the accident were the pilot's use of an aircraft that was not certified for aerobatic flight and possible distraction (diverted attention) when the engine momentarily lost power due to fuel starvation during inverted flight.

Comments

The NTSB summary, quoted almost verbatim above, provides little personal data about the pilot. A separate narrative report on the accident, however, states that he had a private pilot certificate, obtained in 1995, and a total of approximately 350 hours. Earlier in 1995, still as a student at the Spartan School of Aeronautics, he videotaped aerobatic maneuvers he performed during a solo training flight and gave the tape to his flight instructor, telling the instructor he thought the instructor would be interested in it. The school convened a board of inquiry to review the incident, and on July 17, 1995, the pilot was put on academic probation. In January 1996, he was observed performing acrobatic maneuvers in a Cessna 152. The FAA suspended his certificate for 90 days for performing acrobatic maneuvers contrary to the operating limitations specified in the aircraft's flight manual and for performing acrobatic flight within 4 nautical miles of a federal airway's centerline.

His flying history suggests a pattern of irresponsibility and lack of judgment. This, coupled with the fact that he consumed the drugs found in his blood and urine, was bad enough, but then to try to fly when under the influence of marijuana, codeine, and morphine made almost certain the tragic ending of this brief flight. Distorted awareness and bravado ("Let me see if I can't scare the guys to death") won out over any semblance of good sense, and if the "guys" weren't already scared to death, the eventual plunge into the lake achieved the pilot's ultimate "objective."

The distorting effect of drugs and alcohol, individually or in combination, is drastic enough when one is driving a car. In the relatively rarefied atmosphere of flight, the distortion is even more dramatic and debilitating. If you tend to use alcohol or drugs, that's your business, but don't mix either with flying. You're playing with your life, the lives of any others with you, and the lives of innocent people on the ground who fall victim to an out-of-control aircraft. Also, the FAA comes down *very* hard on violators of its substance abuse regulations. To show how far it goes, if you're convicted of driving a car under the influence, you *must* report the violation to the FAA Civil Aviation Security Division in Oklahoma City not later than 60 days after the motor vehicle action [FAR 61.15(e)]. What the FAA then decides may be harmful to your flying aspirations. Intelligence and good judgment say, Lay off the stuff. Be smart and don't disregard what that small inner voice of reason tells you—or should be telling you.

Case 7

Date: 08/31/86
Location: Kansas
Aircraft: Piper PA-28-140
Aircraft Damage: Destroyed
Fatality: 1

The student pilot intended to fly from his home airport to a nearby airport where he was receiving flight instruction. No record of a weather briefing was found. Local authorities said there were low clouds and fog in the area at the time of the accident. No one saw the aircraft take off, but the pilot was seen in a local restaurant a short time before the accident. The aircraft crashed on the municipal golf course about 100 feet from two residences. An occupant of one of the residences saw the aircraft crash and said it was descending nearly vertical just before impact. He also said the engine noise increased just before impact.

Probable cause(s)

Preflight planning and preparation inadequate; lack of instrument time; VFR flight into IMC weather; airplane control not maintained; spatial disorientation. All causes are directly attributable to the pilot in command.

Comments

There's not much more to say about this case. Disregarding VFR weather minimum regulations, the noninstrument pilot lost control of his airplane once low ceilings and fog obscured any reference to the ground. Until you have that instrument ticket, don't lose sight of the ground and don't get caught on top of an overcast (you're going to have to come down through it, which is both illegal and dangerous).

Case 8

Date: 09/07/95
Location: Midland, Texas
Aircraft: Grumman American AA-5A
Aircraft Damage: Destroyed
Fatalities: 2

The recently certified pilot received his private pilot certificate on August 8, 1995, and had only 8 hours of flying time in the accident aircraft. Nonetheless, he and the passenger/owner of the airplane were en route to Alaska on a 3-week hunting and fishing trip. After topping off at their first fueling stop at the Midland, Texas, Airpark, the pilot taxied to runway 29[*(290°). This synopsis heading has to be in error. The comparable runways at Midland Airpark are 25 (250°) and 7 (70°).*] and held while another plane landed into the wind on runway 7. The Grumman plane took off on runway 29 (?) with an 18-knot tailwind, gusting to 24 knots. After a "long" takeoff run, as the airplane came within 500 feet of the departure end of the 4380-foot runway, a "very steep" angle of climb was established and the airplane cleared the ground. After clearing commercial buildings off the airport, the pilot lost control of the airplane and impacted a single-story residence. The winds were reported from 070 degrees at 18 knots, gusting to 24 knots, the temperature 92°F, and the density altitude was calculated as 5300 feet. (The Midland Airpark field elevation is 2802 feet MSL.) At the time of takeoff, the airplane was calculated to be 118 pounds over its maximum gross weight.

Probable cause(s)

The pilot's selection of a downwind runway for takeoff. Contributing factors were the tailwind, the density altitude, and the overloading of the airplane.

Comments

Yes, the principal cause was the downwind takeoff, but what prompted that takeoff decision? Didn't the pilot know the wind direction and its velocity? If not, why not? Didn't he understand the effect a downwind takeoff would have on lift and takeoff run? Was he aware that the density altitude was equivalent to that of an airport at 5300 feet? Or did he know these things but disregard them in an aura of personal invincibility? Also, did he consider the risks to which he was exposing other aircraft that might have been on or turning to the final approach for landing, as he flew directly toward them in his futile effort to get airborne? Finally, did he know the aircraft was 118 pounds over its maximum gross weight? If he did, he was taking a chance, even if he had taken off into the wind. One other question: Did he even know how to compute the weight and balance of the aircraft? These are unanswered but inevitable questions when one sees or reads about such unnecessary accidents and lost lives.

Case 9

Date: 02/01/97
Location: Alaska
Aircraft: Piper PA-22
Aircraft Damage: Destroyed
Fatalities: 3

The non-instrument-rated private pilot received a weather briefing from the Kenai Flight Service Station at 1113 on February 1, 1997, for a flight from Port Alsworth to Anchorage's Merrill Field. At the same time, he also filed a VFR flight plan for a 1200 departure, with an en route time of 2½ hours to his destination and 3 hours of fuel on board. The weather briefing indicated low fog and stratus clouds over Cook Inlet and the Kenai Peninsula, with pockets of IFR conditions. The forecast was for improving weather, with VFR conditions along the route of flight after 1200. The pilot and his two family member passengers took off at 1200, as scheduled.

At about 1350, the pilot was on top of an overcast at 10,000 feet MSL and contacted the Anchorage Approach Control facility for assistance in determining his position. He told the controller that he thought he was a few miles from Anchorage, but with the help of Approach controllers and Flight Service Station specialists, at 1415 his position was determined to be about 124 miles northwest of Anchorage. Meanwhile, the pilot had said that his only electronic navigation instrument aboard, a loran, was not reliable and that there was a large disparity between the readings of his wet (magnetic) compass and his directional gyro. At 1413 the controller asked if he could see the ground at all, to which the pilot responded, "Ah no, that's a negative." At 1414, he added, "I can't see anything now. I'm not exactly sure where we are, but we need to do something quick." A minute later he said he was at 10,100 feet at the cloud tops and going through some "right now." When a Flight Service Station specialist offered a heading to the west side of the Alaska range near McGrath, where there were VFR conditions, the pilot said he didn't have enough fuel to fly over the range.

Radio contact was lost at 1424. At 1521, an emergency locator transmitter (ELT) was received from the accident airplane. Rescue workers, however, couldn't reach the site until February 5. The airplane was discovered crashed in a near-vertical position on a glacier. Postaccident inspection disclosed no mechanical anomalies with the airplane and a functional loran. About 5 to 6 gallons of fuel was remaining in the wing fuel tank.

Probable cause(s)

The pilot's continued VFR flight into instrument meteorological conditions and subsequent failure to maintain control of the airplane. Factors associated with the accident are the pilot's inadequate weather evaluation, his becoming lost or disoriented, and spatial disorientation.

Comments

What else is there to say? Even with a preflight weather briefing, the pilot got caught above the overcast, was lost and low on fuel, and then became totally disoriented as he flew into IFR conditions—conditions with which he was unable to cope. When he saw the overcast ahead of him, instead of trying to climb above it to maintain VFR, why didn't he turn 180° and get out of there, especially when he had to keep going ever higher to stay out of the overcast? We'll never know the answers to many such questions, but this is just another case with at least a couple of meaningful messages: For one, until you're IFR-qualified, *never* allow yourself to get caught above an overcast. You might have to come down through it, and that could spell much trouble. Another message: Centers, Approach Controls, and Flight Service Stations are there to help you, but their potential services are greatly limited if your fuel gauge needles are bouncing on empty when you first contact them. *Don't* wait until you're really in trouble before you call one of the facilities. By then, it may be too late.

As for the pilot himself, he was 27 years old and held a private pilot certificate with an airplane single-engine-land-rating. His pilot and medical certificates indicated he was prohibited from night flying. It is estimated that his total time was approximately 120 hours. An autopsy simply noted that cause of death was "blunt impact injuries."

Case 10

This case is not from the NTSB records but appeared in an issue of *Flyer,* a biweekly newspaper published in Tacoma, Washington. It has a happier ending than the others, but as it is still in the various hearing stages, I'm omitting all names, aircraft N numbers, and potentially identifying data. I've also capsulized the *Flyer* article in the interests of space and brevity.

The incident began at 9:30 in the morning when a non-instrument-rated pilot of a Bonanza A-35 requested flight following from a Center while over the Sierra mountains. All seemed routine until the pilot climbed without approval to 20,000 feet to get above the clouds that were building up ahead of him. As the *Flyer* article stated, the controller contacted the Bonanza and learned that the pilot (1) was not instrument-qualified and (2) had no oxygen on board.

Seeing the potential of a problem on the horizon, another controller, who was also an instrument-rated commercial pilot, took over the controlling responsibilities. As he did, other Center personnel tried to find breaks in the overcast through which the Bonanza might descend. With no autopilot on board, those involved in the efforts to help feared that the VFR-only pilot would lose control of the plane if he had to descend through a thick overcast. There were no breaks, though, and after about an hour in the rarefied 20,000-foot altitude, the pilot's speech was becoming slurred because of hypoxia (the lack of oxygen). And, of course, with hypoxia, judgment, problem-solving abilities, and normal motor skills begin to fail. Then, unless followed by counteraction of some nature, unconsciousness and ultimately death are inevitable. With the first hypoxia symptoms showing, it was clear to the controllers that the Bonanza would have to start down through the overcast—now.

After turning him toward the airport, the instrument-rated controller began a continuous communication with the pilot, directing him to reduce power, keep his wings level, and begin a descent to 12,000 feet. Taking him through the overcast, the pilot descended until he broke into the clear at 14,500 feet. The drama, intense for several minutes, was over.

Shortly afterward, the Bonanza landed safely, with the pilot left with nothing more than a headache for his time in the relatively rarefied atmosphere. Following engine shutdown, he phoned the Center to express his appreciation for the help the controllers gave him.

The *Flyer* article closes with this paragraph: "How long those good feelings for the FAA will last is unknown. An FAA spokesman said the pilot is now under investigation and possibly facing sanctions for departing an assigned altitude without ATC clearance and for operating at altitude without supplemental oxygen."

Comments

The case speaks for itself. Apart from the sanctions for the violations cited, other questions might be asked: Did the pilot contact a Flight Service Station for a preflight briefing? Was he aware of the cloud cover, its floor, its ceiling, and the conditions within the overcast, such as icing, turbulence, rain, lightning? Did he file a flight plan? Why did he allow himself to get caught on top of the cloud cover? Why didn't he make a 180° turn and get back to where the weather had been clear?

These several questions should be answered. At the same time, though, the Center controllers deserve hearty kudos for what they did to escort the pilot through a 6000-foot overcast into clear air and an eventual incident-free landing. This is one example of what ATC can do for you when you get into trouble and of why VFR pilots should learn to use and then take advantage of the FAA services at their disposal. It does seem fair to mention, though, that this pilot, with no instrument rating, had to have done a good job to descend safely through almost 6000 feet of overcast. Not many untrained instrument pilots would have been as fortunate, as skilled, or perhaps as lucky.

If you read the history of most aircraft accidents, one fact will probably hit you: It's a rare accident that is caused simply and solely by a mechanical failure which the pilot could not anticipate or take action to prevent. It's rare that a well-maintained, properly serviced engine just up and quits, and it's even rarer that a plane crashes because some part of the airframe failed or broke off. Yes, engines do quit and airframe failures have happened; but more than anything, accidents, fatal or otherwise, serious or minor, are mostly the result of pilots doing something they shouldn't or not doing something they should. It's almost that simple. The best air traffic control system and the most complete list of regulations will never make aviation accident-free. They will go a long way in that direction, but nothing will replace the pilot's exercise of good judgment and self-control as she or he operates within the overall system.

This leads us now to an overview of the ATC system, followed by a more detailed look at the various functions within the system that make it so effective.

4
The ATC system: An overview

AS I SAID IN CHAPTER 2, MANY NON-INSTRUMENT-RATED PILOTS SHY away from using some of the ATC facilities available to them for any number of reasons, perhaps the primary one being a plain lack of knowledge about the overall system and how it functions. This being the case, let's begin to attack it right now with a broad-brush simulation of a cross-country flight. This will be just an introduction to the principal facilities with which you would typically communicate or monitor, but it will include those you *must* contact, those you *should* contact, and the sequence in which the communications should be established. As such, it will hopefully give those unfamiliar with the air traffic system a feeling for what it is and the roles its various facilities play.

A SIMULATED FLIGHT AND THE ATC CONTACTS

To set the scene:

- The flight will be nonstop from the Kansas City Downtown Airport to the Memphis, Tennessee, International Airport, via the Victor 159 Airway, which runs generally southeast/northwest over Springfield, Missouri, and Walnut Ridge, Arkansas.

- You're going to file a flight plan with the Columbia, Missouri, Flight Service Station (FSS) that serves Kansas City, and close it on arrival with the Jackson, Tennessee, AFSS, serving Memphis. (I should note here that Flight Service Stations are a part of the air traffic system but do not control traffic in any respect, at any time.)
- Kansas City Downtown Airport lies under, not in, the Kansas City Class B airspace. The floor of the Class B airspace is 3000 feet over the airport and 5000 feet a few miles to the south.
- Kansas City Departure Control is located in the Kansas City International Airport tower, 15 miles northwest of Downtown Airport.
- You intend to request en route VFR traffic advisories from the Kansas City Air Route Traffic Control Center and Memphis Center.
- Memphis International is in a Class B airspace, which means that radar contact with Memphis Approach Control and specific radio clearance into the airspace is mandatory.
- As the Downtown Airport and Memphis International are both under or in Class B airspaces, all aircraft operating within 30 nautical miles of the primary airports must be equipped with altitude-reporting transponders (Mode C). The transponder must be on, and the switch must be in the ALT (altitude) position.

Filing the flight plan

The first facility to contact is the Columbia FSS for a weather briefing. Unless you happen to be at an airport that has a Flight Service Station (FSS) on the property, or have computer access to a briefing service, obtaining the weather briefing is done by telephone. For the most complete briefing, the FAA recommends a certain sequence of initial information to give to the specialist. The sequence is summarized in the Flight Service Station chapter.

Satisfied that the weather is no problem, you give the briefer the balance of the information necessary to enter the flight plan. All done through a computer, the flight plan is then stored in the FSS until you radio the facility just before takeoff and ask that the flight plan be opened.

Pretakeoff: Automatic Terminal Information Service

You've completed the preflight check and started the engine. What's next?

With radios on and the transponder in the Stand By (SBY) position (warming up), the first job is to tune in the frequency for the *Automatic Terminal Information Service* (ATIS). The ATIS is a locally recorded message, updated hourly, that provides in sequence the following local airport information:

- Airport name
- Information code (phonetic alphabet: Alpha, Bravo, Charlie, and so forth) of the current report

- UTC time (24-hour coordinated universal time) of weather observations, such as "1355 Zulu weather"
- Sky conditions
- Visibility
- Temperature and dew point
- Altimeter setting
- Instrument approach in use
- Current runway(s) in use
- Information code repeated (phonetic alphabet)

Additional information might be included, such as reports of severe weather, Notices to Airmen (NOTAMs), warnings of construction work near the runway (obstructions, such as cranes), or other conditions of concern to the pilot. The fact that you have monitored the current ATIS must be communicated to Ground Control before you taxi out and in the initial contact with the tower or Approach Control when you land.

Pretakeoff: Clearance Delivery

At those airports where the service is provided, your initial call should go to Clearance Delivery (CD) on its published frequency. After you advise CD of your location on the airport, the fact that you have the current ATIS report, that you're operating VFR, your destination, and intended cruising altitude, CD will coordinate that information with the local tower and, if applicable, with Departure Control. Once the coordination has been completed, CD will call back to confirm your clearance into the Class B or C airspace, the altitude(s) to fly in the airspace, the Departure Control frequency to use, and the transponder code to enter in your transponder.

These are brief radio exchanges, but this preliminary service to VFR as well as IFR operations saves radio communicating time and expedites departures from the busy Class B and C airport environments.

Pretakeoff: Ground Control

If Clearance Delivery, as such, does not exist at the departure airport, Ground Control (GC) may well provide the same service. At any rate, GC represents the next or, if there is no CD, your first radio contact with ATC.

The ground controller operates from the tower itself and is responsible for directing all aircraft and ground equipment movements on the taxiways or when crossing active runways. If you're just shuttling your plane around the ramp, you can do that all day long without anyone's permission. Before your wheels touch a taxi strip, however, you must contact Ground Control for clearance to proceed.

The departure call to Ground Control is usually very brief. Basically, after establishing contact with Ground Control, you simply give your aircraft type and N number; where you are on the airport; that you have Alpha, Bravo, or whatever the current ATIS information happens to be; and that you have received clearance from Clearance Delivery. GC will then authorize you to taxi to the active runway.

Even though cleared to taxi out, it's important to stay tuned to the GC frequency. You're still under the controller's jurisdiction and will be until you are at the runway hold line and ready to contact the tower. In a word, Ground Control is to be monitored from the ramp until at the runway hold line, prior to contacting the tower, and after landing, from a point past the hold line to the ramp. Them's the rules.

Pretakeoff: Flight Service Station

You've taxied to the run-up area, completed the pretakeoff checks, and are ready to go. First, though, it's time to open the flight plan. This involves a change to one of the published FSS frequencies, and the call is both simple and brief. One thing to keep in mind, though: The call is addressed to "——Radio," not "——Flight Service." *Radio* is the standard term for all radio communications with any FSS. The one exception arises when you want to contact an FSS flight watch specialist for a weather update while in flight. That call is addressed to "——Flight Watch."

Something else is important: Include in this and all other FSS radio calls the frequency you're calling on and, if different, the frequency you're receiving on, as well as your location. In the automated FSSs, the in-flight specialist staffing the radio might have up to 48 frequencies to monitor, with certain frequencies duplicated. Unless you announce which frequency you're on and where you are, the specialist might find it impossible to respond (more on this in Chapter 10).

With the flight plan opened, taxi to the hold line.

Control tower

At the hold line—and not before—change frequencies and contact the tower for takeoff clearance. Include in the call the intended direction of flight. Just don't make this call when you're back in the run-up area, maybe 100 feet away. You're not ready to go that far from the runway. Get up to the yellow hold line so that when the tower clears you, you're in a position to move without delay.

Prior to the beginning of the takeoff roll, change the transponder from the SBY position to ON or ALT. The latter puts the unit in the altitude-reporting mode (a Mode C transponder). There's no choice. FAA regulations say that if the aircraft is transponder-equipped, the set must be turned to the ON or ALT position. And from here on, like it or not, when you're within radar range of any controlling agency, an image representing your aircraft will be on the radar screen.

Airborne: Departure Control

Since this is a Class D airport underlying a Class B airspace, the next service, if you want it as a VFR pilot and had not requested same from the tower before takeoff, involves traffic advisories from Kansas City Departure Control. Assuming that you do want the service, when airborne and in an established climb, ask the tower to approve a frequency change. The controller might tell you, "Stay with me for a while," if the local traffic in the vicinity is heavy; but otherwise, he'll come back with, "Frequency change approved."

When you hear that, switch to the Departure Control frequency; establish contact; identify yourself, your present heading, and destination; and request traffic advisories. If the controller's workload permits, perhaps he'll give you altitude or heading directions and advise you of other traffic in your line of flight. Regardless of what you're told or not told, your continuing responsibility is simple: Keep your head out of the cockpit, watch for other traffic, listen, acknowledge advisories or instructions, and do what the controller says.

In a short while, Departure will tell you that you're leaving the Class B airspace, and he might or might not turn you over to the Kansas City Center for flight following. A *handoff,* as it is called, however, is not an automatic procedure; the controller may simply tell you, "Radar service terminated. Squawk one two zero zero. Frequency change approved. Resume own navigation."

Airborne: Air Route Traffic Control Center (ARTCC, or Center)

Because you do want flight following, your first responsibility, after tuning to the Center frequency, is to *listen* to be sure the air is clear before you make the initial radio contact. If it is clear, merely address the call to such and such Center and give your aircraft and N number. No more "Kansas City Center, Cherokee 1234 Alpha." After Center has responded, give your present position, altitude, destination, the numerical code in your transponder, such as "1-2-0-0," and your request for flight following. The Center controller, if his or her workload permits, will give you a different code to enter in the transponder, after which the controller will respond, "Radar contact."

Once you hear that, your progress will be monitored by a facility, which, in the case of Kansas City, is physically located in Olathe, Kansas, about 25 miles southwest of the Downtown Airport. This is one of 21 Centers in the contiguous United States. Each Center is responsible for the control of IFR traffic over its assigned area and, when conditions permit, provides traffic advisories to VFR aircraft.

As you move down the airway toward Springfield, along with some possible advisories of traffic, the controller tells you to "Contact Kansas City Center on—— frequency." This means that you're leaving that controller's sector of responsibility and are being turned over to another controller, perhaps sitting only a few feet away, who will be monitoring your progress in his or her sector and on a different frequency. All you do now is to acknowledge the instruction, repeat back the new frequency (to be sure you've copied it correctly), enter it in the radio, and contact the new controller: "Kansas City Center, Cherokee Eight Five One Five November with you. Level at seven thousand five hundred."

As you near Springfield, Center will tell you to contact Springfield Approach Control on a certain frequency. Why Springfield? You're not going to land there. No, but you'll be passing through the airspace for which that Approach Control is responsible and will thus be under the facility's surveillance. Once you are out of that airspace, Springfield will probably turn you over to Center again, assuming Center's workload in that sector will be able to handle you.

Depending upon the length of the flight, this process of transfer could happen several times, until, in the example we're using, you get about 50 miles southeast of Springfield. At that point, Kansas City will come on the air and tell you to contact Memphis Center on a certain frequency. You're now in Memphis' territory, and future advisories will come from them.

Regardless of the Center, you might hear at any time something like this: "Cherokee Eight Five One Five November, traffic at one o'clock, three miles, also southeast, altitude unknown." The controller has spotted another aircraft on the screen at your one o'clock position and is alerting you to its presence. First acknowledge that you've received the call, and if you see the aircraft, tell the controller. "Roger, Center, Cherokee One Five November has traffic." If you haven't spotted it, the response goes, "Roger, Center, Cherokee One Five November no contact. Looking." If you sight the traffic in a minute or so, advise the controller: "Cherokee One Five November has traffic." Controllers appreciate that information.

Airborne: Memphis ATIS

About 40 or so miles out of Memphis, tune to the Memphis ATIS for the latest weather information and the runway(s) in use. Knowing the active runway this far out gives you time to visualize and plan the probable traffic pattern you'll fly.

Airborne: Approach Control

About 30 miles out, Center turns you over to Memphis Approach Control for vectors (headings) and advisories into the Class B airspace surrounding the airport. Remember that you *must* contact Approach before entering any Class B airspace, whether you've been in contact with Center or not, and you *must* receive specific clearance into it. Once entrance is approved, if you're unfamiliar with the location of an airport, don't be afraid to tell Approach. The controller will give you the vectors that will lead you straight to it.

Airborne: Control Tower

Finally, when you are within a few miles of the airport, Approach tells you to contact Memphis International Tower on a certain frequency. This is the last lap as the tower sequences you into the traffic pattern and gives the clearance to land.

Postlanding: Ground Control

Once you are on the ground and clear of the runway, the next call is to Ground Control for taxi clearance to whatever location or fixed-base operator you've selected. In real-life situations, if you're not sure where to go or how to get there, ask Ground Control for progressive taxi instructions.

Postlanding: Flight Service Station

When you are parked at the ramp, the final radio call is to Jackson Flight Service to close out the flight plan. You can do this by dialing 1-800-WXBRIEF in the operator's facility;

but it's a good idea to make the call as soon as you've shut down the engine. It's an easy call to forget, and if you do forget, the FSS will start looking for you 30 minutes after your estimated arrival. A needless search does not make for happy authorities.

In that same vein, if you find in a real-life situation that headwinds or other factors are slowing you down and that you're going to miss your estimated time of arrival (ETA), contact the nearest FSS in flight and revise the ETA. Or perhaps a favorable tailwind is pushing you along faster than expected, and you determine that you've got enough fuel to reach another airport farther down the airway. The same principle applies. Radio the nearest FSS; advise it of the destination change, your new ETA, and the hours of fuel remaining.

In a word, don't keep Flight Service in the dark if you've filed a flight plan. Search procedures will be started unless those folks know what's going on.

By way of summary

In sequence, the 14 FAA service and controlling facilities involved in this example are

- Flight Service (telephone)
- ATIS
- Ground Control
- Flight Service
- Tower
- Departure Control
- Kansas City Center
- Springfield Approach
- Memphis Center
- ATIS
- Approach Control
- Tower
- Ground Control
- Flight Service

With an absolute minimum of one telephone call and 13 radio-frequency changes, you might get the impression that you have been a little busy. Were they all mandatory? No. Going VFR, you are required to listen to the Kansas City ATIS, contact Ground Control and the tower, monitor the Memphis ATIS, contact Memphis Approach (because Memphis is in a Class B airspace), Memphis tower, and Memphis Ground Control. Otherwise, filing a flight plan and requesting traffic advisories from Departure (when below the floor of a Class B airspace) and the two Centers is your choice.

If you do request advisory services, keep in mind that the ATC system will be tracking you, as in this simulated flight, across 300+ miles of geography. Somebody will know who you are and where you are at all times. Changing radio frequencies and listening for your aircraft N number are small prices to pay for the added security the system can offer the VFR pilot, when, of course, its workload permits it to handle VFR traffic in addition to IFR operations. Nothing will happen, though, until you pick up the mike and make the first call.

The objective for the preceding scenario is merely to introduce the basic elements of the airspace system and the various FAA agencies that would or could enter the picture on a typical VFR cross-country trip. It is a sketchy overview, but greater thoroughness is reserved for the next chapters and what goes on behind the scenes as we file flight plans, get advisories, and the rest.

What I've outlined, however, is part of the National Airspace System (NAS), which includes operations in controlled as well as uncontrolled environments. So with this as a start, the next logical step is to take a closer look at the system and the regulations pertaining to it.

5
A closer look at the airspace system

AS I SAID IN THE INTRODUCTION, REVIEWING OR DESCRIBING THE airspace system in the 1990s has certain risks. What is valid today might be invalid tomorrow. Changes are in the wind or are already blowing across the pilot's horizon. The rash of midair collisions and reported near-misses has stirred the Department of Transportation and its Federal Aviation Administration into a welter of activity uncommon in the bureaucracy. Things are moving rapidly. Regulations are getting tougher; airspace violators are being tracked and punished more severely; and general aviation is finding freedom of the air a diminishing privilege. In the process, it is the general aviation VFR pilot who is bearing the brunt of the increasing restrictions. Some of the prophecies of the 1930s are coming true.

To a certain degree, however, perhaps the VFR pilot population has brought at least a portion of the restrictiveness on itself. While the volume of incidents is relatively small, there have been too many instances of illegal penetration of controlled airspaces and violations of VFR flight regulations, as the cases in Chap. 3 indicate. Whether they are products of carelessness, inattention, or ignorance matters little. The fact remains that federal authorities are taking action to reduce the hazards of the "crowded skies."

That said, pilots still have considerable freedom to go almost anywhere with at least a private license and an aircraft that has the required avionics. They say the freedom is theirs, but freedoms or rights are not always honored because denial or delay of clearances into controlled areas is not a rarity these days. The cause is not all regulatory, although that is certainly a contributor. Until the ATC facilities are fully staffed and the equipment matches today's state of the art, additional regulations might further impinge on the freedoms that remain.

Whatever the future, the basic elements of the airspace system will undoubtedly survive. If that's a reasonable prophecy, let's begin with a general review of the system, followed by a discussion of the special-use airspaces in Chap. 6. Then, in succeeding chapters, we'll look at tower-operated airports more closely, including the control areas that surround an increasing number of the busier terminals.

SOURCES FOR IDENTIFYING AIRSPACES

Before one ventures forth, it's only smart to determine what airspaces will or might be penetrated: controlled, uncontrolled, prohibited, restricted, military operation areas (MOAs), or whatever. Four basic determining sources exist that can be used singly or in combination, depending on the nature of the flight: the sectional aeronautical chart (or just plain sectional), the en route low-altitude chart (ELAC), the *Airport/Facilities Directory* (*A/FD*), and the terminal area chart (TAC) for operating in Class B airspaces.

From beginner on up, the sectional is well known to every pilot. Containing a wealth of surface and terminal information, it's an indispensable flight planning and navigational reference. Published by the National Ocean Service (NOS), 37 geographically designated charts (not maps) cover the 48 contiguous states. Each chart is updated twice per year.

Primarily designed for instrument operations, the ELAC is also an excellent reference for VFR cross-country operations, if it is used in conjunction with the sectional. Unlike the sectional, ground details such as rivers, highways, obstructions, terrain altitudes, towns, and the like are omitted. Instead, the ELAC focuses on radio navigation facilities and includes crucial data not found on the sectional. Combined, the two charts provide about all the information one could want on a cross-country journey. Updated about every 2 months by NOS, 28 individual charts cover the 48 states.

The *Airport/Facilities Directory,* as the name implies, contains data about airport facilities and services, including runways, types of fuel available, communication facilities, frequencies, radio aids to navigation, and other information not readily available elsewhere. Another NOS publication, the *A/FD* is updated six times per year.

The terminal area chart is an enlargement of the Class B surface and airport information depicted on the sectional charts. As an exploded and less cluttered "picture" of the area which lies within the large blue square on the sectional identifying the existence of a Class B airspace, the TAC provides the sort of visual image of the airspace so necessary to operate in a busy airport environment. Similar to the sectional, the TAC is published twice per year.

With any of these sources, be sure to refer to the current issue. Because of changes, what was fact on the last chart or *A/FD* might not be valid today.

HOW THE AIRSPACES ARE DEPICTED

Simply said, the U.S. airspace basically conforms to the worldwide ICAO system in terms of structure and designation. The U.S. system, then, consists of six types of airspace, each identified alphabetically from A through E and then G. (The omission of an F airspace is not a typographic error. That airspace is common overseas, but the United States has no counterpart.) Conceptually, the system is easy to understand, as perhaps Fig. 5-1 illustrates, but more explanation than just a figure is necessary:

The airspaces—a general description

In essence, Class A (Alpha) is the high-altitude (18,000 to 60,000 feet MSL) en route positive control airspace for IFR operations only; Classes B (Bravo), C (Charlie), and D (Delta) are airport terminal airspaces; Class E (Echo), except where these B, C, and D airspaces exist, comprises the en route low-altitude airspace, generally from 1200 feet AGL to 18,000 feet MSL. At the same time and under specified conditions, certain non-B, C, or D airports are identified as Class E; Class G is uncontrolled airspace, which typically rises from the surface to 1200 feet AGL and includes all other airports not justifying a B, C, D, or E classification.

Adding a little more meat to these skeletal descriptions, the following summaries, coupled with reference to Fig. 5-2, may help you to understand the system.

Class A: Positive control areas from 18,000 to 60,000 feet

All operations are conducted under instrument flight rules (IFR) and are subject to ATC clearances and instructions. Aircraft separation and safety advisories are provided by ATC.

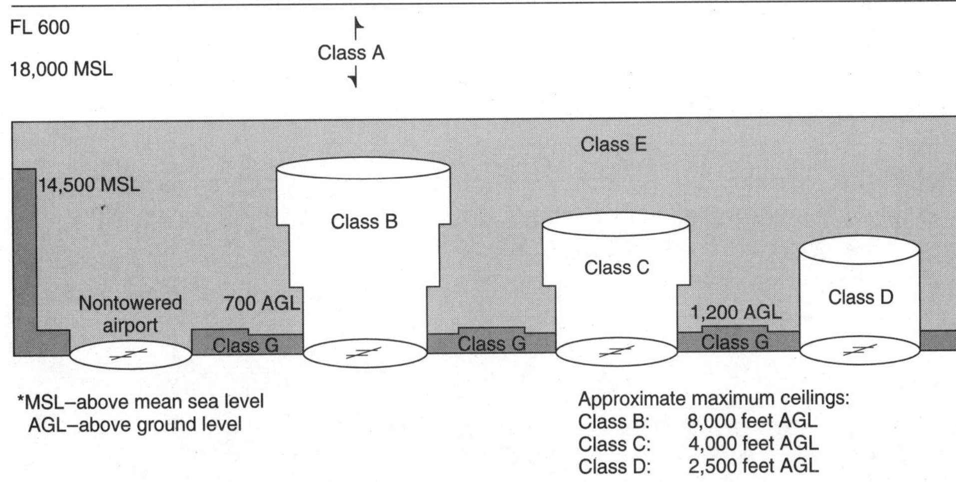

Fig. 5-1 *This commonly seen FAA drawing shows the six types of airspaces from Class A to Class G, with Class A being the most restrictive and Class G the least.*

Airspace Classifications

Airspace features	Class A airspace	Class B airspace	Class C airspace	Class D airspace	Class E airspace	Class G airspace
Operations permitted	IFR	IFR and VFR	IFR and VFR	IFR and VFR	IFR and VFR	IFR and VFR
Entry requirements	ATC clearance	ATC clearance	ATC clearance for IFR. All require radio contact.	ATC clearance for IFR. All require radio contact.	ATC clearance for IFR. All require radio contact.	None
Minimum pilot qualifications	Instrument rating	Private or student certificate	Student certificate	Student certificate	Student certificate	Student certificate
Two-way radio communications	Yes	Yes	Yes	Yes	Yes for IFR	No
VFR minimum visibility	NA	3 statute miles	3 statute miles	3 statute miles	3 statute miles[1]	1 statute mile[2]
VFR minimum distance from clouds	NA	Clear of clouds	500 feet below, 1000 feet above, and 2000 feet horizontal	500 feet below, 1000 feet above, and 2000 feet horizontal	500 feet below, 1000 feet above, and 2000 feet horizontal[1]	Clear of clouds
Aircraft separation	All	All	IFR, SVFR, and runway operations	IFR, SVFR, and runway operations	IFR, SVFR	None
Conflict resolution	NA	NA	Between IFR and VFR operations	No	No	No
Traffic advisories	NA	NA	Yes	Workload permitting	Workload permitting	Workload permitting
Safety advisories	Yes	Yes	Yes	Yes	Yes	Yes

Fig. 5-2 *This abbreviated chart summarizes the operating regulations and ATC services available within the various classifications.*

Class B: The largest and busiest U.S. airports and their surrounding areas, based on the number of instrument flight operations and passenger enplanements.

Operations may be IFR or VFR, but all aircraft are subject to ATC clearances and instructions. ATC provides aircraft separation and safety advisories.

Class C: The medium to large airports, again based on the number of instrument operations and passenger enplanements, and their surrounding areas.

Operations may be either IFR or VFR, and all aircraft are subject to radio contact with ATC and instructions. ATC provides aircraft separation between IFR/IFR and IFR/Special VFR (SVFR) aircraft. VFR operations are given traffic advisories and, on request, collision resolution instructions.

Class D: Tower-controlled airports which have fewer instrument flight operations and passenger enplanements than Class C or B airports and the immediate surrounding areas.

Operations may be either IFR or VFR, with all aircraft subject to radio contact with ATC and subsequent instructions. ATC separation service is provided IFR aircraft only, but all aircraft are given traffic advisories.

Class E: Typically, nontowered airports with weather-reporting sources and approved for Part 135 commuter and on-demand flight operations. Also, Class E represents all the controlled airspace aloft, rising typically from 700 or 1200 feet AGL to 18,000 feet MSL but excluding Class A, B, C, and D airspaces.

On a sectional chart, the Class E airport is surrounded by a segmented magenta circle or cookie-cutter figure (representing what is called a transition area) which establishes the airspace designed to protect arriving or departing IFR aircraft during IMC (instrument meteorological conditions) weather. Within the "design," VFR operations are excluded or limited when IMC prevail. In all other Class E airspace outside the airport environment, operations may be IFR or VFR. Separation service is provided to IFR aircraft only, but to the extent practical, traffic advisories to VFR aircraft are provided, if so requested.

Class G: Nontowered airports without weather-reporting sources and not approved for Part 135 commuter or on-demand operations. Also, most airspace outside the airport vicinity up to 1200 feet AGL.

Operations may be IFR or VFR, but no ATC service is available.

Again, Fig. 5-2 provides additional information, in summary form, about the features and operating requirements within each of the airspaces.

"SUBJECT TO AIR TRAFFIC CONTROL"

Before I proceed, and perhaps to remove present or future confusion, the meaning of a pilot being "controlled by ATC" or "subject to ATC clearances and instructions" warrants clarification. Under instrument flight rules, either expression implies that the IFR pilot, among other things, files a flight plan, receives clearances or amended clearances from ATC, is subject to ATC instructions while in flight, makes required position reports, varies aircraft airspeed if so directed (within safe operational limits), maintains approved altitudes and flight routes, requests altitude or heading deviations, and, barring extenuating circumstances, adheres to and coordinates with ATC all flight operations or instructions.

These overall responsibilities do not imply that the IFR pilot has no control over the management of the flight. The pilot always has the ultimate control. The ATC system, directly administered to the pilot by the controller, is charged with the orderly flow and separation of all traffic in the controlled airspaces. If that is to be achieved, pilot adherence to a planned operation, to approved deviations, and to ATC instructions is essential.

The VFR pilot, on the other hand, whether having filed a flight plan or not, is under no such constraints—with one very important exception. That exception exists when he or she is operating within the confines of a Class B, Class C, or Class D environment.

CONTROLLED AIRSPACE

Logic would have it that the airspace either is controlled or isn't. In one sense, however, that isn't quite true, because if you're flying VFR, you may well be in a controlled area but not literally under the control of any ATC facility. On the surface, that statement doesn't make a lot of sense, but Part 1.1 of the Federal Aviation Regulations tends to clarify the issue—at least partially:

> *Controlled airspace* means an airspace of defined dimensions within which air traffic control service is provided to IFR flights and to VFR flights in accordance with the airspace classification.
>
> NOTE: Controlled airspace is a generic term that covers Class A, Class B, Class C, Class D, and Class E airspace.

What this means, in essence, is that IFR aircraft are subject to air traffic control in all five airspaces. VFR aircraft cannot operate in Class A airspace, but they are subject to control in Classes B, C, and D (the terminal environments that have operating control towers).

As to Class E operations, control in that airspace is a different matter. For example, you're on a VFR cross-country trip and have contacted an Air Route Traffic Control Center for traffic advisories. If the workload permits, the Center controller will provide this service and also alert you to potentially hazardous conflict situations. You're still flying VFR, however, and are thus free to change altitudes or directions, as long as you adhere to VFR flight regulations. (Be sure, though, to advise the controller before making such changes.) You are thus being helped by ATC, but are not under its control.

Here is another VFR cross-country situation: You're flying an airway in the Class E airspace, but you haven't called Center for traffic advisories. Despite being in a controlled environment, you can climb, descend, change headings, or do whatever you want as long as you adhere to the VFR altitude, operational, and cloud separation regulations.

So, to make it simple, you're never under ATC control when flying VFR in the controlled Class E airspace.

UNCONTROLLED AIRSPACE (CLASS G)

As far as uncontrolled airspace is concerned, Class G is the airspace in which no ATC service to either IFR or VFR aircraft will be provided (other than possible traffic advisories when the ATC workload permits and radio communications can be established).

Class G is quite limited, though. As the shaded area in Fig. 5-1 illustrates, the ceilings of the uncontrolled airspace are 700 feet AGL, 1200 feet AGL, and 14,500 MSL. That's well and good, but it still leaves a fair number of questions unanswered. Finding the answers is where the sectional chart comes into play.

If you check any sectional, as I mentioned earlier, you'll see a lot of airports surrounded by magenta designs that identify "transition areas." Most of these designs are circular; others are irregular in structure. The sectional legend flap implies, but doesn't state as such, that within the areas bounded by the magenta, the ceiling of the uncontrolled airspace is 700 feet AGL. It further implies, but doesn't state, that outward from the magenta design, the ceiling of the uncontrolled airspace is 1200 feet AGL.

The fading or fuzziness indicates that everywhere inside the magenta, the 700-foot ceiling prevails, except at those airports where a segmented circle or design in magenta defines this Class E airspace. By the same token, the airspace outside the magenta identifies the geography where the 1200-foot ceiling prevails. Accordingly (other than for any intervening prohibited or restricted areas), in the open country between any airport with magenta and any other airport with magenta, the uncontrolled Class G ceiling is 1200 feet AGL.

Fine, but what about the uncontrolled airspace that goes up to 14,500 feet, per the shaded area at the extreme left in Fig. 5-1? As a general rule, the 1200-foot AGL ceiling or floor exists over most of the United States. It's a different story, however, in the mountainous regions of the west.

For example, look at the excerpt from the Phoenix sectional (Fig. 5-3). This is just a segment of a Victor airway, but you'll notice that the outside lines of the airway (shaded on the sectional here; in blue in full-color versions) are sharp, while the shading fades inward toward the airway center line. This means that the controlled airspace starts at 1200 feet above the ground everywhere within the 8-nautical-mile width of the airway. Outside the airway, however, and beyond the sharp demarcation lines, it's a different story. In these areas, the airspace is uncontrolled up to the 14,500-foot level.

Remember, though, that this symbology is peculiar only to the mountainous areas in the western United States. Elsewhere, the Victor airways are simply narrow blue lines on a sectional.

CONTROLLED AIRSPACE, CLASSES A AND E

Disregarding airports and their immediate surroundings for the moment, Fig. 5-1 depicts the other two controlled airspaces: Classes A and E. To operate in the Class A airspace, regardless of the weather, you must file an IFR flight plan and adhere to all IFR regulations and procedures. Control by ATC from 18,000 to 60,000 feet is, indeed, positive.

As to Class E except in Hawaii, where there are no vertical limits, the normally 8-nautical-mile width of airspace along federal airways, from 1200 up to 18,000 feet, is

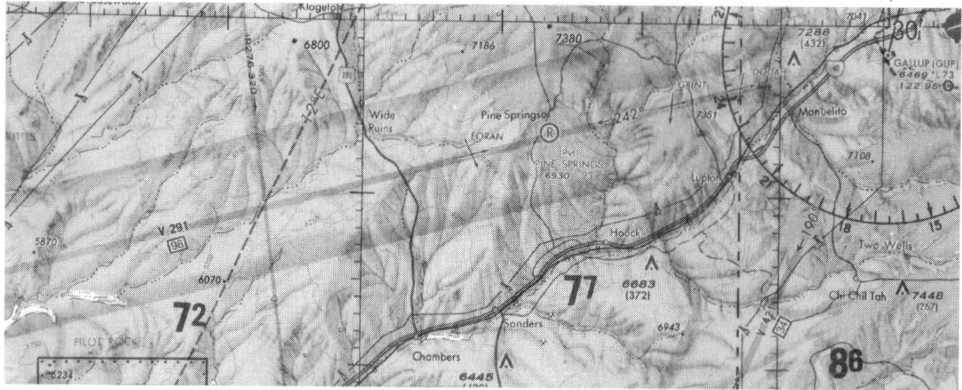

Fig. 5-3 *In this excerpt from the Phoenix sectional, controlled airspace begins at 1200 feet above ground level between the boundaries of the airway. Outside those boundaries, the airspace is uncontrolled from the surface up to 14,500 feet MSL.*

identified as *controlled.* To repeat, though, if you are flying an airway on a VFR flight plan, or no flight plan at all, you're in a controlled airspace but are not under ATC's influence. You might have established contact with a Center for traffic advisories, and if so, you'll probably have several communication exchanges with Center or Approach Control personnel as you proceed along the airway; however, you're still VFR in VFR conditions. Accordingly, if you have been receiving advisories, your only responsibilities are to adhere to the VFR regulations, to advise Center if you are going to change altitudes or deviate from your announced route of flight, and to keep your eyes open.

Until you near a Class B, Class C, or Class D airspace, you can fly the airways all day and never call or be in contact with any controlling agency. That's not a necessarily good idea, but it's still the VFR pilot's privilege.

VFR REGULATIONS

With the basic structure of the airspace out of the way (except for the Class B, C, and D airports), a brief review of the altitude, visibility, and cloud separation regulations affecting VFR pilots is in order. These might be well known, but no discussion of operating within the airspace system would be complete without at least a short summary.

Flying VFR places that old and oft-repeated responsibility on the pilot: See and avoid, whether the airspace is controlled or uncontrolled. That's as applicable in the open country as in the vicinity of a tower-operated airport. In a controlled environment, such as around an airport, you might be given advisories that you "...have traffic at two o'clock," but the ultimate responsibility for conflict avoidance is still yours.

Despite that obvious fact, the skies would be chaotic and infinitely more dangerous if pilots were allowed to roam about completely at will, relying solely on the hope that the other pilot will see and avoid. Consequently, and to minimize the potential of conflict, regulations have been established governing altitudes to be flown as well as visibility and cloud separation minimums that must be observed.

Altitudes.

First, let's look at the altitudes, again from *AIM,* as illustrated in Fig. 5-4. The chart is self-explanatory, but an easy way to remember whether the VFR altitude should be in odd or even thousands of feet is to use the acronym WEEO: westbound even, plus 500; eastbound odd, plus 500. Note, though, that those altitude requirements don't apply when you're flying at 3000 feet AGL or below.

If everyone adhered to the prescribed altitudes, we'd have a lot fewer near-misses. Evasive action is too frequently necessary when you're at the correct altitude, and some sightseer barrels toward you head-on at the same altitude. This often happens above 3000 feet AGL within 30 or 40 miles of an airport where, for some reason, altitude adherence seems less important.

And then there are cases when both aircraft are going by the book, but one is headed southeast and the other northeast. Unless at least one pilot has alert and roving eyes, a disaster is in the making. If you have your head in the cockpit much more than 10 seconds, instead of scanning the surrounding atmosphere, you ought to be getting a little nervous. The rate of closure, even between light aircraft, will not tolerate inattention to the outside world.

Visibility and cloud separation.

Now let's look at the visibility and cloud separation minimums. Figure 5-5 tells the story, and there's not much to add. Okay, you're at the proper altitude, but the visibility is decreasing or there's a bunch of puffy clouds up ahead. Again, to see and avoid, the FARs are very specific about visibility minimums and separation from clouds or overcasts.

Have trouble remembering the numbers? Follow this sequence: feet below, feet above, feet laterally. Then double the figures as you go: 500 feet below, 1000 feet above, 2000 feet laterally. Just don't forget that 2000 feet from one cloud also means 2000 feet from the next, for a 4000-foot separation between those billowing whites.

Despite the regulations, for some the desire to skim along a few feet above or below a cloud layer is irresistible. It's a great way to get the sensation of speed, while others

VFR flight altitudes

If your magnetic course (ground track) is	More than 3,000' above the surface but below 18,000' MSL, fly
0° to 179°	Odd thousands MSL, plus 500' (3,500, 5,500, 7,500, etc.)
180° to 359°	Even thousands MSL plus 500' (4,500, 6,500, 8,500, etc.)

West Even—East Odd : plus 500'

Fig. 5-4 *The required VFR flight altitudes above 3000 feet AGL.*

Basic VFR Weather Minimums

Airspace	Flight Visibility	Distance from Clouds
Class A	Not Applicable	Not Applicable
Class B	3 statute miles	Clear of Clouds
Class C	3 statute miles	500 feet below 1,000 feet above 2,000 feet horizontal
Class D	3 statute miles	500 feet below 1,000 feet above 2,000 feet horizontal
Class E Less than 10,000 feet MSL	3 statute miles	500 feet below 1,000 feet above 2,000 feet horizontal
At or above 10,000 feet MSL	5 statute miles	1,000 feet below 1,000 feet above 1 statute mile horizontal
Class G 1,200 feet or less above the surface (regardless of MSL altitude).		
Day, except as provided in section 91.155(b)	1 statute mile	Clear of clouds
Night, except as provided in section 91.155(b)	3 statute miles	500 feet below 1,000 feet above 2,000 feet horizontal
More than 1,200 feet above the surface but less than 10,000 feet MSL.		
Day	1 statute mile	500 feet below 1,000 feet above 2,000 feet horizontal
Night	3 statute miles	500 feet below 1,000 feet above 2,000 feet horizontal
More than 1,200 feet above the surface and at or above 10,000 feet MSL.	5 statute miles	1,000 feet below 1,000 feet above 1 statute mile horizontal

Fig. 5-5 *This excerpt from the* Aeronautical Information Manual *specifies the VFR visibility and cloud separation minimums for flight within the various airspaces.*

have trouble overcoming the temptation to burst into a nice puffy cloud just for the fun of it or to see if they really can fly on instruments.

Are you a gambler or a Russian roulette devotee? That's what it's all about. Some other character might also be testing his new-found instrument skills in the same cloud. Or a perfectly legitimate IFR aircraft may be climbing or letting down through the cloud layer. Suddenly there's the IFR aircraft and there you are. The other pilot is legal, you're not, but that won't make much difference if the dreaded midair collision becomes reality.

The old saying that "There are old pilots and there are bold pilots, but there are no old bold pilots" is a time-worn adage, but age hasn't dimmed its validity. Violating the rules might give some people a sense of bravado and make for good hangar talk. In those cases, though, bravado is named stupidity.

UNCONTROLLED AIRPORTS

Fundamentally, the existence or nonexistence of an operating tower and a qualified weather-reporting source on an airport property determines whether an airport is classified as controlled or uncontrolled. If there is no tower at all, the airport is uncontrolled in the sense that no one is directing the routine flow of traffic in the traffic pattern or within the general 5-statute-mile radius of the airport proper. Also, many airports have control towers, but the towers operate only part-time, say, from 7:00 A.M. to 11:00 P.M. When closed, the airport reverts to an uncontrolled status, again in the sense that there is no external control of traffic within the immediate airport environment. All told, more than 87 percent, or roughly 4450 out of 5132, airports in the United States available for unrestricted public use, excluding heliports and seaplane bases, fall into this description of *uncontrolled.*

There's another aspect, however, to this matter of controlled versus uncontrolled. If you check almost any sectional, you'll see a fair number of magenta nontowered airports surrounded by a segmented magenta circle or design. This design indicates that in IMC weather either a Center or a nearby Approach Control facility will provide control of arriving IFR aircraft down to the surface and of departing IFR aircraft from the surface to the aircraft's eventual assigned en route altitude. These generally are the Class E airports which, in the FAA context, are thus controlled.

At many of the other magenta airports, as I pointed out earlier, where there is no segmented circle, you'll note a solid magenta design—again, basically circular or cookie-cutter in form—surrounding the airport. This symbol, which becomes fuzzy as it fades inward, indicates that the floor of the Class E airspace, normally 1200 feet AGL, is 700 feet AGL within the confines of the symbol, and that ATC control of IFR aircraft in IMC will be provided down to or up from that AGL altitude. Keep in mind, though, that these designs and altitudes apply only in IMC. In VMC, you can figuratively erase them from the sectional.

A caution about operating VFR in these so-called uncontrolled airports: Being uncontrolled does not mean that you have total freedom to operate as you please in or around these many airports. The FAA visibility and cloud separation minimums still apply, as do radio communication responsibilities and the traffic pattern procedures.

Class G airports

The Class G airports are typically the least complex in terms of operating and communicating requirements. As a general rule, but certainly not exclusively, these are the small, low-volume airports that are unattended and probably with no air-to-ground radio facilities at all. Once again, such airports are easily identified on the sectional chart by the magenta coloring of the airport symbol and the information about the airport, its elevation, runway data, and radio frequency.

To be more specific, refer to the Warren, Arkansas, example in Fig. 5-6.

The airport data block says that the field elevation is 235 feet, the runway length is "38" (3800 feet), and the frequency is the italicized *122.9,* followed by the C in the solid circle. This symbol, whether in magenta or blue (blue for controlled airports), always identifies the CTAF (common traffic advisory frequency) for that airport. Incidentally, the L does not indicate runway length, but implies that at single- or multiple-runway airports at least one

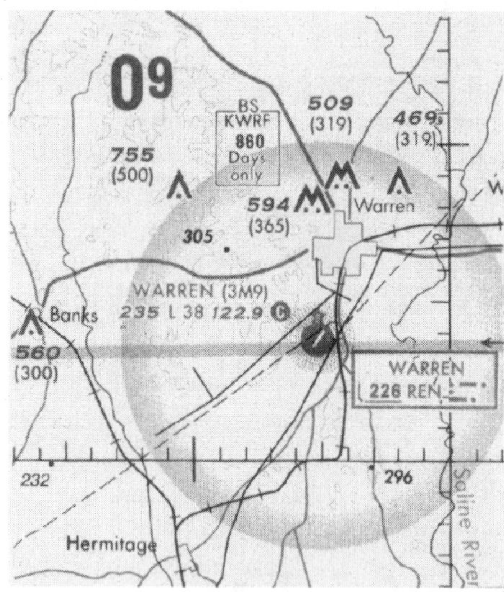

Fig. 5-6 *Warren airport, as shown on the sectional, is a Class G multicom airport with the aircraft-to-aircraft 122.9 CTAF.*

runway can be lighted for night operations. An asterisk before the L would mean that the lights are pilot-activated by depressing the microphone button a certain number of times. (Refer to the *A/FD* to determine how many times to press the mike button at a given airport.)

By inference, then, Warren has no tower, no Flight Service Station, no unicom. It is uncontrolled in every sense, which means that

- You can operate in and around the airport at will, observing only the basic rules of traffic pattern flying.
- If you maintain an altitude of 1200 feet AGL or less, the visibility must be at least 1 statute mile and you must be able to remain clear of any clouds.
- To operate above 1200 feet, the visibility must be at least 3 miles, with the standard cloud separation of 500 feet below, 1000 feet above, and 2000 feet horizontally maintained.
- Radio position reports and intentions are always communicated on the 122.9 CTAF, and all calls are addressed to "(Airport name) traffic"—or, in this case, to "Warren traffic."

CLASS E AIRPORTS

A Class E airport is something like a chameleon in that it can change "colors" depending on the existence or nonexistence of certain conditions. For example:

- An airport has no tower, but a qualified weather-reporting source, either human or automated, such as ASOS or AWOS, exists on the property. As long as that source is on duty or functioning, the airport is a Class E. When weather information is not available (the human source goes home for the night and there is no ASOS or AWOS), the airport reverts to a Class G.

- Another airport has a tower plus a weather-reporting source on duty. This, then, is a Class D airport. The tower, however, closes, say, from 1900 hours local to 0700 hours. If the weather-reporting source is still available, the field becomes Class E during those 12 hours of downtime. Should both the tower and the weather source go off duty simultaneously, the airport drops to a Class G.

As is apparent, the existence or nonexistence of an operating tower and a weather-reporting source is the determining factor. Depending on what is available, the airport is a Class E or D; without either, it is a Class G. To simplify the discussion here, however, let's focus solely on the typical Class E airport which has weather reporting but no tower.

Identifying a Class E airport

To identify a Class E, do as you did with a Class G: First find an airport on the sectional that is depicted in magenta with a segmented magenta circle surrounding the airport. One of many examples is Minnesota's Grand Rapids Gordon Newstrom Field, illustrated in Fig. 5-7. Also, as part of the airport data block, check the italicized radio frequency. If the frequency is *122.7, 122.8,* or *123.0,* as is so commonly the case, you have further evidence that the airport is a Class E and provides unicom radio service. Then for additional details about the airport, refer to the *Airport/Facilities Directory* (Fig. 5-8). This establishes the fact that the airspace is indeed Class E and provides service from 1100 to 0300Z Monday through Saturday and 1400 to 0300Z Sunday. At other times, it reverts to Class G.

From an operating and communicating point of view, the advantage of unicom is that when contacted for a field advisory, a unicom operator (typically an employee of a fixed-base operator) will give you the current wind direction and velocity, the favored runway in use, and the existence of any reported traffic in the pattern or area. In no way, however, is unicom a controlling agency. It is merely a field advisory service.

In addition to field advisories, the fixed-base operator (FBO), upon request, can call a taxi, make a phone call for you, relay messages to people waiting for you, alert a mechanic for repairs, and so on. These services are available wherever unicom exists, whether the airport is controlled or uncontrolled.

To obtain either those services or a field advisory at any nontower airport, the initial radio contact is addressed to "(Airport name) unicom." All subsequent calls reporting your position or intentions are then addressed to "(Airport name) traffic" on the airport's same published unicom frequency.

Airports with closed towers

The next possibility is an airport with unicom and a tower that operates part-time, say, from 0700 to 1900. When the tower is open, the airport is controlled and the rules for

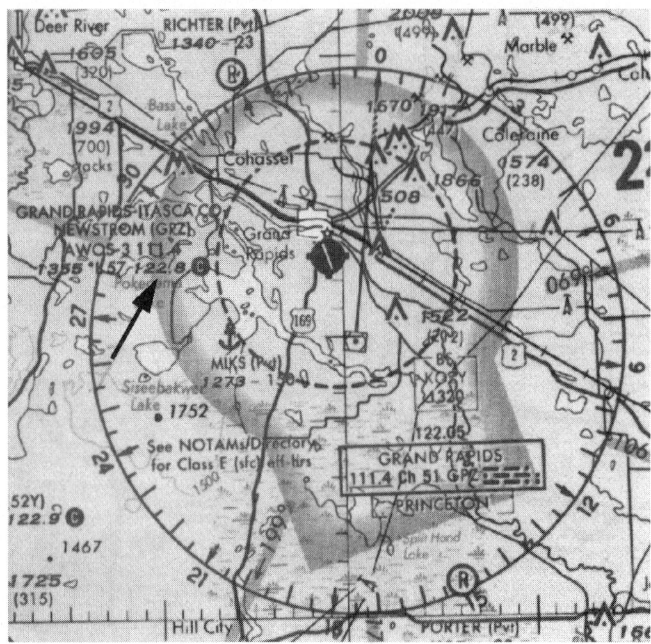

Fig. 5-7 *Grand Rapids, Minnesota, is a non-towered Class E airport, identified in part as such by the 122.8 CTAF.*

GRAND RAPIDS/ITASCA CO GORDON NEWSTROM FLD (GPZ) 2 SE UTC–6(–5DT) **TWIN CITIES**
N47°12.67′ W93°30.59′ **H–1E, 3G, L–10G**
1355 B S4 **FUEL** 100LL, JET A OX 2 ARFF Index A **IAP**
RWY 16–34: H5755X100 (ASPH–PFC) S–23, D–38, DT–78 HIRL 1.0% up SE
RWY 16: REIL. VASI(V4L)—GA 3.0° TCH 50′. Thld dsplcd 423′. Tree.
RWY 34: MALSR. VASI(V4L)—GA 3.0° TCH 50′.
RWY 04–22: 2968X135 (TURF)
RWY 04: Trees. **RWY 22:** Trees.
RWY 10–28: 2470X100 (TURF)
RWY 10: Trees. **RWY 28:** Trees.
AIRPORT REMARKS: Attended dalgt hrs. Rwy 04–22 and Rwy 10–28 CLOSED to wheel acft winter months. Deer and gulls on and invof arpt. Rwy 16–34 has a 582′ paved area north end of rwy. Rwy 16 REIL omni directional. ACTIVATE HIRL Rwy 16–34, VASI Rwy 16 and Rwy 34, REIL Rwy 16 and MALSR Rwy 34—122.8.
WEATHER DATA SOURCES: AWOS–3 111.4 (218) 326–8337.
COMMUNICATIONS: CTAF/UNICOM 122.8
PRINCETON FSS (PNM) TF 1–800–WX–BRIEF. NOTAM FILE GPZ.
RCO 122.05 (PRINCETON FSS)
Ⓡ **MINNEAPOLIS CENTER APP/DEP CON** 127.9
→ **AIRSPACE: CLASS E** svc Mon–Sat 1100–0300Z‡, Sun 1400–0300Z‡ other times CLASS G.
RADIO AIDS TO NAVIGATION: NOTAM FILE GPZ.
(L) VORW/DME 111.4 GPZ Chan 51 N47°09.82′ W93°29.31′ 337° 3.0 NM to fld. 1400/6E.
VOR portion unusable 120°–192° byd 12 NM blo 5000′.
DME portion unusable 140°–215° byd 20 NM blo 3000′.
215°–045° byd 20 NM blo 3500′.
GALEX NDB (LOM) 272 GP N47°07.82′ W93°28.88′ 344° 5.0 NM to fld.
ILS 110.1 I–GPZ Rwy 34. LOM GALEX NDB.

Fig. 5-8 *The* Airport/Facilities Directory *provides more information about the Grand Rapids airport and the services available.*

operating within at least a 5-mile radius apply (subsequently explained in greater detail). When the tower is closed, though, the airport essentially becomes Class E or G airspace. The only difference, in radio use, is that field advisories would be obtained by first contacting unicom on its frequency (assuming the FBO is open) and then addressing position reports to "(Airport name) traffic" on the tower frequency, even though the tower is closed.

How do you know whether a tower is open full- or part-time? The sectional will tell you, as will the *A/FD*. First, find a blue airport on any sectional. If there is a star or asterisk immediately following the tower frequency, the tower is part-time. For example, look at Fig. 5-9 and Sioux City's Sioux Gateway Airport. The star to the right of the frequency—CT 118.7*—is the clue. Now turn to the inside flap of the sectional and the table data under the control tower frequencies (Fig. 5-10). Along with other information, you'll see that the tower is in operation from 0600 to 2400 local time. During those hours, the airport is controlled. At all other times, it is Class E and, as far as local traffic is concerned, uncontrolled. Unicom, however, can be reached on 122.95, as indicated by the italicized frequency on the sectional.

Here is another variation. A part-time tower and a Flight Service Station are on the airport (although this is becoming a matter of history as more and more FSSs have been consolidated into regional locations). With the tower closed, the FSS provides the airport advisories on the tower frequency, not 123.6 or any of the published FSS frequencies. For emphasis, however, at no time is a Flight Service Station a controlling agency. Other than being capable of providing more accurate and complete weather information, an on-field FSS functions basically as unicom, as far as flight operations are concerned, but it will not provide personal message services.

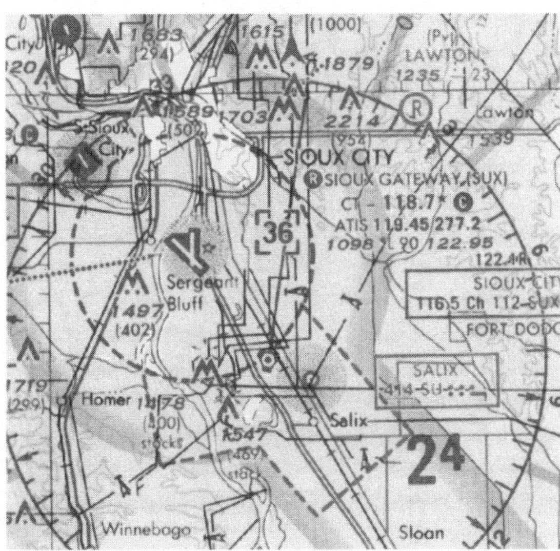

Fig. 5-9 *A star to the immediate right of the tower frequency and just before CTAF symbol identifies the tower as part-time.*

CONTROL TOWER FREQUENCIES ON OMAHA SECTIONAL CHART

Airports which have control towers are indicated on this chart by the letters CT followed by the primary VHF local control frequency. Selected transmitting frequencies for each control tower are tabulated in the adjoining spaces, the low or medium transmitting frequency is listed first followed by a VHF local control frequency, and the primary VHF and UHF military frequencies, when these frequencies are available. An asterisk (*) follows the part-time tower frequency remoted to the collocated full-time FSS for use as Local Airport Advisory (LAA) during hours tower is closed. Hours shown are local time. Ground control frequencies listed are the primary ground control frequencies.

Automatic Terminal Information Service (ATIS) frequencies, shown on the face of the chart are primary arrival VHF/UHF frequencies. All ATIS frequencies are listed below. ATIS operational hours may differ from control tower operational hours.

ASR and/or PAR indicates Radar Instrument Approach available.

"MON-FRI" indicates Monday thru Friday.

CONTROL TOWER	OPERATES	TWR FREQ	GND CON	ATIS	ASR/PAR
CENTRAL NEBRASKA REGIONAL	0700-1900	118.2 388.2	121.9 388.2	127.4	
DES MOINES INTL	CONTINUOUS	118.3 257.8	121.9 348.6	119.55 283.0	ASR
EPPLEY	CONTINUOUS	132.1 256.9	121.9	120.4	
FOSS	0500-2300	118.3 257.8	121.9 348.6	126.6	ASR
LINCOLN	0530-2400	118.5 253.5	121.9 275.8	118.05 302.2	
OFFUTT AFB	CONTINUOUS	123.7 348.4	121.7 275.8	126.025 273.5	ASR/PAR
→ SIOUX GATEWAY	0600-2400	118.7 254.3	121.9 348.6	119.45 277.2	

Fig. 5-10 *Another source for determining a tower's period of operation is the reverse side of the sectional's legend panel.*

Whom do you call when, and what frequency do you use? There are a lot of possible combinations; Fig. 5-11 on pages 72 and 73 might help clarify the situation.

CONTROLLED AIRPORTS, CLASS D

A step up from the Class G and E uncontrolled airports are those airports that are controlled and fall under the Class D airspace category. Such an airport has an operating control tower which, besides controlling traffic within the airspace, typically has Ground Control, perhaps what is called Clearance Delivery, unicom for nonoperational requests, and a weather-reporting source, whether human or automated, such as ASOS or AWOS.

To repeat just for emphasis: If an airport has an operating tower, then the airport is controlled and every pilot is under the jurisdiction of ATC. If there is no tower or if the tower is closed, then the airport becomes Class E or G where the VFR weather and operating regulations apply and there is no ATC control of local traffic pattern operations.

Radiating out from Class D airports is an airspace with a 4.3-nautical-mile radius that defines the outer limits of that airport's control. If Fig. 5-12 (see page 74) were in color, you could easily spot Nantucket Island Memorial as a towered airport by the blue airport symbol, the airport data block, and the segmented circle. Additional information in the data block includes "CT" (obviously meaning Control Tower) and the tower's CTAF frequency of 118.3, which is followed by an asterisk, indicating that the tower is part-time. The data block further tells us that ATIS can be monitored on 126.5, the field elevation is 48 feet MSL; the longest runway is 6300 feet and is lighted. Finally, 122.95 is the Nantucket unicom frequency. One other bit of information about the airspace itself is its ceiling. At about the four o'clock position southeast of the airport symbol, you'll see the number 25 inside a segmented box. This represents the AGL ceiling of Class D at Nantucket (these ceilings do vary slightly from Class D to Class D, but 2500 feet AGL is the standard across the country).

For additional information about the airport, the *A/FD* covering the northeastern United States is the logical source (Fig. 5-13, page 75). As the Nantucket example illustrates, many more details are provided, including fuel available, runway and lighting data, airport physical and operating information, communications, the type of airspace, and navigational radio aids. With this further wealth of information available, one going into Nantucket, or indeed any airport, would be foolish not to refer to the appropriate *A/FD* as part of the flight planning process.

It's undoubtedly evident by now that any pilot intending to take off, land, or transit this cylinder of controlled airspace has certain responsibilities to fulfill before penetrating it or operating within it—a few of which include the following:

- Two-way radio contact with the tower must be established before you operate in any part of the Class D airspace, and radio contact must be maintained while in this airspace.
- You are expected to comply with the control tower instructions, unless doing so would cause you to violate a VFR regulation or create a potentially hazardous situation. In such instances, you must immediately so advise the tower.
- Controller instructions are to be tersely acknowledged in a few words that tell the controller you have received the message and understand what is expected of you. Merely "Rogering" an instruction does not necessarily communicate understanding.
- Permission to transit the airspace at altitudes below the 2500-foot ceiling of the airspace must be obtained from the tower controller before you enter the area. Above that ceiling, you're out of Class D, and no radio contact is required.
- You do not report on downwind, base, or final, as at an uncontrolled field, unless the tower requests you to do so. The controller knows where you are, and those calls only needlessly consume airtime and the controller's attention.

It's obvious that if a tower exists, the airport has enough activity to warrant such a traffic controlling agency. Consequently, permission to take off is required, and the initial contact before entering the airspace, for either landing or transiting, should be established at least 10 or 15 miles from the field. In the latter cases, merely identify your aircraft (type and N number), position, altitude, the fact that you have monitored the current ATIS (if this service exists on the airport), and your intention (to land or to transit). For instance: "Billard Tower, Cherokee 8515 November over Perry Dam at four thousand five hundred with Charlie (the current ATIS report), landing Billard."

If you're below the ATA's ceiling and merely want to fly through the area, the call goes: "Billard Tower, Cherokee 8515 November over Perry Dam at two thousand three hundred. Request approval to transit your area to the west." From then on, it's just a matter of acknowledging and following the controller's instructions.

Now let's assume that instead of specifically authorizing you to enter the airspace for landing or transiting, the controller calls you back with this: "Cherokee eight five one five November, stand by." What should you do? Answer: Keep right on going. The

Tower status	On-site FSS status	On-site RCO	FBO Status	Field advisories type/radio frequency	Radio frequency for self-announce position reports (CTAF)	ATC radio frequency
Tower Open						Tower
Tower Closed	FSS Open			AAS/Tower[5]	Tower	
Tower Closed	FSS Closed	RCO	FBO Open	UFA/UNICOM[1]	Tower	
Tower Closed	FSS Closed	RCO	FBO Closed	FFA/RCO	Tower	
Tower Closed	FSS Closed	RCO	No FBO	FFA/RCO	Tower	
Tower Closed	FSS Closed	No RCO	FBO Open	UFA/UNICOM	Tower	
Tower Closed	FSS Closed	No RCO	FBO Closed	Not Available	Tower	
Tower Closed	FSS Closed	No RCO	No FBO	Not Available	Tower	
Tower Closed	No FSS	RCO	FBO Open	UFA/UNICOM[1]	Tower	
Tower Closed	No FSS	RCO	FBO Closed	FFA/RCO	Tower	
Tower Closed	No FSS	RCO	No FBO	FFA/RCO	Tower	
Tower Closed	No FSS	No RCO	FBO Open	UFA/UNICOM	Tower	
Tower Closed	No FSS	No RCO	FBO Closed	Not Available	Tower	
Tower Closed	No FSS	No RCO	No FBO	Not Available	Tower	
No Tower	FSS Open			AAS/123.6[3]	123.6[2]	
No Tower	FSS Closed	RCO	FBO Open	UFA/UNICOM[1]	123.6[2]	

No Tower	FSS Closed	RCO	FBO Closed	FFA/RCO	123.6[2]	Tower
No Tower	FSS Closed	RCO	No FBO	FFA/RCO	123.6[2]	
No Tower	FSS Closed	No RCO	FBO Open	UFA/UNICOM	123.6[2]	
No Tower	FSS Closed	No RCO	FBO Closed	Not Available	123.6[2]	
No Tower	FSS Closed	No RCO	No FBO	Not Available	123.6[2]	
No Tower	No FSS	RCO	FBO Open	UFA/UNICOM[1]	UNICOM	
No Tower	No FSS	RCO	FBO Closed	FFA/RCO	UNICOM	
No Tower	No FSS	RCO	No FBO	FFA/RCO	122.9[4]	
No Tower	No FSS	No RCO	FBO Open	UFA/UNICOM	UNICOM	
No Tower	No FSS	No RCO	FBO Closed	Not Available	UNICOM	
No Tower	No FSS	No RCO	No FBO	Not Available	122.9[4]	

[1] Last hour's official weather observation available from FSS over RCO if weather observer is on duty.
[2] Or as listed in A/FD.
[3] Where available. Some AFSSs may not offer this service.
[4] MULTICOM.
[5] FSS will reply on tower frequency.

AFSS - Automated Flight Service Station
ATC - Air Traffic Control
FBO - Fixed - Base Operator with UNICOM
FSS - Flight Service Station (All AFSSs are open 24 hours.)
RCO - Remote Communications Outlet
AAS - FSS Airport Advisory Service (winds, weather, favored runway, altimeter setting, reported traffic within 10 miles of airport)
FFA - FSS field advisories (last hour's winds, weather, and altimeter setting, if observver is on duty at airport)
UFA - UNICOM field advisories (winds, favored runway, known traffic, altimeter setting [at some locations])

Fig. 5-11 *This chart summarizes the facilities and frequencies to use for field advisories (winds, reported traffic, favored runway, and, in some cases, weather observations) and for self-announce position reports. Check the A/FD, though, for exceptions.*

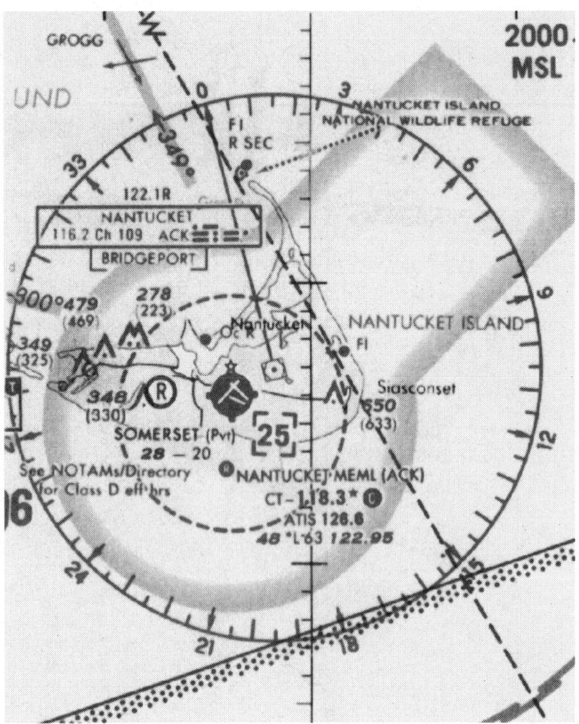

Fig. 5-12 *The segmented circle around Nantucket's airport identifies the Class D area of control.*

fact that the controller has included your N number in his or her response to your call means that radio communications with Billard tower have been established and despite the instructions to stand by, you are clear to enter the airspace.

But suppose the response to your initial call is this: "Aircraft calling Billard, stand by." Or "Aircraft calling Billard, remain outside the Class D airspace and stand by." In these cases, your N number was not included in the response. Therefore, radio communications have not been established, and you must remain clear of the airspace until you have reestablished contact.

By the same token, ground movements around the airport that would put you on any taxiway or runway require approval of Ground Control. In sum, whether transiting, landing, taxiing, departing, or shooting touch-and-gos at a controlled airport, radio contact with the tower personnel, including Ground Control, is mandatory.

That's all well and good, but what happens if the tower is part-time and closed when you want to take off or land? In that case, the airspace reverts to a Class E or Class G and radio calls are just like those at a unicom-only uncontrolled airport.

To be more specific about that, refer again to Fig. 5-11 and take the example with the arrow where there is no FSS on the field, no *remote communications outlet* (RCO) to an FSS, and the FBO is open. For field advisories, you'd call the FBO on the unicom frequency; and for position reports, you'd transmit and listen on the tower frequency. Or if there is no FSS, no RCO, and the FBO is closed or none exists, you wouldn't be able to get a field advisory unless you heard other traffic in the pattern making routine position reports and stating the runway in use: "Beetown Traffic, Cessna zero zero zero alpha left downwind, landing two four Beetown."

Regardless of what facility is open, is closed, or doesn't exist at a tower airport, the only operational position-reporting frequency you would use is the tower's. This is illustrated in Fig. 5-11, along with the several potential tower-closed variables you might encounter.

MORE ON CLASS D AND E AIRSPACE PURPOSES AND DESIGNS

Some further discussion is in order relative to the blue and magenta designs, segmented or otherwise, that surround Class D and E airport symbols. While I have partially explained the purposes of these designs elsewhere, I don't believe that all questions that a curious reader might ask have been answered. Should that be the case, even while recognizing the possibility of some repetition, we dig a little more deeply.

NANTUCKET MEM (ACK) 3 SE UTC−5(−4DT) N41°15.18′ W70°03.61′ **NEW YORK**
48 B S4 **FUEL** 100LL, JET A ARFF Index A **H–3J, L–25D**
RWY 06–24: H6303X150 (ASPH) S–75, D–170, DT–280 HIRL CL 0.3%up NE. **IAP**
RWY 06: MALSF. VASI(V4L)—GA 3.0°. Thld dsplcd 539′. **RWY 24**: SSALR. TDZL.
RWY 15–33: H3999X100 (ASPH) S–60, D–85, DT–155 MIRL
RWY 15: REIL. Building. **RWY 33**: REIL. VASI(V4R)—GA 3.0°TCH 43′.
RWY 12–30: H3125X50 (ASPH) S–12
RWY 12: Trees. **RWY 30**: Trees.
AIRPORT REMARKS: Attended continuously. Be aware of hi-speed military jet and heavy helicopter tfc vicinity of Otis ANGB. Deer and birds on and invof arpt. Rwy 12–30 VFR/Day use only aircraft under 12,500 lbs. Arpt has noise abatement procedures ctc Noise Officer 508–325–6136 for automated facsimile back information. PPR 2 hours for unscheduled air carrier ops with more than 30 passenger seat, call arpt manager 508–325–5300. When twr clsd ACTIVATE MALSF Rwy 06; SSALR Rwy 24; HIRL Rwy 06–24; MIRL Rwy 15–33 and twy lgts—CTAF. Rwy 24 SSALR unmonitored when arpt unattended. Twy F prohibited to air carrier acft with more than 30 passenger seats. Fee for non-commercial acft parking over 2 hrs or over 6000 lbs. NOTE: See Land and Hold Short Operations Section.
WEATHER DATA SOURCES: ASOS (508) 325–6082. LAWRS.
COMMUNICATIONS: **CTAF** 118.3 **ATIS** 126.6 (508–228–5375) (1100–0200Z‡) Oct 1–May 14, (1100–0400Z‡) May 15–Sept 30. **UNICOM** 122.95
BRIDGEPORT FSS (BDR) TF 1–800–WX–BRIEF. NOTAM FILE ACK
RCO 122.1R 116.2T (BRIDGEPORT FSS)
® **CAPE APP/DEP CON** 126.1 (1100–0400Z‡) May 15–Sept 30, (1100–0300Z‡) Oct 1–May 14.
BOSTON CENTER APP/DEP CON 128.75 (0400–1100Z‡) May 15–Sept 30, (0300–1100Z‡) Oct 1–May 14.
TOWER 118.3 May 15–Sep 30 (1100–0300Z‡), Oct 1–May 14 (1130–0130Z‡).
GND CON 121.7 **CLNC DEL** 128.25
AIRSPACE: **CLASS D** svc May 15–Sep 30 1100–0300Z‡, Oct 1–May 14 1130–0130Z‡ other times CLASS G.
RADIO AIDS TO NAVIGATION: NOTAM FILE ACK.
(H) VOR/DME 116.2 ACK Chan 109 N41°16.91′ W70°01.60′ 236°2.3 NM to fld. 100/15W.
WAIVS NDB (LOM) 248 AC N41°18.68′ W69°59.21′ 240° 4.8 NM to fld.
NDB (HH–ABW) 194 TUK N41°16.12′ W70°10.80′ 115° 5.5 NM to fld.
ILS/DME 109.1 I–ACK Chan 28 Rwy 24. LOM WAIVS NDB. ILS unmonitored when twr clsd.

Fig. 5-13 *The* A/FD *for Nantucket provides much more information about the airport and the facilities and services available.*

What do the various segmented designs mean or represent?

In addition to establishing the 4.3-nautical-mile radius of Class D airspace, the blue segmented design around Class D airports indicates that all traffic within that design is controlled from the surface to the ceiling of the airspace—approximately 2500 feet AGL. At the same time, when IMC or marginal VFR weather exists, ATC has the authority to limit or prohibit entirely VFR operations within that segmented airspace.

While most Class D airports have perfectly cylindrical airspace designs, many have built-in or added-on segmented extensions. The purpose of these extensions is simply to expand the areas of ATC of IFR aircraft arriving during periods of IMC weather as they make the transition from Class E airspace to the Class D airport environment. And, quite logically, the same principle applies in reverse to departing IFR aircraft in IMC weather.

If a given extension reaches out 2 nautical miles or less from the core segmented circle, the extension appears in blue on the sectional as an integral part of the circle. It is thus part of the Class D controlled airspace that exists from the surface to the Class D ceiling. Operationally, this means that pilots must contact the tower before entering one of those extensions—just as they would prior to penetrating any other portion of Class D airspace. The Pendleton, Oregon, airport (Fig. 5-14) illustrates this extension that lies just west of the airport symbol on the sectional.

Often, though, a longer extension than just 2 nautical miles of controlled airspace is needed for instrument approaches or departures. In those cases, the extension is *added*

Fig. 5-14 *This Pendleton, Oregon, excerpt from the Seattle sectional shows how a Class D airspace extension—the keyholelike design to the west of the airport symbol—is charted.*

to the Class D circle but appears in magenta rather than blue. That color change identifies the extension as Class E airspace, signifying that control within the area runs from the surface up to the floor of the next-higher overriding airspace, be it Class A, B, or C. Tennessee's McKeller-Sipes Airport (Fig. 5-15) illustrates this addition, although, of course, it shows up in black here instead of the sectional's magenta. Since this transition area is Class E airspace, pilots flying VFR in VFR weather are *not* required to contact the control tower prior to entering or operating in that portion of the airspace. Radio contact with the Class D tower is, of course, still required before the pilot penetrates any portion of the blue segmented Class D airspace itself.

Keep in mind that the purpose of these Class E magenta designs and symbols in the Class D airport environment is to define the areas in which ATC of IFR aircraft exists *during periods of IMC weather.* In VFR conditions, you can dismiss those magenta designs as though they faded off the sectional. That doesn't mean, however, that VFR flight regulations have also faded away. Far from it. The visibility and cloud separation regulations continue in place, as do those affecting radio communications and traffic pattern operations.

How can there be control at nontower Class E airports?

That's a valid question. To a large extent it depends on geography. At Class E airports located near a Class B or C airspace, the B or C Approach Control facility, through its radar facilities, would assume the controlling responsibility. On the other hand, should the nontower airport be beyond the radar coverage of any Approach Control facility but near a Center remote outlet, then the Center would provide the necessary radar coverage and instructions, probably down to the final approach.

To determine if a Class E airport has radar Approach Control, check the appropriate *A/FD.* It will tell you one of three things:

1. There is the symbol ® in the left margin, followed by "(blank) APP/DEP CON" or "(blank) Center APP/DEP CON." This tells you that radar service is provided to the airport in question by either an Approach Control or a Center facility.
2. Only one of the two facilities—"...APP/CON" or "...Center"—is listed, but no ® symbol precedes the listing. The implication here is that that facility will provide radar service to IFR aircraft down to a certain altitude. Because of lack of radar coverage below that altitude, however, the facility will apply nonradar, or "manual," control of landing or departing aircraft. To do so requires ongoing radio communications between controller and pilot relative to the aircraft's position and altitude, as well as pilot compliance with the controller's instructions. To ensure separation of participating aircraft, the *Air Traffic Control* manual 7110.65J for controllers contains many procedures and instructions that controllers are to follow to maintain the necessary lateral, longitudinal, vertical, and visual separations of aircraft for safe operations in IMC weather.

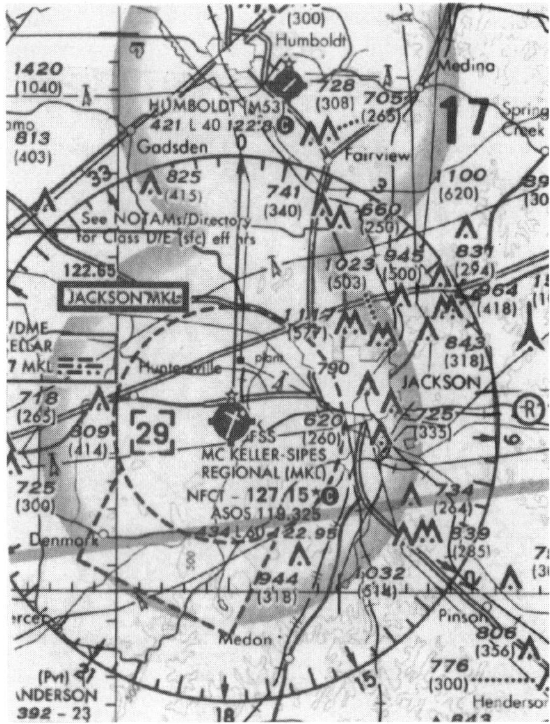

Fig. 5-15 *A Class E extension (southwest of the airport) to a Class D airspace is illustrated in this McKeller-Sipes (Tennessee) airport. Note that the Class D segmented circle is closed and the Class E extension is added on, whereas in Fig. 5-14, the circle is not closed and the entire area within the segmented design is Class D airspace.*

3. If neither "(blank) APP/DEP CON" nor "(blank) Center APP/DEP CON" appears in the *A/FD* legend, you can be sure that no controlling service is available at the airport in question.

What is required for an airport to be Class E?

There may be several factors, but at least one of the following must be located on the airport:

- An operating control tower with a qualified weather observer on duty
- A Flight Service Station
- A federally designated qualified weather observer
- A National Weather Service office

The basic requirement is the on-field resource qualified to report accurate and current weather data. If such a source is part-time and the airport is without any weather-reporting capability, it then becomes Class G.

What are the solid magenta designs for that surround so many airports, large and small?

You may recall the earlier discussion of these designs and that whatever their shape—circular, keyhole, or a cookie-cutter pattern—the inside of the design becomes fuzzy as the magenta fades inward toward the airport. These structures, called *transition areas,* exist to contain and protect IFR aircraft during IMC weather as they make the transition from en route flight to arrival and, conversely, departure to an in-flight status. The inward fading of the magenta indicates that the floor of the Class E airspace within the design is now 700 feet AGL rather than the usual 1200-foot floor that generally prevails outside the design. However, when the airport is Class D or E, with the segmented blue or magenta circle around the airport proper, the 700-foot floor exists only to that segmented design. At that point and inward, the floor of the controlled airspace drops from 700 feet down to the surface.

Outside those solid magenta shapes around so many airports, however, and beyond the design's sharp external edge, the floor of the Class E airspace returns to the normal 1200-foot AGL altitude that prevails throughout so much of the United States. In other words, barring interruptions by any Class B, C, or D airspaces, the open-country geography between all solid magenta designs around airports is Class E airspace, wherein all Class E operating rules and regulations in terms of flight altitudes, visibility, and cloud avoidance minimums apply.

How much are VFR pilots affected by all this?

In general terms, only marginally. To operate VFR, you must have at least 3-mile visibility and a 1000-foot ceiling. In addition to meeting those standard minimums, you are required to make contact with the Class D tower well before you penetrate any portion of the airspace identified by the blue segmented circle or design on the sectional. This requirement applies whether you plan (1) to land at the primary airport; (2) to enter the airspace below the published ceiling of 2500 feet AGL just to transit a portion of it; or (3) to land at a satellite airport that lies within the Class D airspace. Otherwise, in VFR weather, you can disregard any segmented magenta add-ons to the Class D structure as well as the solid magenta transition area(s) that surround the Class D airport environment.

Similarly, if you're operating into or out of a Class E nontowered airport and the weather is VFR, don't worry about the segmented magenta design around the airport, the transition areas, or the magenta 700-foot floor symbol. These have no meaning for VFR pilots *when* VFR visibility and ceiling conditions prevail. They exist solely to provide protection and control of IFR aircraft in IMC weather.

SPECIAL VFRs (SVFRs)

I've mentioned Special VFRs in passing but have never explained what they are and how they can be obtained. So now is the time to be more specific.

Let's assume that you are not IFR-qualified and that you want to depart from an airport where the current weather is below the 3-mile, 1000-foot visibility and ceiling VFR minimums. From various weather-reporting sources, however, you do know that once you get out of the immediate airport area, conditions are VFR to your intended destination. Now is the time to request an SVFR, with the hope that ATC will approve same.

The SVFR weather minimums and general regulations

If the visibility is at least 1 mile and you are able to remain clear of clouds, you can request an SVFR clearance from the controlling ATC facility. As a rule, however, only one fixed-wing (FW/SVFR) aircraft at a time is permitted within the horizontal and vertical boundaries of the surface-based controlled airport airspace. Approval will depend on the existing traffic and whether granting an SVFR would interfere with IFR operations. Also, as I just implied, the SVFR is valid only within the established limits of the controlled airspace. Beyond those limits, the pilot must be able to adhere to the basic VFR minimum ceiling and visibility regulations, both below and above the 700- and 1200-foot floors.

Regardless of IFR traffic, no SVFR would be approved unless the following minimum safe altitudes stated in FAR 91.119 could be met:

- No pilot may operate an aircraft over any congested area of city, town, or settlement, or over any open-air assembly of persons, below 1000 feet above the highest obstacle within a radius of 2000 feet of the aircraft.
- The minimum altitude for fixed-wing aircraft, while flying over other than congested areas, is 500 feet AGL, except over open water or sparsely populated terrain.

Thus, if the ceilings are such that these portions of the FARs would be violated, a request for an SVFR would be denied. By the same token, however, these minimums must not be violated by fixed-wing aircraft, no matter what the weather. (The FARs are a little more lenient for helicopters.)

What about night SVFRs?

These are prohibited between sunset and sunrise unless the pilot is instrument-rated and the aircraft is equipped for IFR flight.

Can SVFRs be obtained at all airports?

No. Some of the busy, high-density Class B and C airports will not approve SVFRs. The ban, where it exists, is indicated on the sectional chart by the notation "No SVFR." Typically, the notation is located just above the airport data block, as Fig. 5-16 illustrates. Also, the specific airports imposing the ban are listed in FAR Part 91, Appendix D, Section 3.

How is an SVFR obtained at a Class E airport?

In nontower locations, the SVFR is requested through the Flight Service Station, operating tower, Approach or Departure Control, or Air Route Traffic Control Center responsible for serving the area.

Why contact an FSS? It's not a controlling agency.

True, but the FSS will relay the SVFR request to the appropriate ATC facility, such as Approach Control or Center. That facility will approve or disapprove the request, based

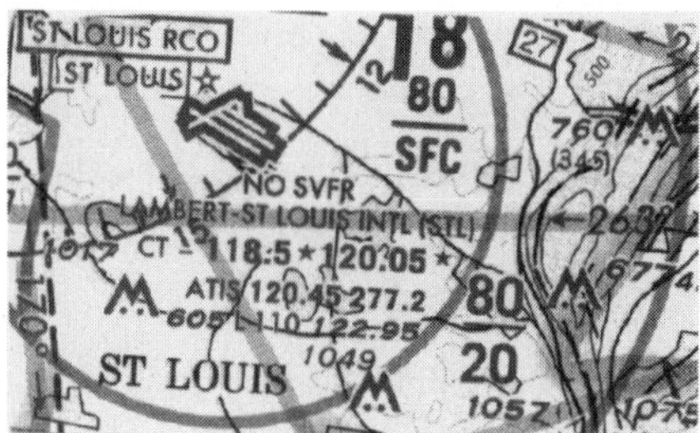

Fig. 5-16 *The "No SVR" directly above the name of the airport indicates just that—no special VFR clearances are permitted at St. Louis Lambert Field.*

on existing traffic, and will inform the FSS accordingly, which, in turn, will inform the pilot. Although it's an abbreviated example of the radio call, the phraseology, after establishing contact with the FSS, would go something like this:

> Pilot: Jonesville Radio, Cherokee one two three four echo requests Special VFR out of the Jonesville Class E surface area for VFR northwest to Smithtown via Victor four zero zero. Departure time immediate upon approval of request. Three four echo.

There will be a period of silence while the FSS specialist contacts the responsible controlling facility and then reports back:

> FSS: Cherokee 34 echo, ATC clears Cherokee one two three four echo out of the Jonesville Class E surface area for northwest departure on Victor four zero zero for Smithtown. Maintain Special VFR conditions at or below three thousand while in the Class E surface area. Report leaving the area.

What facility would you contact in other situations?

That depends on where you are geographically and the facilities that are on or off the airport. Generally speaking, however, here are some broad guidelines on whom to call for an SVFR clearance:

Departing:

- Class E airport with no facility physically on the airport: Call the nearest FSS, the Approach or Departure Control, or Center responsible for traffic control in the Class E airport airspace.
- Class B, C, or D airports: *AIM* says call the tower. Alternatives are Ground Control or Clearance Delivery. If uncertain, make the first call to Ground Control and ask if it is the facility that initiates the SVFR request. Ground Control will then either tell you whom to contact or will handle the request itself.

Arriving or Transiting. (You are flying VFR but have learned from ATIS or an FSS that your destination airport is below the VFR minimums of 3000 feet and 1 mile. Just be sure to call 15 to 20 miles out so that there will be time to receive the SVFR approval *before* you inadvertently penetrate a controlled airport airspace.) Your destination airport is a

- Class E. Call the FSS, Center, or Approach Control responsible for the Class E traffic control.
- Class D with tower but no Approach Control. Call the tower.
- Class D, C, or B with tower and Approach Control. Call Approach Control.
- Satellite airport lying within the surface-configured Class D airspace of the primary airport or the core area of a Class C or B airspace. Call the Class D Approach Control, if such exists, or the Class D tower. Call Approach Control if the primary airport is Class C or B.

Some of this talk about the airspaces and SVFRs undoubtedly gets confusing at times, and perhaps I've belabored the subject(s) to the extreme. They're all part of the system, though, and thus must be understood by those who use the airspaces. I would suggest, however, whether you are a student or VFR, IFR, private, or commercial pilot, that you master the airspace concepts and stay on top of whatever changes may be forthcoming. Currency here, as well as in all other aspects of flying, not only could be, but is, essential to your well-being.

TEMPORARY FLIGHT RESTRICTIONS

Curiosity and/or morbidity is rather common in humans. A major fire is raging; an explosion has devastated a wide area; a tornado has wiped out a portion of a town; a major sporting event is underway. Whatever the incident, many of us are tempted to get airborne and see what's going on from above. Before we do so, it would be wise to do a little checking.

If there is an incident that warrants temporary flight restrictions, the restrictions are established by the area manager of the Air Route Traffic Control Center that has jurisdiction over the area in which the incident has taken, or is taking, place. Then, through FAA procedures, a NOTAM is issued stipulating what restrictions are in effect. Largely, these are designed to bar sightseers from the area and to prevent interference with emergency, rescue, or disaster relief measures.

Normally, the restricted airspace extends to 2000 feet AGL within a 2-nautical-mile radius of the event. These dimensions can vary, however, with the seriousness of the occurrence and the rescue or relief operations involved. The NOTAM fully explains the restrictions, how long they will be in effect, what aircraft are permitted within the area, and the military or federal agency responsible for coordinating emergency activities.

FARs state the restriction regulations, and *AIM* provides further explanation. Recognizing the occasional tendency to be ambulance chasers or just plain gawkers, we should review current regulations, plus check for NOTAMs that might have been issued, before giving into that tendency, should it exist; it could keep us out of trouble.

AUTOMATED WEATHER-OBSERVING SYSTEM (AWOS) AND AUTOMATED SURFACE OBSERVATION SYSTEM (ASOS)

If you glance at the airport data blocks on almost any sectional chart, you'll find a goodly number that are equipped with AWOS (automated weather-observing system) or ASOS (automated surface observation system). A "goodly" number is probably not very descriptive, however, because estimates, including those from the National Weather Service ASOS Program Office in Silver Spring, Maryland, put the current installations in excess of 1000, with many additional systems underway or projected.

The advantages of an automated system are many, ranging from minute-to-minute real-time observations; to more consistent information, undiluted by human judgment, interpretation, vision-blocking obstructions, or darkness; to greater economic use around the clock of airport personnel. In addition to these advantages is the obvious safety factor. Particularly with ASOS's more extensive observations and reports, pilots, when approaching an unattended Class E or G airport, will have a much clearer picture of the current conditions than would otherwise be possible or probable. And, in a similar vein, AWOS or ASOS on the field opens the airport to increased local and transient traffic, ultimately resulting in a more profitable operation for the community.

Much has been written describing and justifying both AWOS and ASOS. For our purposes here, however, a brief summary of the two systems and the data they transmit would seem more to the point. Consequently, what follows focuses on what the systems are, what they do, and what they don't do.

AWOS and ASOS: General

As the National Weather Service's *Tool Box* (a summary of automated surface observations for ASOS trainers) puts it, both AWOS and ASOS are composed of "electronic sensors, connected to a computer, that measure, process, and create surface observations every minute. These systems provide 1-minute, 5-minute, hourly, and special observations 24 hours a day." Through computer-generated voice subsystems, the minute-by-minute observations are transmitted over discrete VHF radio frequencies and can be received up to 25 nautical miles from the airport as well as up to 10,000 feet AGL. Transmissions may also be over the voice portion of a local navigational aid. Whichever the vehicle, the weather message is 20 to 30 seconds long and is updated each minute. Consequently, if you monitor the reports from a given airport over a reasonable period of time, you can develop a picture of the prevailing conditions and whether they are degenerating, improving, or remaining static.

Although AWOS and ASOS would seem to have a close-cousin relationship, there are differences that make ASOS the more complete system and the system that is in the gradual process of replacing AWOS. Neither system, however, is likely to eliminate entirely the need for human observations, if only because the electronic systems are limited in their horizontal coverage and cannot forecast weather trends.

They only report what *is* happening—not what *will* happen. Of course, as I said, if you listen to enough consecutive reports of what is going on now at an airport, you'll be able to detect or establish a weather pattern trend. That trend, though, is a product of deduction, not prognostication.

There is another factor related to human involvement: The automated systems report only the weather that exists directly above the sensors. They have no ability to accumulate and digest conditions that might be surrounding or approaching the airport. For example, the observing system reports highly favorable conditions at a given airport in terms of ceiling, visibility, winds, temperature, density altitude, dew point, and the like—in essence, perfect flying weather. But only a couple of miles or so off the airport property, a raging thunderstorm has blackened the sky. The automated observing systems will not report that storm because they're not capable of processing horizontal or diagonal weather. Despite all their data-collecting capabilities, the current systems have a built-in vertical tunnel vision which, at times, requires human intervention, or "augmentation," to provide a more complete report of present and/or anticipated conditions. Whenever this augmentation by a qualified observer is considered necessary, it is, as *AIM* puts it, "identified in the observation as *observer weather.*"

Location of the sensors on the airport is important. Generally speaking, the chosen site is near the touchdown point of the principal instrument runway; but also to be considered in that decision are local conditions such as nearby lakes, rivers, an ocean, or terrain that could adversely affect accurate observations. If such potentially distorting elements exist, additional sensors could be installed to produce more accurate reports.

Of the two systems, AWOS is the older, having been around in one form or another for more than 30 years. Despite a continuing pattern of adding information to the system, AWOS does not produce the variety of observations provided by ASOS. Consequently, ASOS is gradually replacing AWOS, and AWOS will presumably disappear from the scene within the next few years.

AWOS, in brief

Four levels make up the AWOS:

1. AWOS-A: Only reports altimeter setting.
2. AWOS-1: Reports altimeter setting, winds, temperature, dew point, and density altitude.
3. AWOS-2: Reports the information provided by AWOS-1, plus visibility.
4. AWOS-3: Reports the information provided by AWOS-2, plus cloud and ceiling data.

In addition to the radio transmissions, most AWOS messages can be monitored on the ground via telephone. For the level of an AWOS at a given airport, plus the radio frequency and telephone number, consult the appropriate *A/FD*. If AWOS or ASOS is on the field, you'll see in bold print an *A/FD* entry similar to this: Weather Data Sources: AWOS-3 133.8 (814) 443-2114.

ASOS, in brief

The ASOS program, which is the primary surface weather-observing system, is a joint effort of the National Weather Service, the Department of Defense, and the FAA. The system, as *AIM* puts it, provides "continuous minute-by-minute observations and performs the basic observing functions necessary to generate an aviation routine weather report (METAR) and other aviation weather information." Equipped with at least one sensor for each unit, a given ASOS, as the National Oceanic and Atmospheric Administration (NOAA) describes it, will be able to "observe" and report these conditions:

- Cloud height and amount (clear, scattered, broken, overcast) up to 12,000 feet
- Visibility (to at least 10 statute miles)
- Precipitation identification (type and intensity for rain, snow, and freezing rain)
- Barometric pressure and altimeter setting
- Ambient temperature and dew point temperature
- Wind direction, speed, and character (gusts, squalls)
- Rainfall accumulation
- Selected significant remarks such as variable cloud heights, variable visibility, precipitation beginning and ending times, rapid pressure changes, pressure change tendency, wind shift, and peak wind

Figure 5-17 is a NOAA illustration of the principal elements and sensors of an ASOS installation.

With all its positive features, however, ASOS is *not* designed to report

- Clouds above 12,000 feet
- Tornadoes
- Funnel clouds
- Ice crystals
- Drizzle
- Freezing drizzle
- Blowing obstructions (snow, sand, or dust, snowfall and snow depth)

To paraphrase the NWS *Tool Box,* data related to many of these latter conditions are, or can be, provided by other sources. Meanwhile, NWS adds that "...new sensors will be added to measure some of these weather elements."

As a reminder again, these automated systems provide 24-hour observations of weather conditions within 2 to 3 miles of the sensor site. Beyond those limits, lateral

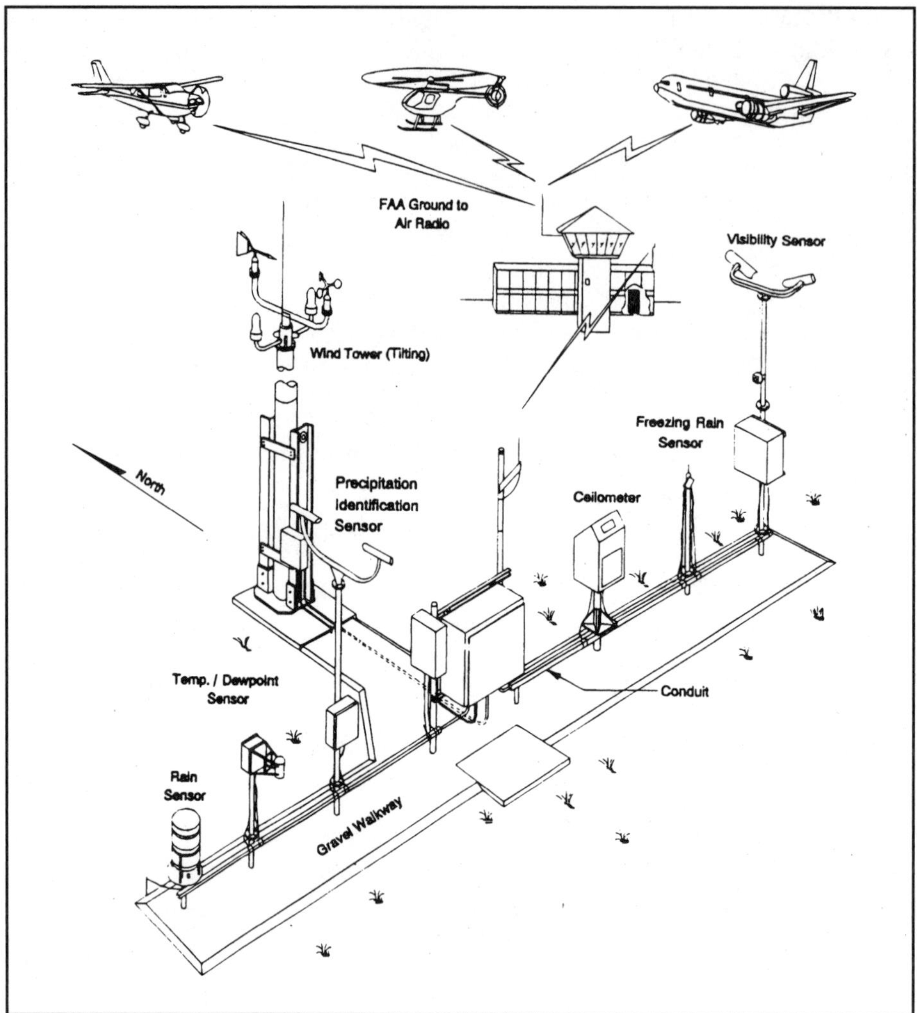

Fig. 5-17 *The elements of an ASOS airport installation.*

coverage is not possible. Keep in mind, though, that observing systems are really in their infancy, despite the fact that AWOS has been around since the 1960s. As new sensors are developed and computer technology advances, improvements in the systems are inevitable.

These, then, are some of the AWOS and ASOS basics, although there's more that could be said about this electronic weather data processing system. I felt, however, that an overview of what the systems do and can't do would be more meaningful than a technical discussion of their components, the application of mathematical logic (algorithms), or why human augmentation is often an essential supplement to the automated report. But like so many other aspects of aviation, this is just one more subject or area in which the proficient pilot keeps him- or herself informed. If you tend to do most of your flying in Class E or G airport environments where 24-hour automated weather broadcasts may be available, knowledge of the system, what it's telling you, and its limitations could be especially important. There will be changes—mostly for the good—as time moves along, so staying on top of these safety-enhancing systems should be a high-priority project for every pilot, whatever his or her rating or experience level.

6
Special-use airspace

GLANCING AT ALMOST ANY SECTIONAL REVEALS A VARIETY OF lines and designs that depict airspaces set aside for special use. In all cases, these are blocks of space established for purposes of national security, welfare, and environmental protection, plus military training, research, development, testing, and evaluation (military training/RDT&E). Although the airspace reserved for security, welfare, and the environment could require flight detours or altitude changes, their size and sparseness make them relatively minor obstacles to VFR and IFR operations. Not so, though, with the areas designed for military training/RDT&E, which provide space for all sorts of flight training maneuvers, bombing runs, missile launching, aerial gunnery, or artillery practice.

It's thus apparent that unauthorized or careless penetration of active special-use airspace (SUA) could be somewhat hazardous to the unwary pilot. That being the case, let's start with a summary of the policy behind this airspace, followed by the various types of SUA and the VFR pilot's responsibilities relative to them.

MILITARY OPERATIONS REQUIREMENTS

The FAA has a controller's handbook titled *Special Military Operations* (7610.4G) that summarizes the basic FAA policy relative to military operations requirements. In essence, the policy recognizes that the military has a continuing need to conduct certain training as well as research, development, testing, and evaluation activities, and that these activities should take place in airspaces large enough to contain the planned activity and should be as free from nonparticipating aircraft as is practical. Accordingly, four types of special-use airspace exist primarily, but not exclusively, for military purposes: *restricted areas* (R), *military operations areas* (MOAs), *alert areas* (A), and *warning areas* (W). In addition, but not considered special-use airspace, there are the *Air Defense Identification Zones* (ADIZs) and cross-country low-level VFR and IFR *military training routes* (MTRs).

The one other type of SUA, classified as *prohibited areas* (P), is established for national security, national welfare, or environmental protection. As mentioned, however, these are relatively few in number and small enough in area to be of only infrequent concern to the pilot. Prohibited areas, along with MTRs, ADIZs, and the varieties of military SUA, are depicted on sectional and other aeronautical charts.

As a further matter of policy, the government agency, organization, or military command responsible for establishing SUA must specify the proposed area's

- Vertical limits
- Horizontal limits
- Hours of use, plus notations indicating whether the use is continuous, intermittent, by NOTAM, or otherwise

The policy also states that

- The SUA will be limited to the minimum area(s) necessary to support operational requirements.
- The area will be designed to conduct the maximum number of different types of military activity in the same airspace area.
- The military shall provide procedures for joint-use scheduling in the area (joint use meaning use by both participating and nonparticipating aircraft).

Does the military just grab a chunk of airspace that it decides it needs? Hardly. Take the case of a MOA. The only aspect of the process occasionally subject to whimsy is the MOA's name. From the time the Air Force determines the need for the airspace until the FAA headquarters in Washington issues the final approval, eight or nine steps have intervened. These include reviews by, and coordination with, the military's regional office, the Air Route Traffic Control Center responsible for the area in which the SUA will be established, the FAA's regional office, interested entities on whom the airspace might have impact (such as airport managers, pilot organizations, and pilots themselves), and if military activities are proposed below 3000 feet AGL, the Environmental Protection Agency (EPA). Above 3000 feet, a *categorical exclusion* exists, and the EPA does not become involved. What with consultations, negotiations, and the need to follow the military and government chain of command, it can easily take up to 2 years from start to finish to establish a military SUA.

Moreover, once the SUA comes into being, each using agency (as subsequently defined) must submit annual reports on the previous 12 months' activity. In the case of restricted areas, this includes the usage by daily hours, days of the week, and the number of weeks during the year that the space was released to the controlling agency for public use. In effect, the report justifies the existence of the space as it stands or reflects the need for revisions.

Some definitions might help in understanding the basic policy:

Using agency
This refers to the agency or military unit that is the primary user and scheduler of the particular airspace.

Controlling agency
This is the FAA facility, almost always the ARTCC, in which the airspace is located. Depending on a variety of factors, Center might exert direct control of military traffic operating within that airspace.

Participating aircraft
These aircraft, usually but not necessarily military, are involved in the training/RDT&E.

Nonparticipating aircraft
These are aircraft for which a Center has separation responsibility (meaning IFR aircraft) but which have not been authorized by the using agency to operate through or in the SUA.

Before we discuss SUA in a little greater detail, let's examine the three basic areas that fall under the broad heading of SUA.

Prohibited
Throughout the country, certain geographic areas have been set aside to protect wildlife and recreational properties. In these prohibited areas, either flight is banned completely or aircraft must observe the established minimum altitude. If you check the sectional charts or the ELAC (en route low-altitude chart), you'll find a few such areas, one example being located in the arrowhead portion of Minnesota on the U.S.-Canadian border. The minimum altitude over the areas identified as P-204, P-205, and P-206 is 4000 feet AGL.

Other types of prohibited territory include those that are considered important in terms of national security or history. Examples are the White House and government buildings, mostly along the Mall; Mount Vernon, Virginia; Kennebunkport, Maine (former President Bush's family residence); Camp David; the Naval Support Facility near Thurmont, Maryland; and a Department of Energy nuclear facility in Amarillo, Texas.

Restricted
Approximately 180 restricted areas exist across the country, with many composed of subsegments, such as A, B, and C. The subsegments, however, are not counted as part of the 180 total.

Military operation areas
There are also approximately 180, with each specific MOA counted as a single area, regardless of the number of subsegments.

Finally, you who fly exclusively in Connecticut or Rhode Island are lucky. Those are the only two states of the 50 that have no special-use airspace within their borders.

SPECIAL-USE AIRSPACE: TYPES

Now for a closer look at the types of SUA, why they exist, and the restrictions, if any, they place on the VFR pilot.

Prohibited areas (P)

These areas are identified in sectional charts as illustrated in Fig. 6-1. The Camp David area is depicted on the Washington sectional by the inward-pointing shaded lines (in blue in the full-color originals) and the "P-40" identification. The SUA table on the sectional (Fig. 6-2) states that flight below 5000 feet is prohibited, the ban is continuous, and there are no air-ground communications in the area.

The same principles apply in other such areas. From the surface to whatever altitude is specified, the area is prohibited, and that means prohibited: no ifs, ands, or buts. Prior approval is required and must be properly obtained to penetrate any of this space.

Fig. 6-1 *How the sectional chart depicts a prohibited area.*

SPECIAL USE AIRSPACE ON WASHINGTON SECTIONAL CHART

Unless otherwise noted altitudes are MSL and in feet; time is local.
Contact nearest FSS for information.
†Other time by NOTAM contact FSS

The word "TO" an altitude means "To and including."
"MON-FRI" indicates "Monday thru Friday"
FL – Flight Level
NO A/G – No air to ground communications

U.S. P–PROHIBITED, R–RESTRICTED, A–ALERT, W–WARNING, MOA–MILITARY OPERATIONS AREA

NUMBER	LOCATION	ALTITUDE	TIME OF USE	CONTROLLING AGENCY**
P-40	THURMONT, MD	TO BUT NOT INCL 5000 (UNDERLIES R-4009)	CONTINUOUS	NO A/G
P-56	WASHINGTON, DC	TO 18,000	CONTINUOUS	NO A/G WARNING - AVOID THIS AREA
P-73	MOUNT VERNON, VA	TO BUT NOT INCL 1500	CONTINUOUS	NO A/G
R-4001 A	ABERDEEN, MD	(1) UNLIMITED (2) TO 10,000	(1) 0700-2400 (2) 0000-0700 HIGHER ALTITUDES BY NOTAM 24 HRS IN ADVANCE	ZDC CNTR
R-4001 B	ABERDEEN, MD	TO 10,000	INTERMITTENT BY NOTAM 24 HRS IN ADVANCE HIGHER ALTITUDES BY NOTAM 24 HRS IN ADVANCE	ZDC CNTR

Fig. 6-2 *The special-use airspace box on the sectional summarizes the SUA flight restrictions and times of use.*

Restricted areas (R)

More common, and larger in territory, are the restricted areas. These blocks of space, when active, pose serious and often invisible hazards to nonparticipating aircraft and those not specifically authorized to enter the area. What sort of hazards? Well, how about artillery fire, missiles, aerial gunnery, or bombing as examples? That should be enough to discourage violation of the area by any VFR pilot when it's active.

The areas are easy to spot on the sectional because of the vertical (formerly diagonal) blue lines that establish the horizontal perimeters. Figure 6-3 illustrates two areas located near Brookfield, Kansas, identified as R-3601A and R-3601B. The table on the Wichita sectional (Fig. 6-4) provides further information about the altitudes within which military activity can be conducted, the time(s) of use, and the controlling agency. In this case, it is ZKC, which is the Kansas City ARTCC.

You're flying VFR at 7500 feet and would like to cross through R-3601B going west to east. Can you do it without permission or clearance? Yes. The area's altitude of use is from the surface to and including 6500 feet MSL. Above that altitude, R-3601B doesn't exist; thus, no approval to transit the airspace is required, and there is no threat from ground or airborne military activities.

Transiting R-3601A is a different story. This airspace extends from the ground up to FL180, and during the hours of use, ZKC (Kansas City Center) would route even IFR aircraft around or above the area. Obviously, VFR flight should not even be contemplated.

During the published hours of use, the using agency is responsible for controlling all military activity within the R area and determining that its perimeters are not violated. When scheduled to be inactive, the using agency releases the airspace back to the controlling agency (Center), and, in effect, the airspace is no longer restricted.

By the same token, it's entirely possible that no activity will be scheduled during some of the published hours of use. In those instances, the using agency again releases the space to the controlling agency for nonmilitary operations during that period of inactivity.

From a VFR point of view, then, the pilot's responsibility is rather apparent:

- When you are plotting a VFR flight and the route crosses a restricted area, determine from a current sectional the altitudes of activity and the days and hours of use. If the flight would penetrate the area when it is active, there's only one admonition: Stay out. An active R area is a land for no man. Furthermore, if you should wander into such an area intentionally or carelessly, anticipate a chat with the FAA and a resulting violation filed against you.
- If the flight is planned during a period when the area is published as inactive, don't plod ahead in blind confidence. Note the likely statement "O/T by NOTAM," meaning possible use at times other than stated. When this occurs, the using agency notifies the controlling ARTCC (16 hours in advance, in the cases of R-3601A and B). Center then advises all Flight Service Stations within 100 miles of the area, and a NOTAM is issued by those FSSs reflecting the nonpublished activation of the area. So, even though you're planning to head out

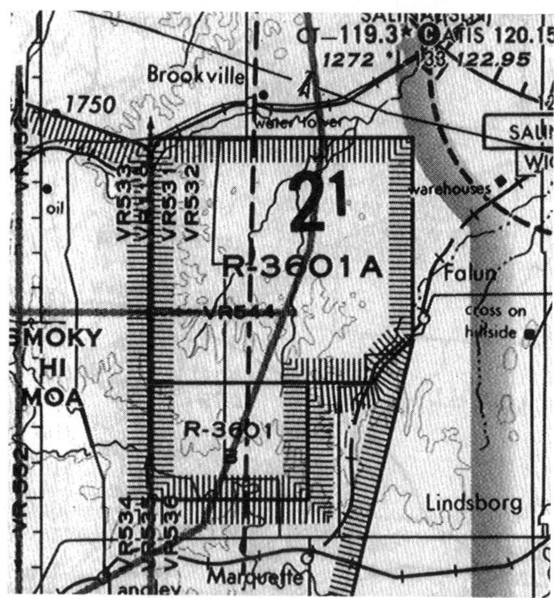

Fig. 6-3 *Restricted areas on the sectional are identified by the R number and the border lines (in blue on the original).*

SPECIAL USE AIRSPACE ON WICHITA SECTIONAL CHART

Unless otherwise noted altitudes are MSL and in feet; time is local.
Contact nearest FSS for information.
†Other time by NOTAM contact FSS

The word "TO" an altitude means "To and including."
"MON-FRI" indicates "Monday thru Friday"
FL – Flight Level
NO A/G – No air to ground communications

U.S. P-PROHIBITED, R-RESTRICTED, A-ALERT, W-WARNING, MOA-MILITARY OPERATIONS AREA

NUMBER	LOCATION	ALTITUDE	TIME OF USE	CONTROLLING AGENCY**
R-3601 A	BROOKVILLE, KS	TO FL 180	0800-1800 MON, WED, FRI, SAT, 0800-2230 TUES, THURS, †24 HRS IN ADV	ZKC CNTR
R-3601 B	BROOKVILLE, KS	TO 6500	0800-1800 MON, WED, FRI, SAT, 0800-2230 TUES, THURS, †24 HRS IN ADV	ZKC CNTR
R-3602 A	MANHATTAN, KS	TO 29,000	CONTINUOUS	ZKC CNTR
R-3602 B	MANHATTAN, KS	TO 29,000	CONTINUOUS	ZKC CNTR
A-562 A	ENID, OK	TO 10,000	SR-3 HR AFTER SS MON-FRI	NO A/G
A-562 B	ENID, OK	TO 10,000	SR-SS MON-FRI	NO A/G
A-683	WICHITA McCONNELL AFB, KS	TO 4500	0800-1900 MON-FRI	NO A/G

**ZKC-Kansas City

Fig. 6-4 *Another example of the SUA data summary in the sectional chart.*

on a Sunday morning or any other time when an R area is apparently not in use, don't do so until you have contacted the appropriate FSS. Then specifically ask if there is a NOTAM stating that the R area will be active at the time you will pass through it. If there is such a NOTAM, you again have only one choice: Reroute and stay out; an R area is not to be fooled with.

- Even though a chart might indicate that a military-related R area is effective 8 a.m. until noon, Monday through Friday, it doesn't mean that the area is always active during that period. If the military is not using the airspace and has released it to the controlling agency, you might get permission from the controlling agency (usually Center) to pass through the R area. All it takes is a telephone or radio call, and it can save you time and money. Be sure you call, though, within 2 hours of your estimated transit through the area, to make sure that the military does not intend to reactivate it on short notice.

Military operations areas

Military operations areas pose the largest potential obstacle to direct VFR flight between two points because of their relative size and number. This is not always the case, of course, but it happens frequently enough to cause diversions or detours when a MOA is active.

What is a MOA? It's the vertical and horizontal chunk of airspace established to segregate certain military flight training exercises, such as combat maneuvers, aerobatics, and air intercept training, from nonparticipating IFR traffic. While activity in a restricted area is described as potentially *hazardous* to nonparticipating aircraft, the same adjective is not employed in describing a MOA. Perhaps that's a matter of semantics, however. An F-16 barreling straight up or straight down could be considered somewhat hazardous to an aircraft that had penetrated an active MOA.

To draw a clearer distinction between a restricted area and a MOA, restricted areas are established primarily for artillery, missiles, lasers, ground-to-ground and air-to-air gunnery, bombing practice, and similar training/RDT&E exercises. Because of the nature of the activities, the ground and airspace above a restricted area are, in effect, "deeded" to the military by the government and made a matter of record in the *Federal Register.*

A MOA, on the other hand, is designed for the flight training exercises cited above. Furthermore, the airspace might be requested by the military (Air Force, Navy, or Air National Guard), but it is the FAA in the final analysis that agrees to establish a MOA. In other words, one might say that a MOA comes into being only at the discretion of the FAA.

Identifying MOAs

Undoubtedly familiar to every pilot are the vertically striped magenta bands on the sectional that block off those large chunks of terrain and the airspace above them. Designed as they are with consideration for both military and nonmilitary operations, the length and width of an active MOA could add miles and certainly minutes to a VFR flight. (As an aside, *hot* is the usual pilot jargon to refer to an active MOA or restricted area, as in "Demo 2 MOA is hot.")

As just one example of size, take the Ada West MOA in central Kansas (Fig. 6-5). It's not unusually large, but it does stretch 40 nautical miles east to west and 18 to 30 nautical miles north to south. That could be a fair piece of geography to circumnavigate if the MOA were hot.

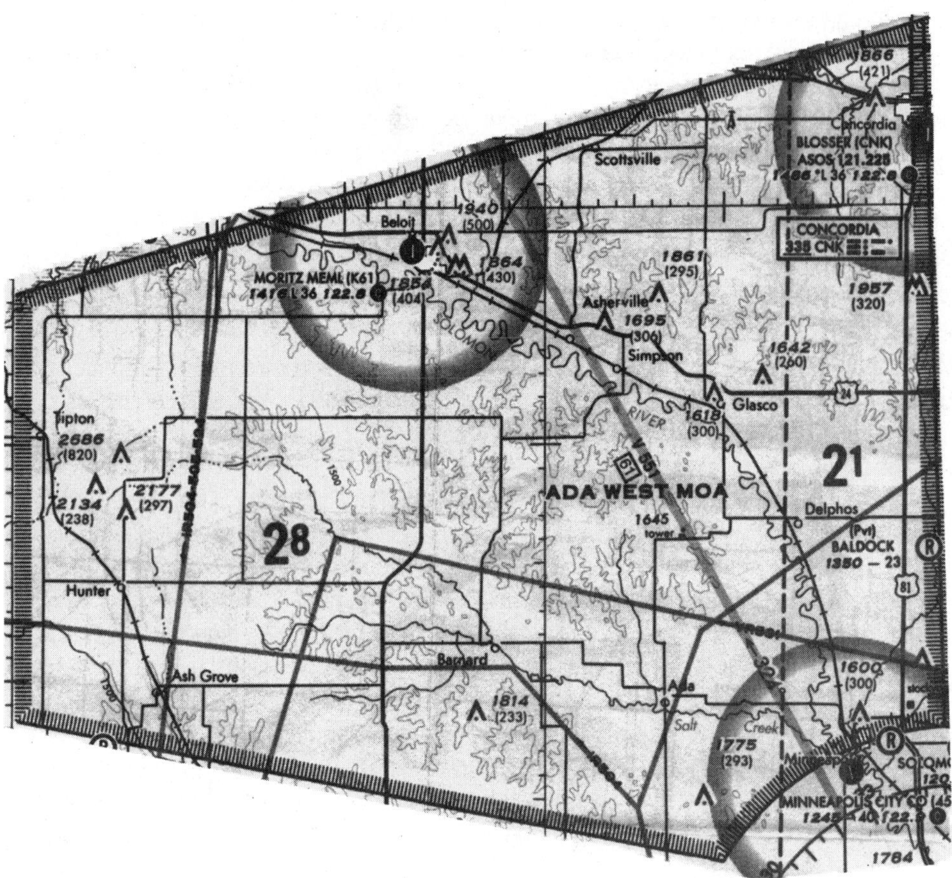

Fig. 6-5 *An excerpt from the Wichita sectional shows the expanse of the Ada West MOA.*

Should you or should you not avoid a MOA? First, check the sectional table (Fig. 6-6). Printed in magenta on the original is the MOA name, altitudes of use, time(s) of use, and controlling agency. Note particularly the Ada West altitudes of use: 7000 feet. This means that the MOA can be active from 7000 to flight level 180 (18,000 feet), as per the asterisk footnote, and the time of use is from sunrise (SR) to sunset (SS) Monday through Friday. As a matter of general information, MOAs may extend vertically above FL180 through the designation of the airspace as an *ATC assigned airspace* (ATCAA).

The time of use raises a point. These are the "published" periods during which the MOA is most likely, but not necessarily, active. Said another way, these are the times that the using agency has identified as the "probable" periods of activity based on operations schedules, availability of aircraft, pilots, and similar considerations. The area's using agency, let's say an Air Force unit, has, in each case, a scheduling office that is responsible for establishing a real-time activity schedule for the MOA and forwarding it, as well as any subsequent changes, to the controlling ARTCC. That office is also responsible for developing procedures with other Air Force user units to ensure that those units notify the scheduler as soon as possible of any periods (1 hour or longer) of MOA nonuse after the initial schedule has been established. The purpose, of course, is to permit the scheduling office to return complete control of the airspace to the responsible ARTCC for nonmilitary use. As with restricted areas, however, "O/T by NOTAM" (other times by NOTAM) also applies to the MOAs.

Consequently, keep in mind that the time of use only establishes the hours during which the using agency is free to schedule activity. Through its scheduling office, however, that agency must advise the ARTCC on a daily basis of the planned schedule, as well as changes in that schedule that might occur. Otherwise, the MOA cannot be used for its designated purposes.

MOAs and the VFR pilot

Can you, as a VFR pilot, enter any MOA at any time, whether active or not? Yes. It is not a prohibited or restricted area. Should you enter? If the area is hot at your intended altitude, the answer is an absolute no. It's like cloud-busting—you're playing Russian roulette.

For one thing, an active MOA might be full of fighters zipping around you at close to Mach 1 speeds. Also, military training involves acrobatics and abrupt maneuvers. To permit such training, participating aircraft in a MOA are exempt from FAR 91 which states

> No person may operate an aircraft in acrobatic flight...within a control zone or a Federal airway...[or] below an altitude of 1,500 feet above the surface....

Freed of these regulations, you could have aircraft going straight up, straight down, inverted in flight, or whatever, while you're plodding along in their training airspace. To compound the risk, despite the fact that military pilots are probably far better trained in the see-and-avoid concept than the typical civilian, they are often very busy while

MOA NAME	ALTITUDE OF USE*	TIME OF USE†	CONTROLLING AGENCY**
ADA EAST	7000	SR-SS MON-FRI	ZKC CNTR
ADA WEST	7000	SR-SS MON-FRI	ZKC CNTR
BISON	1000 AGL	0830-1130 & 1330-1600 MON-FRI & ONE WEEKEND PER MONTH	ZKC CNTR
KIT CARSON A	100 AGL TO BUT NOT INCL 9000	INTERMITTENT BY NOTAM	ZDV CNTR
KIT CARSON B	9000	INTERMITTENT BY NOTAM	ZDV CNTR
LINCOLN	8000	BY NOTAM (NORMALLY 0900-1600 TUE-SUN)	ZMP CNTR
MT. DORA EAST, NORTH, WEST HIGH	11,000	BY NOTAM	ZAB CNTR
MT. DORA EAST, NORTH, WEST LOW	1500 AGL TO BUT NOT INCL 11,000	BY NOTAM	ZAB CNTR
PINON CANYON	100 AGL TO 10,000	INTERMITTENT BY NOTAM	ZDV CNTR
SMOKY	500 AGL TO BUT NOT INCL 5000	0900-1700 MON-SAT	ZKC CNTR
SMOKY HIGH	5000	0900-1700 MON-SAT	ZKC CNTR
VANCE 1A	10,000	1 HR BEFORE SR-1 HR AFTER SS MON-FRI	ZKC CNTR
VANCE 1B	7000	1 HR BEFORE SR-1 HR AFTER SS MON-FRI	ZKC CNTR

*Altitudes indicate floor of MOA. All MOAs extend to but do not include FL 180 unless otherwise indicated in tabulation or on chart.
†Other time by NOTAM contact FSS.
**ZAB-Albuquerque, ZDV-Denver, ZKC-Kansas City, ZMP-Minneapolis.

30'

Fig. 6-6 *The MOA data in the sectional detail the altitudes, times of use, and controlling agency—in this case, ZKC (Kansas City Center).*

maneuvering in a MOA and can't devote much time or attention to looking for nonparticipating aircraft.

Here is a point of clarification: Participating aircraft are exempt from FAR 91 only when they are operating between the published MOA floor and ceiling. In the Ada example, from 7000 feet MSL to FL180, the FAR doesn't apply; however, below 7000 feet, participating aircraft must abide by all FARs. The rules for them are the same as for any pilot, VFR, IFR, airline, or general aviation.

So, once again, how do you know whether you should or shouldn't penetrate a MOA? Let's go back to the Ada West example (Fig. 6-5). If you planned a daylight trip during the week and wanted to cruise at any altitude above 7000 feet MSL through the area, you'd be wise to forget it. Make a flight plan for a lower altitude or detour the whole MOA. Not that you are prohibited from cruising at 7500 or 8500 feet, but you're likely to encounter activity anywhere between 7000 and 18,000 feet. Unless, within a few hours of your departure, you can determine from a Flight Service Station that no operations have been scheduled, despite the published time of use, it's just not worth the risk.

However, suppose you want to venture forth on a weekend. Presumably the MOA will be quiet, per the sectional, and a flight through it at any altitude would pose no problem. But don't be too sure. A call to your Flight Service Station is in order. During the briefing, if the information is not volunteered, specifically ask if any NOTAMs have been issued about activity in the Ada MOAs.

Assuming no NOTAMs have been issued, you're probably in good shape. But let's say that your last phone call to the FSS was 4 or 5 hours ago. Now you're airborne, and what was fact then might not be fact now. The using agency could have scheduled an activity in the interim. If so, you ought to know about it. So what do you do? As you're flying along and approaching the MOA, get on the radio and call the controlling Air Route Traffic Control Center—in the Ada case, Kansas City Center. If you have not been in contact with Center for traffic advisories up to now, the call is simple:

You: Kansas City Center, Cherokee Eight Five One Five November.
Center: Cherokee Eight Five One Five November, Kansas City Center, go ahead.
You: Center, Cherokee One Five November is about twenty north of Ada West, level at seven thousand five hundred. Can you advise if the area is hot?
Center: Cherokee One Five November, negative. There is no reported activity at this time and no NOTAMs issued.
You: Roger, center. Thank you. Cherokee One Five November.

If the area is hot, Center will confirm that fact and probably tell you the type of activity that's going on.

Instead of contacting Center, why not call the nearest FSS? Although both Center and the FSS will have the same schedule of activity, only Center has the most accurate reading of what participating aircraft are actually in the area and where they are; thus, Center is the best source for determining the current, real-time MOA activity.

Let's say the MOA is hot. Who provides any control of the participating aircraft? (*Participating* means the aircraft authorized and scheduled to be in the MOA.) An ATC facility, such as Center, might assume the responsibility when requested by the military.

Otherwise, when certain conditions are met and a letter of agreement exists, control of a MOA, or any other ATC Assigned Airspace (ATCAA), can be transferred to a *military radar unit* (MRU). It is now the MRU's responsibility to keep its aircraft within the altitudes and boundaries of the airspace, to provide traffic advisories to participating aircraft, to separate participating aircraft, and to advise Center immediately when participating aircraft cannot remain within the allocated airspace. So, in this case, there is control, but it is of the military, by the military.

Suppose, going VFR, you have been warned by a Center that a MOA is hot, but you choose to enter it anyway. What can you expect from Center? First, Center would probably advise the military radar facility that a VFR aircraft had penetrated the MOA. Center then *might* give you advisories of potential conflicting military traffic, but don't count on it! If the controller has told you that the MOA is hot but you decide to drive on into it anyway, much more likely is a call saying that "Radar service is terminated. Frequency change approved. If you want later flight following, contact Center when clear of the MOA." The wording may differ somewhat, but that's the gist of what the controller will probably transmit to you.

The common concern of controllers about committing to giving advisories in this situation is the very good possibility that they won't be able to maintain continuous radar contact with the military aircraft during their maneuvering and constant altitude changes. And yet the controllers potentially could be held responsible, should a midair incident occur. It's a logical concern. Traffic advisories are meaningful only when the traffic can be seen on the radarscope and its altitude verified.

So don't rely on much, if any, help from Center in an active MOA. Center will provide separation between nonparticipating IFR aircraft cleared into all MOAs or ATCAAs, but it's a different matter when VFR aircraft are involved. You've been warned that the MOA is hot. You're within your rights to enter the area, but you have to assume the risk and the responsibility to see and avoid. Is the risk really worth the miles and minutes you're saving? You be the judge.

MARSA

Here's an acronym with which many pilots might not be familiar: MARSA, or *military assumes responsibility for separation of aircraft.* This means that when an agreement between the military and the FAA controlling agency has been reached (via letter or otherwise), the military using agency has the right to invoke MARSA. Depending upon the conditions or purposes for doing so, separation and control of participating aircraft become the responsibility of the military radar units, *airborne radar units* (ARUs); or it might be nothing more than visual separation and the pilots' responsibility to see, avoid, and stay within the confines of the assigned airspace.

One example cited by Lt. Col. John Williams, formerly Air Force representative to the FAA's Central Region, was the Williams MOA, just east of Phoenix, Arizona. Designed for extensive pilot training, the MOA was divided into several horizontal and vertical internal segments, with one aircraft assigned to a specific segment. Albuquerque Center, through radar coverage, was responsible for keeping each aircraft within its assigned segment to ensure proper separation. The problem was that the

Center controllers, trying to do their jobs, were on the air so much with the participating aircraft that the flight instructors found it difficult to communicate with their students. Consequently, an agreement was engineered with Center that MARSA would automatically be in effect during student training exercises.

Another example is aerial refueling operations. MARSA begins when a tanker and receiver are in the *air refueling airspace* and the tanker advises ATC that it is accepting MARSA. From then on, until MARSA is terminated, the tanker and receivers are responsible for their own separation.

This is from the FAA's *Special Military Operations* handbook, paragraph 1-33:

> The application of MARSA is a military service prerogative and will not be invoked indiscriminately by individual units or pilots.... ATC facilities do not invoke or deny MARSA. Their sole responsibility concerning the use of MARSA is to provide separation between military aircraft engaged in the MARSA operations *and other nonparticipating IFR aircraft.* (Author's italics)

This is perhaps a matter of little concern to the VFR pilot, but if you should be considering entering a MOA or flying along a military training route (we'll discuss those in a moment), recognize that MARSA might have been invoked, and that the military is assuming responsibility for the separation of its aircraft and its aircraft alone. ATC is now out of the picture entirely, other than separating its nonparticipating IFR aircraft from those of the military.

That's pretty much the MOA story. Of all special-use airspace, MOAs typically offer the largest obstacle to a direct flight between two points; however, the VFR pilot can penetrate them safely if he chooses between two safe courses of action:

- Fly above or below the altitudes of scheduled activity.
- Determine from the FSS the extent of activity, if any, within the assigned altitudes by asking for MOA NOTAMs, and then establish contact with the controlling Center for current activity updates.

Otherwise, be wise. Stay out of MOAs if you don't know what's going on within those magenta boundaries.

Alert areas

Now we come to a slightly different breed of SUA. Except for prohibited areas and air defense identification zones, alert areas are the only type of special-use airspace that exists for other than just military operations. Alert areas might contain a high volume of pilot training or unusual types of aerial activity, neither of which is classified as hazardous to aircraft. While most SUAs do indicate military pilot training, those near Miami, Wichita, and along the Texas and Louisiana Gulf Coast, for example, denote heavy civilian flying activity. In essence, they exist to "alert" pilots to areas of high-density air traffic.

As with the other areas discussed, the alerts are depicted on the sectional by the familiar vertically striped bands (in blue on the original) that define the perimeters

(Fig. 6-7), and the areas are further detailed on the sectional table (Fig. 6-8), outlining location, altitudes of use, and time(s) of use. Underneath the Controlling Agency section is a "No A/G" notation (*no air-ground communications*), which means that no controlling agency is dedicated specifically to the alert area, and no special frequency is assigned for operations within the area.

That might require a little more explanation. Take the case of alert area A-562B, located just a few miles north of Enid, Oklahoma's, Woodring Airport and Vance Air Force Base. If you were coming from the north for landing at Woodring, it might be faster and perhaps more logical to fly straight ahead through the alert area, despite the density of student training. Once in the area, you'd undoubtedly hear all sorts of radio communications, especially to and from the Woodring Class D tower—including the tower's response to your call requesting landing instructions. So, yes, there are air-ground communications in these alert areas, but none of it from the ground relates to control of the operations or traffic within the area itself. So in that context, "No A/G" is absolutely correct.

Unlike the other military-use airspace, the type of activity in the alert area is stated on the sectional. An example is "high-density student training" in A-562B, or perhaps "high volume of helicopter and seaplane traffic," or whatever the reason for existence of the area might be.

Okay, but what's the difference between this and the other areas described? First, participating aircraft in an alert area are governed by all FARs, including the ban on

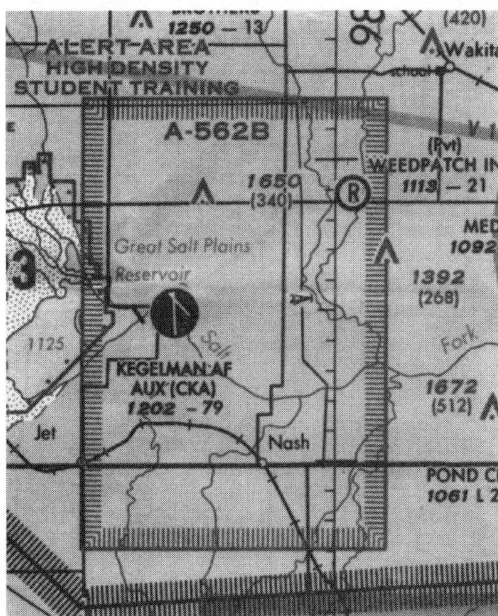

Fig. 6-7 *The alert area at Enid, Oklahoma, is identified by A-562B and the inward-directed lines.*

SPECIAL USE AIRSPACE ON WICHITA SECTIONAL CHART

Unless otherwise noted altitudes are MSL and in feet; time is local.
Contact nearest FSS for information.
†Other time by NOTAM contact FSS

The word "TO" an altitude means "To and including."
"MON-FRI" indicates "Monday thru Friday"
FL – Flight Level
NO A/G – No air to ground communications

U.S. P–PROHIBITED, R–RESTRICTED, A–ALERT, W–WARNING, MOA–MILITARY OPERATIONS AREA

NUMBER	LOCATION	ALTITUDE	TIME OF USE	CONTROLLING AGENCY**
R-3601 A	BROOKVILLE, KS	TO FL 180	0900-1700 MON-SAT †6 HRS IN ADV	ZKC CNTR
R-3601 B	BROOKVILLE, KS	TO 6500	0900-1700 MON-SAT †6 HRS IN ADV	ZKC CNTR
R-3602 A	MANHATTAN, KS	TO 29,000	CONTINUOUS	ZKC CNTR
R-3602 B	MANHATTAN, KS	TO 29,000	CONTINUOUS	ZKC CNTR
A-562 A	ENID, OK	TO 10,000	SR TO 3 HRS AFTER SS MON-FRI	NO A/G
A-562 B	ENID, OK	TO 10,000	SR-SS MON-FRI	NO A/G
A-639 A	USAF ACADEMY, CO	3000 AGL TO 12,000	SR-SS MON-FRI EXC HOL †DAYLIGHT ONLY	NO A/G
A-639 B	USAF ACADEMY, CO	3000 AGL TO 12,000	SR-SS MON-FRI EXC HOL †DAYLIGHT ONLY	NO A/G
A-683	WICHITA MC CONNELL AFB, KS	TO 4500	0800-1900 MON-FRI	NO A/G

** ZKC-Kansas City

Fig. 6-8 *Another example of how the sectional denotes altitudes and times of use of an alert area.*

acrobatics on a federal airway and below 1500 feet AGL. Second, no permission is required to enter an alert area. Third, participating as well as nonparticipating aircraft are equally responsible for collision avoidance. Because no agency (other than routine FAA or military air traffic control) is issuing traffic advisories or alerts, or providing any sort of separation between aircraft within the area, whether IFR or VFR, *alert* is thus a good adjective to describe the area.

Warning areas (W)

Another chunk of special-use airspace are the warning areas (Figs. 6-9 and 6-10); however, these areas should be of little concern to the typical VFR pilot because they're located offshore. Actually, there is almost no difference between warning and restricted areas in terms of the types of activity and the hazards to nonparticipating aircraft.

Nonregulatory warning areas.

These areas are designated over international waters in international airspace beyond 12 nautical miles from the U.S. coast, and thus they cannot legally be regulated by the FAA. However, for any nonparticipating pilot, the admonitions about penetrating a restricted area apply equally when the area is active: Said simply, Stay out.

Regulatory warning areas.

These areas extend from 3 to 12 nautical miles from the U.S. coast (over areas now considered U.S. territorial waters) and contain the same form of hazardous activity as nonregulatory warning areas and restricted areas. They serve to warn nonparticipating pilots of the potential dangers. Within regulatory warning areas, pilots must abide by the operating rules of FAR Part 91.

Air Defense Identification Zones (ADIZs)

Finally, we have these offshore areas called Air Defense Identification Zones (ADIZs). Unlike the airspace reserved for training, research, development, testing, and evaluation, these areas fit better under the national security category. More specifically, an Air Defense Identification Zone (ADIZ) is an area of airspace over

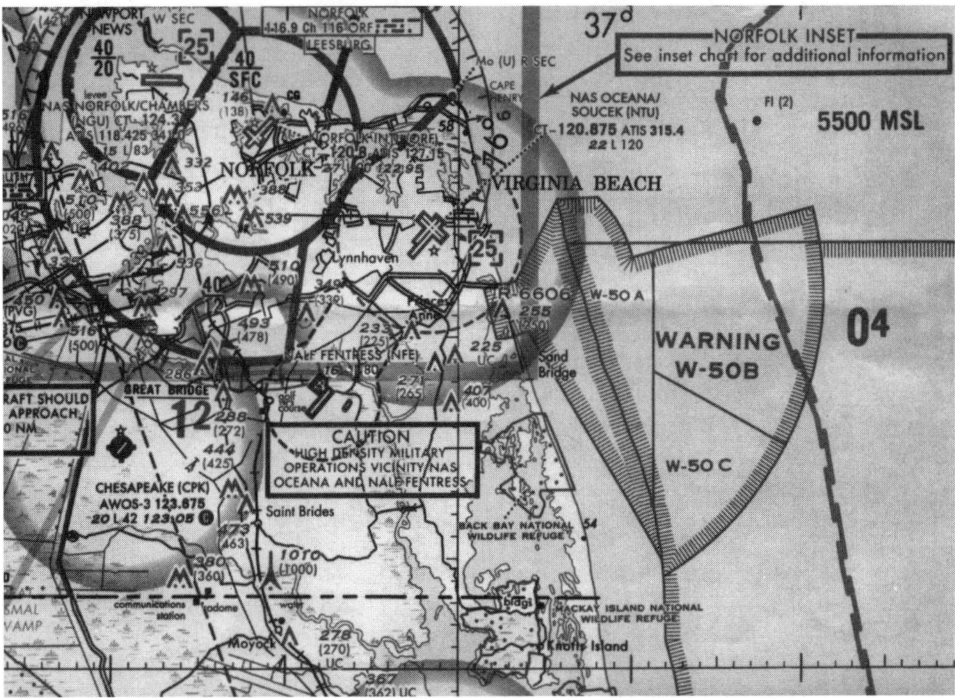

Fig. 6-9 *The W-50 warning areas off the Atlantic coast at Norfolk, Virginia.*

R-6611 A	DAHLGREN COMPLEX, VA	TO 40,000	0800-1700 MON-FRI †48 HRS IN ADVANCE	ZDC CNTR
R-6612	DAHLGREN COMPLEX, VA	TO 7000	0800-1700 MON-FRI †48 HRS IN ADVANCE	ZDC CNTR
R-6613 A	DAHLGREN COMPLEX, VA	TO 40,000	0800-1700 MON-FRI †48 HRS IN ADVANCE	ZDC CNTR
A-220	MC GUIRE AFB, NJ	TO 4500	0800-2200	MC GUIRE RAPCON
W-50 A, B, C	DAM NECK, VA	TO FL 750	INTERMITTENT BY NOTAM	ZDC CNTR
W-72 A	NORTH CAROLINA	E OF 75°30′00″ UNLIMITED, W OF 75°30′00″ TO BUT NOT INCL 2000	INTERMITTENT	ZDC CNTR
W-72 B	NORTH CAROLINA	UNLIMITED	INTERMITTENT	ZDC CNTR
W-105 B	NARRAGANSETT, RI	TO BUT NOT INCL FL 180	INTERMITTENT	ZBW CNTR

Fig. 6-10 *More information about W-50 from the sectional.*

land or water in which the ready identification, location, and control of civil aircraft is required in the interest of national security.

Flight regulations

Considering the purpose of an ADIZ, specific regulations pertain to operations into and within one of these security areas (excerpts), In brief,

- Aircraft must have a functioning two-way radio and a transponder with altitude-reporting equipment. The only exception to the radio requirement pertains to procedures for aircraft without two-way radios and operated on a defense VFR (DVFR) flight plan.
- An IFR or DVFR (defense VER) flight plan must be filed.
- IFR and DVFR position reports are required.
- Flight plan deviations by IFR aircraft in uncontrolled airspace, and by DVFR aircraft, are prohibited unless the appropriate aeronautical facility has been notified prior to the deviation.
- Radio failures must be reported to the proper facility as soon as possible.

These few regulations make it rather clear that unauthorized penetration of an ADIZ could be a serious matter. The whole ADIZ concept, however, shouldn't concern most of us. With only a few exceptions, the areas begin 20 or more nautical miles off the coasts, and other than for those pilots who fly aircraft equipped for extensive overwater flight, the ADIZs lie a little far offshore for the average general aviation plane or pilot. Despite that, no discussion of the special-use airspace would be complete without at least a brief mention of ADIZs and some of the rules pertaining to them.

Controlled firing areas

This area is one I haven't mentioned for a couple of reasons. First, although the activities within the controlled firing area could be hazardous, those activities are suspended immediately when radar, spotter aircraft, or ground lookout positions detect an approaching aircraft. Second, because of this feature—and the fact that they do not cause nonparticipating aircraft to alter their flight route—the areas are not identified on any aeronautical chart. They pose no problem to either VFR or IFR flight, but just be aware that such things exist.

If some of what I've said about the SUA is a little confusing, perhaps Fig. 6-11 on pages 106 and 107 will provide a more succinct summary.

MILITARY TRAINING ROUTES

No review of the airspace system would be complete without a brief discussion of those thin gray lines on the sectional or the brown lines on the en route low-altitude charts that identify the military training routes (Fig. 6-12). (They're shown in pink on VFR wall planning charts.)

What they are

Similar to special-use airspace, MTRs exist because of the recognized need for high-speed, low-altitude military pilot training in the interest of national security. A Department of Defense and FAA joint venture, MTRs come in two forms: IFR, which is charted as IR, and VFR, which is charted as VR.

How they are identified

All routes flown exclusively below 1500 feet AGL are assigned a four-digit number, such as IR 1221 or VR 1756. Routes with one or more segments flown above 1500 feet have three numbers: IR 804. Thus, a route with, say, three segments below 1500 feet and only one above will have a three-digit identification.

As Fig. 6-13 indicates, the numbers are allocated in blocks and identify the FAA region in which the route's entry point is located. Three-digit numbers are not used in the Southern Region.

Route structures

Another aspect of the structure is the small arrows adjacent to the route numbers, indicating the direction of flight along the route (Fig. 6-12). And related to this is the fact that a given numbered route always has one-way traffic. As Fig. 6-12 illustrates, VR 1522 is a southwest route flown under 1500 feet; IR 506, also southwest, is flown above 1500 feet; and VR 1523 is a northeast route under 1500 feet—three different numbers for the same track over the ground. The example further illustrates that a given route can have two-way traffic flowing on it, but when it does, the reciprocal is always given a different route number. This is unlike the Victor airways where the airway number is the same regardless of the direction in which it is flown.

When an MTR is indeed one-way traffic throughout, it does have a couple of advantages for the nonparticipating pilot. If you're crossing or paralleling the route, you at least know the flow of the military traffic and in which direction to keep your eyes peeled. Also, in planning a cross-country trip, if your route coincides with a one-way MTR, you'd be wise to plot your course well to the right or left of the MTR centerline, especially if you're traveling in the same direction as the potential traffic. A jet coming up behind you at 250+ knots might find you a little hard to spot if you're in its direct line of flight—and unless you've got a rear-view mirror and a swivel neck, you'd probably never see him at all. This is just another reason for getting a thorough FSS briefing and maintaining contact with the ARTCC for en route traffic advisories. Those are the folks who can help keep you out of trouble.

Whether IR or VR, the routes below 1500 feet are structured to skirt uncontrolled but charted airports by at least 3 nautical miles or 1500 foot altitude. Similarly, the routes are designed to avoid populated areas and controlled airport areas, and to cause as little disturbance as possible to people and property on the ground.

Although the sectional and the ELAC depict an MTR with the thin colored line, do not let the thinness deceive you. The actual width of an MTR can be considerably greater

SPECIAL USE AIRSPACE MATRIX

Type of airspace	Purpose/activity	Dimensions	Designated hours of operation	Nonparticipating aircraft permitted during designated hours?	Chart / publication
Prohibited Area	To prohibit flight over a surface area in the interests of national security or national welfare.	VERT: Min. required FLOOR: Surface HORZ: As required	Continuous	No	Sectional/WAC ELAC IFR Planning *Federal Reg.*
Restricted Area	To confine or segregate activities considered hazardous to nonparticipating aircraft. Guns and bombs	VERT: As required FLOOR: As charted HORZ: As required	Charted times	No[1]	Sectional/WAC ELAC IFR Planning *Federal Reg.*
Warning Area (Nonregulatory)	To contain activity that may be hazardous to nonparticipating aircraft. Guns and bombs	Defined dimensions over international water outside 12-nautical mile limit	Charted times	Yes[2]	Sectional/WAC ELAC IFR Planning *Federal Reg.*
Warning Area (Regulatory)	To contain activity that may be hazardous to nonparticipating aircraft. Guns and bombs	Defined dimensions between 3 and 12 nautical miles offshore	Charted times	Yes[2]	

SPECIAL USE AIRSPACE MATRIX

Type of airspace	Purpose/activity	Dimensions	Designated hours of operation	Nonparticipating aircraft permitted during designated hours?	Chart/ publication
Military Operations Area	To contain nonhazardous training activity in airspace as free as possible of nonparticipating aircraft Acrobatics, maneuvers	VERT: As required to FL180 FLOOR: Normally 1200' HORZ: As required	Charted times	Yes[2]	Sectional/WAC ELAC IFR Planning
Alert Area	To alert nonparticipating pilots of high volume nonhazardous activity. Fixed-wing, oil rigs helicopter training, etc.	VERT: To FL180 FLOOR: Surface HORZ: Avoid airways airports	Charted times	Yes[3]	Sectional/WAC ELAC
Controlled Firing Area	Hazardous to nonparticipating aircraft. Rockets, blasting, field artillery	VERT: 1000' above highest altitude activity FLOOR: Surface HORZ: 5 statute miles visibility - 360	By NOTAM	Yes	Not charted

[1] unless airspace has been released to ATC and pilot obtains ATC permission

[2] but not recommended when active

[3] use caution

Fig. 6-11 *This matrix summarizes the types, purposes, and pertinent operating data related to special-use airspaces.*

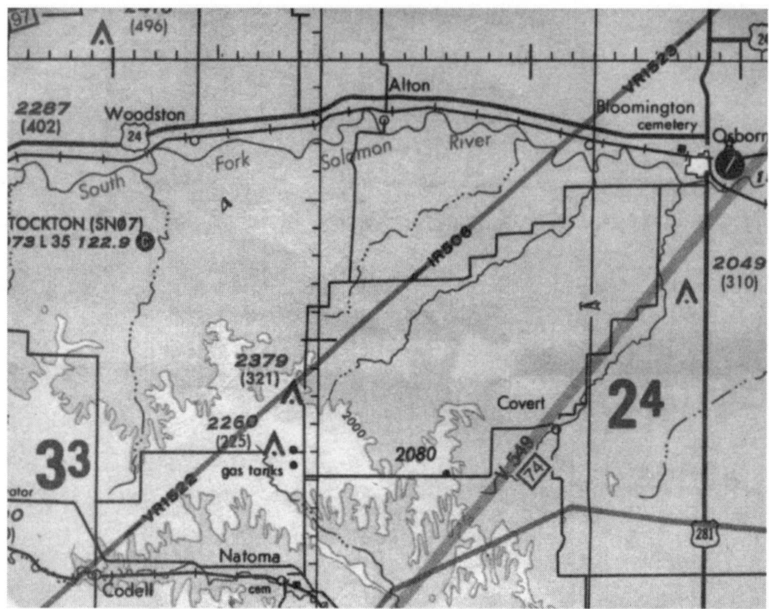

Fig. 6-12 *The thin lines on the sectional identify the VR and IR military training routes. Note the small arrows that indicate the direction of the routes. VR 1522 and IR 506 both are southwest routes, while VR 1523 goes northeast.*

Route Numbers

FAA Region	**One or More Segments above 1500 Feet**	**All Segments at or below 1500 Feet**
Southern	1 thru 99*	1001 thru 1099
Southwest	100 thru 199	1100 thru 1199
Western-Pacific	200 thru 299	1200 thru 1299
	980 thru 999	1980 thru 1999
Northwest Mountain	300 thru 499	1300 thru 1499
Central	500 thru 599	1500 thru 1599
Great Lakes	600 thru 699	1600 thru 1699
Eastern	700 thru 799	1700 thru 1799
New England	800 thru 899	1800 thru 1899
Alaska	900 thru 979	1900 thru 1979

*Leading zeros are dropped

Fig. 6-13 *The MTR numbering system is based on the region in which the route originates.*

than the charts intimate. If there is any standard at all, it is probably 5/5 (meaning 5 miles either side of the centerline).

Don't take that as a rule, though. The variations are considerable. For example, IR 514, originating at Lincoln, Nebraska, varies from 4/4 to 16/25; IR 608, Pensacola, Florida, is 10/10 throughout; VR 1128, Tinker Air Force Base, Oklahoma, is 2/2; and VR 1180, Cannon Air Force Base, New Mexico, fluctuates from 5/5 to 7.5/7.5.

The point for the nonmilitary VFR pilot is that just because you might be a little to the right or left of an MTR centerline doesn't mean the potential for conflict no longer exists. Those B-52s, or what-have-you, could be anywhere within the route's established limits. Once again, vigilance is the key.

Military pilot rules on an MTR

Whether VFR or IFR, the military pilot is responsible for remaining within the confines of the published MTR width and altitude. Flights are to be conducted at the minimum speed compatible with the mission requirements. However, while on the MTR and if below 10,000 feet MSL, military aircraft are not bound by FAR 91, which limits aircraft speed to 250 knots indicated (288 miles per hour) below that altitude. When exiting or before entering an MTR, that FAR does apply, unless the aircraft manual recommends a higher speed for safe maneuverability.

Visual flight rule operations on a VR route are conducted only when weather conditions are better than standard VFR minimums (1000 and 3). More specifically, flight visibility must be 5 miles or better, and flights are not conducted when the ceiling is less than 3000 feet AGL.

If operating IFR, on an IR route, will the military pilot get the standard services and aircraft separation from ATC? Perhaps, but mission requirements, the altitudes flown, or the inability of Center's radar to pick up the target could make those services impossible. In such cases, through a letter of agreement between the scheduling unit and the appropriate ATC facility, the route or routes might be designated for MARSA. Then the military assumes sole responsibility for separation of its aircraft.

Route scheduling

Each MTR has a designated military unit responsible for scheduling all military flights intending to use that route. When it is practical to do so, the scheduling unit, each day and prior to 2400 hours, confirms with the appropriate FSS (the tie-in FSS) the next day's planned route utilization. When that much advance notice is not possible, and barring any other agreement, the scheduling must be accomplished and communicated to the FSS at least 2 hours before use.

The schedule confirmed with the tie-in FSS is the hourly schedule for each IR and VR route, and it includes the route number, aircraft type, number of aircraft on the mission, proposed times when the aircraft will enter and exit the MTR, and altitude(s) to be flown. If a given route is closed or a scheduled aircraft cancels, the scheduling unit is required to relay any changes to the tie-in FSS as soon as possible.

With this information on hand, the Flight Service Station tonight would be able to give you a reasonably accurate briefing on tomorrow's activity. Changes might occur, though, so the closer the briefing to your actual departure time, the more accurate the MTR's status will be.

MTRs and the VFR pilot

A few precautions will minimize the risks of MTRs to the VFR pilot:

- In planning a cross-country trip, note what MTRs will cross or parallel your route of flight.
- When you call the Flight Service Station for a briefing, specifically ask for the scheduled military activity at the approximate time you would be on or crossing an MTR.
- Get an updated activity report from the nearest FSS when you are within 100 miles of the MTR.
- Establish and maintain contact in flight with the appropriate Air Route Traffic Control Center for routine traffic advisories as well as the actual, real-time military activity on the MTRs in your line of flight.
- Keep your transponder on. (If you have one, that's an FAA requirement anyway.) Many military aircraft have airborne radar and could spot you as a target and take evasive action before an emergency arose.
- Stay above 1500 feet AGL. That sounds like an obvious admonition, but remember that there could be a fair volume of high-speed, low-level operations anywhere from 100 feet on up.
- Finally, keep your head out of the cockpit and your eyes open. Military aircraft aren't easy to see. They've been camouflaged to blend in with the sky or the terrain.

MTRs are rarely discussed or considered as potential hazards to the VFR pilot, but they can be. And what perhaps adds to the potential is the MTR's apparent innocence. Unlike the distinct definition of a MOA or a restricted area, there are just those grayish lines on the sectional—nothing to cause us to sit up and take notice. But take notice we should. That empty sky out there could soon be darkened by a stream of B-52s or some other sample of airborne military machinery. A paragraph in the *Aeronautical Information Manual* seems to sum up MTRs:

> Nonparticipating aircraft are not prohibited from flying within an MTR; however, extreme vigilance should be exercised when conducting flight through or near these routes. Pilots should contact FSSs within 100 nm of a particular MTR to obtain current information of route usage in their vicinity. Information (available) includes times of scheduled activity, altitudes in use on each route segment, and actual route width. Route width varies for each MTR and can extend several miles on either side of the charted MTR centerline.…When

requesting MTR information, pilots should give the FSS their position, route of flight, and destination in order to reduce frequency congestion and permit the FSS specialist to identify the MTR routes that could be a factor.

SUAs: A SMALL PRICE TO PAY

Discussions with many pilots, experienced as well as student, tend to point to two principal areas in which initial and refresher training are deficient: radio communications and special-use airspace. The obvious intent of this chapter is to fill in some of the possible gaps in the latter.

SUAs do consume a fair amount of airspace, but it is airspace set aside with the mutual consent of several agencies of the government—and for the best possible purpose: our national defense and security. That purpose can be achieved only through the training, research, development, testing, and evaluation of our defense resources, human and materiel. MOAs, restricted areas, and the like could indeed present barriers to direct-line flight or require altitude deviations, and we might complain silently or loudly about those infringements on our freedom, but they are small prices to pay for the reasons this airspace exists.

7
Transponders

UPCOMING DISCUSSIONS OF CLASS B AND CLASS C CONTROLLED AIRport areas will focus, in part, on the crucial role of the transponder. Without a transponder, or without an understanding of its proper use and the associated terminology, operating in many of the controlled airspaces would be next to impossible. Accordingly, this chapter outlines the radar beacon system, then the transponder and what it does, and finally transponder terminology.

To avoid confusion, it's important to note that the system and the radarscope images discussed here pertain only to terminal Approach Control facilities. This is called an *automated radar terminal system* (ARTS) and is a different system from that used in the en route Centers. ARTS II and ARTS III identify advanced models of the basic system.

AIR TRAFFIC CONTROL RADAR BEACON SYSTEM (ATCRBS)

ATCRBS permits more positive control of airborne traffic and consists of two basic sky-scanning features. The first is called *primary* radar, the other *secondary radar.* Primary radar sweeps its area of coverage and transmits back to the radarscope images of obstacles it encounters, such as buildings, radio towers, mountains, heavy precipitation, or aircraft. The size of the return depends on the reflective surface encountered by the radar sweep. A small fabric-covered aircraft would produce an almost negligible reflection on the radarscope compared to that of an all-metal Boeing 747. Whatever its construction, an aircraft appears on the controller's scope as merely a small blip, showing the aircraft's range (distance) and direction (azimuth) from the radar site.

These limited returns produce a very imprecise means of identification; they only indicate to the controller that there's an airplane out there on a certain bearing and a certain number of miles from the radar site. With such scant data, a controller would be hard-pressed to track, control, separate, or identify traffic in the aircraft's vicinity with any degree of accuracy.

To overcome those limitations, a secondary system exists that incorporates a ground-based transmitter/receiver, called an *interrogator,* along with an operating aircraft transponder. The two radar systems, primary and secondary, then function in unison and constitute the Air Traffic Control Radar Beacon System.

As the two systems make their 360° sweep, the secondary beacon antenna transmits a signal that "interrogates" each transponder-equipped aircraft (or *target,* in controller parlance), and "asks" the transponder to "reply." As the transponder replies, the synchronized primary and secondary signals produce a distinctly shaped image on the radarscope. The image, however, only indicates that the transponder is on and, unless the pilot has been otherwise directed, the transponder has been set to the standard VFR transmitting code of 1200. As the terminology goes, it is "squawking one two zero zero," or "squawking twelve hundred," or "squawking VFR."

But this, too, is limited data—particularly in a heavy-traffic area. For more specific identification, each transponder has a small button that, when the pilot activates it, more definitively identifies that particular aircraft. Thus, when a controller tells you to "ident" and you push the Ident button, the radarscope image changes again, permitting the controller to positively identify your aircraft among all the targets on the screen.

Very superficially, that's the basic principle of the radar beacon system. Figures 7-1 and 7-2, taken directly from *AIM*, illustrate and identify the various ground and airborne images produced by ARTS III. The transponder, however, is the airborne unit that maximizes the system's value in the traffic control process.

TRANSPONDER MODES AND FEATURES

Undoubtedly, most general aviation pilots have at least a speaking acquaintance with the transponder. That acquaintanceship is particularly likely if they have been flying in or around any type of high-density terminal airspace. For other pilots not entirely conversant with the transponder or the regulations pertaining to its use, a few words might be in order.

Transponder modes

Transponders are usually referred to in terms of types or *modes,* of which seven are either in use or available (general aviation interest is currently centered on Modes 3/A and C):

- Modes 1 and 2: assigned to the military
- Mode 3/A: used by both military and civilian aircraft
- Mode B: reserved for use in foreign countries
- Mode C: Mode 3/A transponder equipped with altitude-reporting capabilities
- Mode D: not presently in use
- Mode S: a relatively new mode that may come into use at a later time (S means select, or selective address)

The big advantage of a Mode S–equipped aircraft is that it will permit ATC to selectively interrogate and address that aircraft, even in high-traffic-density situations. In the same vein, it can function in concert with the FAA's TCAS (Traffic alert and Collision Avoidance System). Despite these and other safety-oriented features, however, this element of the FAA's National Airspace System Plan (NASP) has badly missed its intended 1995 implementation date and, at the time of writing, appears to be at a standstill. Even should such a system be mandated, the costs to convert to a Mode S transponder would likely be beyond the reach of those who own or rent the typical general aviation aircraft. The objectives and the value of the overall program are unquestioned; the potential costs, however, raise barriers that may be hard to overcome.

Features

Mode 3/A is the standard transponder that does a reliable job of establishing radarscope identification of a given aircraft. The unit pictured in Fig. 7-3 happens to be an Allied Signal Bendix/King KT 76A, but all makes are basically the same.

The unit is activated by the function selector at the extreme left of the set. The selector positions, as the picture shows, range from OFF to SBY (standby), ON (or NORMAL on some sets), ALT (altitude), and TST (test).

When the engine is started, the selector should be turned to SBY. This allows the set to warm up, which normally takes 2 to 3 minutes, but it does not transmit any signal. At the same time, check to be sure that the transponder has been set to 1200, unless ATC has given you a different code. When you have been cleared for takeoff, turn the selector to ON, if you don't have altitude-reporting capabilities (Mode C). The set is now in the Mode 3/A posture, and after you're airborne, this symbol would appear on the radarscope. (For purposes here, the size of the symbol is considerably exaggerated.)

The symbol, however, will reflect only your relative geographical position in the airspace and the fact that you're transmitting the 1200 code.

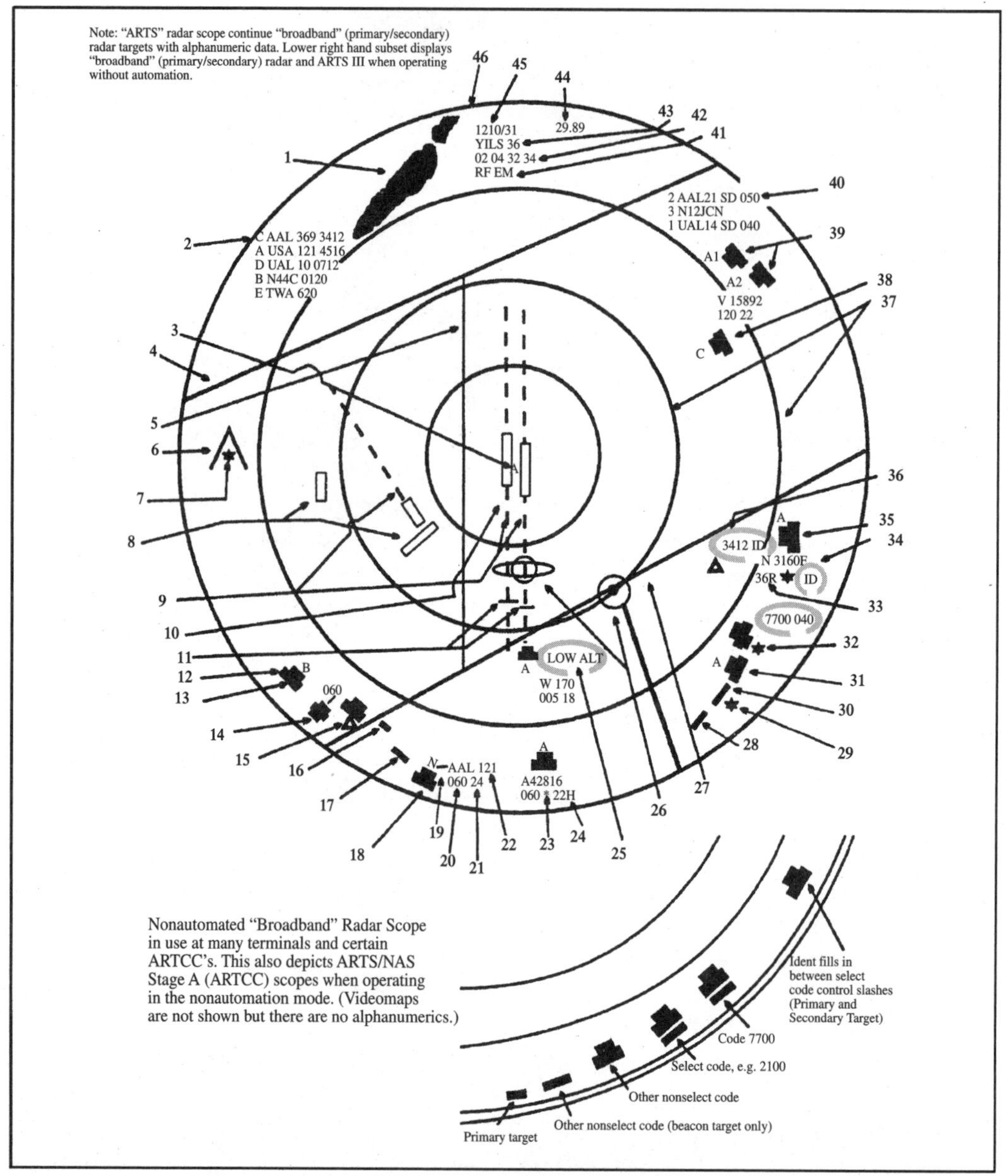

NOTE-

A NUMBER OF RADAR TERMINALS DO NOT HAVE ARTS EQUIPMENT. THOSE FACILITIES AND CERTAIN ARTCC'S OUTSIDE THE CONTIGUOUS U. S. WOULD HAVE RADAR DISPLAYS SIMILAR TO THE LOWER RIGHT HAND SUBSET. ARTS FACILITIES AND NAS STAGE A ARTCC'S, WHEN OPERATING IN THE NONAUTOMATION MODE, WOULD ALSO HAVE SIMILAR DISPLAYS AND CERTAIN SERVICES BASED ON AUTOMATION MAY NOT BE AVAILABLE.

Fig. 7-1 *These are the radarscope symbols and images produced by ARTS III.*

Example–

1. AREAS OF PRECIPITATION (CAN BE REDUCED BY CP)
2. ARRIVAL/DEPARTURE TABULAR LIST
3. TRACKBALL (CONTROL) POSITION SYMBOL (A)
4. AIRWAY (LINES ARE SOMETIMES DELETED IN PART)
5. RADAR LIMIT LINE FOR CONTROL
6. OBSTRUCTION (VIDEO MAP)
7. PRIMARY RADAR RETURNS OF OBSTACLES OR TERRAIN (CAN BE REMOVED BY MTI)
8. SATELLITE AIRPORTS
9. RUNWAY CENTERLINES (MARKS AND SPACES INDICATE MILES)
10. PRIMARY AIRPORT WITH PARALLEL RUNWAYS
11. APPROACH GATES
12. TRACKED TARGET (PRIMARY AND BEACON TARGET)
13. CONTROL POSITION SYMBOL
14. UNTRACKED TARGET SELECT CODE (MONITORED) WITH MODE C READOUT OF 5000'
15. UNTRACKED TARGET WITHOUT MODE C
16. PRIMARY TARGET
17. BEACON TARGET ONLY (SECONDARY RADAR) (TRANSPONDER)
18. PRIMARY AND BEACON TARGET
19. LEADER LINE
20. ALTITUDE MODE C READOUT IS 6000' (NOTE: READOUTS MAY NOT BE DISPLAYED BECAUSE OF NONRECEIPT OF BEACON INFORMATION, GARBLED BEACON SIGNALS, AND FLIGHT PLAN DATA WHICH IS DISPLAYED ALTERNATELY WITH THE ALTITUDE READOUT)
21. GROUND SPEED READOUT IS 240 KNOTS (NOTE: READOUTS MAY NOT BE DISPLAYED BECAUSE OF A LOSS OF BEACON SIGNAL, A CONTROLLER ALERT THAT A PILOT WAS SQUAWKING EMERGENCY, RADIO FAILURE, ETC)
22. AIRCRAFT ID
23. ASTERISK INDICATES A CONTROLLER ENTRY IN MODE C BLOCK. IN THIS CASE 5000' IS ENTERED AND "05" WOULD ALTERNATE WITH MODE C READOUT
24. INDICATES HEAVY
25. "LOW ALT" FLASHES TO INDICATE WHEN AN AIRCRAFT'S PREDICTED DESCENT PLACES THE AIRCRAFT IN AN UNSAFE PROXIMITY TO TERRAIN. (NOTE: THIS FEATURE DOES NOT FUNCTION IF THE AIRCRAFT IS NOT SQUAWKING MODE C. WHEN A HELICOPTER OR AIRCRAFT IS KNOWN TO BE OPERATING BELOW THE LOWER SAFE LIMIT, THE "LOW ALT" CAN BE CHANGED TO "INHIBIT" AND FLASHING CEASES)
26. NAVAIDS
27. AIRWAYS
28. PRIMARY TARGET ONLY
29. NONMONITORED. NO MODE C (AN ASTERISK WOULD INDICATE NONMONITORED WITH MODE C)
30. BEACON TARGET ONLY (SECONDARY RADAR BASED ON AIRCRAFT TRANSPONDER)
31. TRACKED TARGET (PRIMARY AND BEACON TARGET) CONTROL POSITION A
32. AIRCRAFT IS SQUAWKING EMERGENCY CODE 7700 AND IS NONMONITORED, UNTRACKED, MODE C
33. CONTROLLER ASSIGNED RUNWAY 36 RIGHT ALTERNATES WITH MODE C READOUT (NOTE: A THREE LETTER IDENTIFIER COULD ALSO INDICATE THE ARRIVAL IS AT SPECIFIC AIRPORT)
34. IDENT FLASHES
35. IDENTING TARGET BLOSSOMS
36. UNTRACKED TARGET IDENTING ON A SELECTED CODE
37. RANGE MARKS (10 AND 15 MILES) (CAN BE CHANGED/OFFSET)
38. AIRCRAFT CONTROLLED BY CENTER
39. TARGETS IN SUSPEND STATUS
40. COAST/SUSPEND LIST (AIRCRAFT HOLDING, TEMPORARY LOSS OF BEACON/TARGET, ETC.)
41. RADIO FAILURE (EMERGENCY INFORMATION)
42. SELECT BEACON CODES (BEING MONITORED)
43. GENERAL INFORMATION (ATIS, RUNWAY, APPROACH IN USE)
44. ALTIMETER SETTING
45. TIME
46. SYSTEM DATA AREA

Fig. 7-2 *The meanings of the various symbols as numbered in Fig. 7-1.*

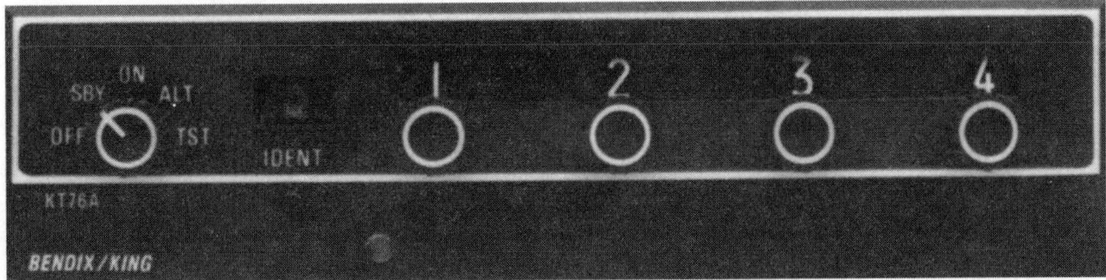

Fig. 7-3 *This is a typical Mode 3/A transponder that can be easily converted to a Mode C altitude-recording unit.*

If the set has altitude-reporting capabilities (Mode C), the switch should be turned to ALT. Then this symbol will appear on the controller's scope, once the aircraft is airborne:

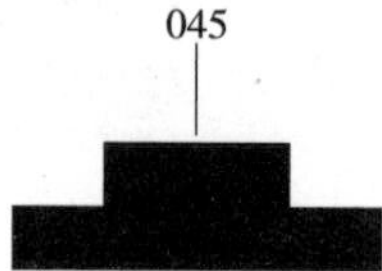

Now the controller can determine your azimuth, range, and current altitude; in this case, 4500 feet.

A firm FAA ruling is that the transponder must be in the ON position, or in the ALT position if it has altitude-reporting capabilities. And it must be left on from takeoff until landing, unless a controller instructs otherwise.

Skipping the ident feature for the moment and moving to the right of the switch positions in Fig. 7-3, we see the next prominent feature is the four CODE windows and the 1-2-0-0 numeric display, plus knobs below each window which change the numbers to whatever code ATC requests. The 1200 code is the standard VFR code and, under normal operating conditions, should never be changed unless ATC so advises. However, a change is likely to be requested if you are in a controlled area, such as Class B or Class C airspace, or in most cases, when you're receiving en route traffic advisories from an Air Route Traffic Control Center on a cross-country excursion. In any of these situations, you may still be flying VFR, but ATC will assign you a specific *discrete* code so that your aircraft can be distinguished from all others in the airspace. That discrete code will be yours alone as long as you are in that ATC facility's airspace and are being controlled or given advisories.

Relative to these codes, reference is often made to a *4096 transponder.* What this means is that each of the four knobs can dial in eight digits from 0 to 7. Combined and multiplied, the four knobs thus produce a total of 4096 (8 × 8 × 8 × 8) different codes. Anticipating what discrete code ATC might assign you is impossible. With only a few exceptions, which I'll review in a moment, the code is selected by a computer according to the *National Beacon Allocation Plan.* It thus could be anything within the block of codes assigned to a given facility.

If ATC asks you to *squawk* (meaning to dial in) a certain code, first write down the numbers so you won't forget them (it's easy to confuse 0465 with 0456 or any other potential combination). Next, repeat the code back to the controller to confirm that you have copied it correctly. Then immediately enter the code in the transponder. When you do, an image similar to this will appear on the radarscope:

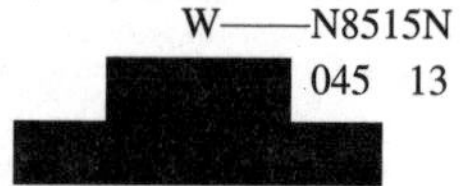

The line is called the *leader line,* and 045 is the aircraft's altitude (based on Mode C's altitude-reporting capabilities). The 13 represents the aircraft's groundspeed of 130 knots, while W indicates that the west sector controller is handling the aircraft.

Going back to the unit itself, located between the function selector and the four code selector knobs are two features, both of which are difficult to see in this photograph—one the reply light and the other the Ident pushbutton.

As to the light, every time the transponder is interrogated by a radar beacon in its 360° sweep, the light blinks momentarily, thus indicating that the set is working properly and is transmitting a signal that represents your aircraft back to the ground unit. In effect, the transponder is "replying" to the interrogator. If the light appears to be blinking almost constantly, it simply means that the transponder is replying to several interrogators that are located within radar range of your present position.

The Ident button comes into play when a controller asks you to "Ident." In effect, he or she wants you to push the button once—and only once. When you do, the four-number code assigned to you "blossoms" on the scope, as the following drawing attempts to illustrate, thus further distinguishing your aircraft from the others in the area. (Also see example 35 in Fig. 7-1.) It's important to stress, however, that you push this Ident button only when instructed to do so. Don't touch it unless you hear something like "Cherokee, Eight Five One Five November, ident." Then push it, but, again, only once.

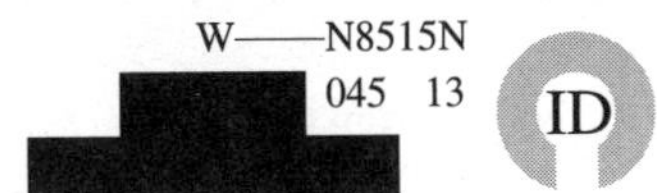

TRANSPONDER CODES

As I've said, the standard VFR code is 1200 and should always be entered in the transponder during normal flight operations, unless ATC directs otherwise. You should, however, be familiar with other select codes.

For instance, if you have a bona fide emergency—a fire, engine failure, loss of control, whatever—and if time permits, immediately enter code 7700. When you do, as the controllers describe it, "Lights light up and bells ring" (example 32, Fig. 7-1). All radarscopes within range will signal an emergency, and controllers at a nearby radar-equipped tower, Center, or Approach Control will be trying to contact you by radio. That won't do much good if you're not on (or monitoring) one of their frequencies or the 121.5 emergency frequency, but at least ATC will be able to follow the track of your aircraft and be in a better position to spot your approximate position, should you go down. That 7700 code, however, is strictly an emergency code, and should never be entered, even momentarily in the transponder window.

Until recently, the transponder code for radio failure was 7700 for 1 minute, followed by 7600 for 15 minutes, and then this sequence repeated. Now, however, the code is simply 7600, and the pilot should leave it there unless advised otherwise by ATC. This change is cited in the *Aeronautical Information Manual,* paragraph 6-4-2, which reads as follows:

> **Transponder operation during two-way communications failure**
>
> **a.** If an aircraft with a coded radar beacon transponder experiences a loss of two-way radio capability, the pilot should adjust the transponder to reply on MODE A/3, Code 7600.

Transponder Code	Type of Flight	When Used
0000*	Military	North American Air Defense
1200	VFR	All altitudes, unless instructed otherwise by ATC
4000*	Military VFR/IFR	In Warning and Restricted areas
7500	VFR/IFR	Hijacking
7600	VFR/IFR	Loss of radio communications
7700	VFR/IFR	In an emergency—"Mayday"
7777*	Military	Intercept operations
Any code	VFR/IFR	When using center or Approach Control and ATC assigns a specific, or "Discrete" code

Note: The starred (*) codes are for military operations only, and never to be used by civilian pilots.

Fig. 7-4 *A summary of the standard military and civilian transponder codes, including the starred codes that civilian pilots should never use.*

b. The pilot should understand that the aircraft may not be in an area of radar coverage.

Figure 7-4 recaps these and other standard codes. The starred codes should never be used by civilian pilots.

A FEW WORDS ABOUT MODE C

In light of the FAA regulations effective in 1989 and 1990, some additional comments about Mode C are essential. Until fairly recently, Mode C for strictly VFR operations was more of a voluntary addition to the Mode 3/A transponder than a necessity. True, it was mandatory for flight above 12,500 feet MSL and in the Class B airspaces, but otherwise it was not a requirement. Times have changed, however.

The rash of midair collisions such as the Cerritos, California, accident cited in Chap. 3, in high-density traffic areas during the latter part of the 1980s triggered that change. Coupled with more and more reported close calls, the public, the media, and congressional pressure forced the FAA to take action. Particularly in terminal areas, the FAA responded by tightening pilot and equipment requirements in controlled airspaces. Mostly, but not exclusively, the tightening related to the transponder and its ability to report aircraft altitudes in those terminal areas. Enter, then, Mode C.

What makes a transponder Mode C?

A regular Mode 3/A transponder becomes Mode C by one of two conversions. The first is to remove the present altimeter and replace it with an *encoding* altimeter. Externally, this looks like any ordinary altimeter; internally, however, there are some modifications. Electronically connected to the transponder, the altimeter aneroid bellows expand and contract with altitude changes, and the changes are converted to coded responses by the transponder. When interrogated by the sweeping radar beacon, the transponder replies by transmitting those responses, which are then decoded on the ground. The process concludes when the target's altitude appears on the radarscope.

The second conversion option is to leave the old altimeter right where it is and to install a *blind encoder.* This unit does just what the altimeter does, differing only in that it is a small black box, usually physically mounted on the firewall or elsewhere under the instrument panel and out of the pilot's sight.

Which is preferable? Operationally, both are equally effective. The blind encoder, however, can be removed for repairs and the airplane is still flyable, except, of course, where Mode C is required.

On the other hand, if the encoding altimeter goes on the fritz, it has to be removed, you'll have no altimeter, and the aircraft is grounded pending repairs. Plus, you've probably replaced a perfectly good altimeter. If you're lucky, you might be able to sell it; otherwise, you're stuck with a reliable but useless instrument.

TRANSPONDER TERMINOLOGY

To round out the transponder picture, the terminology associated with transponder use comes into play. These are the most common terms or expressions (some of which I've already touched on), whether the equipment is Mode 3/A or C.

Squawk

Back in the early World War II days, the Allies had a radar beacon system known as IFF (*identification friend or foe*). Our aircraft were equipped with transmitters that, when queried by the radar sweeps, sent back a sound similar to that of a parrot's squawk, identifying themselves as friends. That squawk has carried over and is used by controllers and pilots alike to mean that the transponder has been turned on and that a certain code has been, or should be, dialed in. When a controller tells you to "Squawk four three two one," he's telling you to enter those digits in the unit. In essence, squawk means transmit. The two words could be used interchangeably, but squawk has hung on, reminiscent of those days 50-plus years ago.

Ident

When you hear "Cherokee One Five November, ident," the controller wants you to push the ident button one time so that your aircraft can be more positively identified on the radarscope. At this point, it's appropriate, but not required, to acknowledge the call with a simple "Roger." Say no more. Just push the button. Saying "Roger, Cherokee One Five November identing" is unnecessary. As the ID on the scope blossoms, the controller will know that you followed the instruction.

Squawk (number) and ident

This instruction means to enter a certain four-digit code in the transponder and then ident. For example, "Cherokee Eight Five One Five November, squawk one two zero zero and ident." If you've already got that standard VFR code in the unit, nothing more needs to be done except the act of identing. If you've been given a different code, say, 4321, then it's proper to read back the code to be sure you understood it. "Roger, four three two one." Now enter it and ident, if the controller told you to. If you don't hear "Ident," don't touch the button.

Stop squawk

This is an instruction to turn the transponder off entirely.

Squawk standby

For whatever reason, the controller says this to have you discontinue transponder replies, but not turn the transponder off. So merely switch from ON or ALT to the SBY position. Replies cease, but the set will still be warm for immediate future use.

Stop altitude squawk

If you hear this, turn the switch to the ON (or in some sets, NORMAL) position, not to OFF. ATC wants you to continue transmitting your position on Mode 3/A, but not your Mode C altitude.

Recycle or reset

Occasionally, a squawk will transmit a questionable signal or one that is the same code given to another aircraft. Also, one of the code numbers might not quite slot into place. Whatever the case, ATC is asking you to reset the four digits so that you are transmitting the assigned code.

Squawk Mayday

If you've reported an emergency of some sort, the controller with whom you've been in contact might tell you to "squawk Mayday," meaning that you are to dial in the 7700 emergency code. (Mayday comes from the French word *M'aidez,* pronounced mayday, meaning "Help me.")

A PASSPORT TO SAFETY

Transponders, Modes 3/A and C, are things of the present and immediate future. More and more aircraft have to have them to operate in any environment other than uncontrolled airports, away from terminal control areas, and below 10,000 feet MSL. The specific requirements, especially for Mode C, are reviewed in Chap. 8.

Requirements aside, the transponders are one more piece of equipment that enhances safety in the air. Without them, ATC would be hard-pressed to direct and separate terminal or en route traffic with any degree of accuracy.

Despite the furor raised by many general aviation interests over some of the FAA's Mode C rulings, the cost to equip an aircraft with altitude-reporting capability is relatively minor when the increased safety factor is considered. It's also a minor price to pay for the privilege of entering and operating in the most strictly controlled airspaces: the airspaces near and surrounding the busy air carrier airports in some 150 major U.S. cities. Those terminal airspaces, along with the associated transponder requirements, are reviewed in Chap. 8.

8
Operating in Class B, Class C, and TRSA airport environments

SOME ASPECTS OF THE CONTROLLED AIRPORT ENVIRONMENTS, INcluding Class D airports, have already been discussed, along with references to Class B and C airspaces. Now, however, it's time to be more definitive about those latter airspace structures and the facilities that manage air traffic in the terminal area. Specifically, I'm talking about the control tower and Approach/Departure Control.

THE CONTROLLED AIRPORT ENVIRONMENT: BE PREPARED!

When the figures are rounded, we have more than 18,000 airports in the United States, including heliports, STOL ports, and seaplane bases. Of that total, some 13,000 are *limited-use* airports, meaning that they are privately owned and access to them requires prior owner approval, and slightly more than 5000 are for public use. Among those 5000, roughly 680 have control towers, 400 of which are FAA-administered; 90 have towers staffed by private contractors, identified on sectional charts as NFCT (nonfederal control tower) in the airport data block (Fig. 8-1); and 175 airports have military towers.

So, again with rounding, more than 5000 airports are for your use and mine, while 680, or 13 percent, are classified as controlled. The remaining 87 percent are Class E and Class G uncontrolled fields requiring only self-announce communications. That gives us a lot of room to roam about, unfettered by the rules, procedures, or requirements involved in operating in the controlled airport environment.

The only problem, if there is a problem, is that these 680 or so aerodromes are located, for the most part, in the more populated areas and the larger cities. Consequently, access to them demands certain pilot qualifications as well as aircraft radio and avionics equipment. It further requires pilot knowledge of what the controlled airspaces are and how to operate within them.

If there is a knowledge deficiency, one of two things will happen: The pilot will go miles out of the way to avoid a Class C or Class B airspace, or he or she will fly unannounced into a controlled terminal area, potentially causing all sorts of havoc. The first alternative is needlessly costly in time and fuel; the second is both illegal and dangerous.

In interviews with many air traffic controllers, one common plea to pilots emerged: Be prepared. Do some homework before you sally forth into a controlled environment. Know the procedures and requirements. Know how and when to use the radio. Know what to say and what you can expect to hear. If you haven't understood an instruction, don't be afraid to ask the controller to "Say again" or "Speak more slowly." Don't just "Roger" an unclear instruction simply because you're reluctant to reveal your uncertainty to the listening audience.

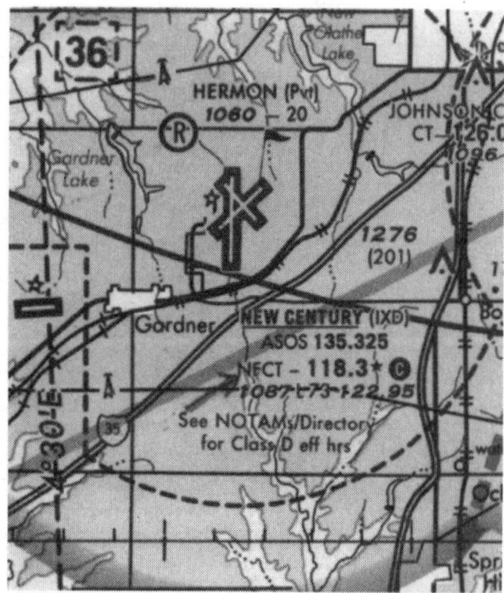

Fig. 8-1 *The "NFCT" located to the left of the tower frequency identifies that tower as nonfederal and thus operated by private contractors.*

And there are other elements in this matter of preparation, such as knowing the tower and ground frequencies of the airport you're entering. One controller cited this as a frequent example of unpreparedness, of which even air carrier pilots are occasionally guilty. As the controller said, "There are three people up there in the front end of a Boeing 727, making pretty good money, and they haven't even taken the time to look up the correct tower frequency."

In another case, a pilot called in for landing instructions and then asked the tower if the airport "was north or south of the river." The controller admitted the temptation to retort that the airport was north of the river, "where it's for 50 years." The controller overcame the temptation, but I wonder how many times controllers have bitten their tongues when questions born of inadequate preparation have come through their headsets. A mere glance at the sectional before departing, or even en route, would have told this pilot exactly where the airport was located.

Still another example: Many airports have navigation aids, such as VOR/DME or nondirectional beacons (NDBs), right on the field; however, controllers say it is not unusual for pilots to contact the tower and ask for vectors or headings to the airport. Of course, if the necessary avionics aren't on board or aren't working properly, the request can be justified. Otherwise, just dialing in the appropriate frequency and centering the needle would lead these pilots directly to their destination. But these same folks probably didn't take a few extra minutes to check the sectional or the *Airport/Facility Directory* before venturing forth.

The lack of preparation arose many times in discussions with controllers, whether based in a tower, Approach Control, or Center, and with specialists at Flight Service Stations. Of course, pilots have to know what they're preparing for, so knowledge becomes the obvious cornerstone. Flying into or out of a controlled environment requires no rare or elusive skill, but it does demand those two basics: knowledge and preparation.

The remainder of this chapter thus briefly reviews the roles of two controlling facilities: the tower and Approach/Departure Control. Then the chapter summarizes the areas that comprise Class C and Class B airspaces including how they're identified, their structure, the pilot and equipment requirements, and finally the operating regulations, particularly the VFR regulations, pertaining to each.

TWO TERMINAL-CONTROLLING AGENCIES

Two facilities are responsible for the orderly terminal arrivals and departures of both IFR and VFR aircraft. One is the air traffic control tower (ATCT), and the other is Approach/Departure Control.

The tower exercises control over only that traffic within the approximate 5-mile radius of the airport. Where it exists, Approach/Departure is responsible for separating aircraft, particularly IFR operations, outward from the airport area to about a 30-mile radius around the primary airport. Vertically, Approach/Departure's airspace rises to the upward limits of its radar coverage responsibility, which might vary from approximately 10,000 feet to 15,000 feet AGL, depending upon the terminal.

Two acronyms identify the most common Approach/Departure facilities: first, is *TRACON,* which means Terminal Radar Control. The other is *RAPCON,* Radar Approach Control. What's the difference? The first is FAA-operated, while the second is a military operation.

TRACON means that the actual facility, with its radar equipment, computers, phones, and personnel, is housed in the control tower structure but not in the glass-enclosed tower cab itself. All the larger airports have TRACON because of the space needed for equipment and personnel.

RAPCON is the Air Force/FAA acronym for Radar Approach Control, and where it exists, it is entirely removed from the civilian airport tower structure. It does, however, provide radar service to nearby civilian airports and civil aircraft, but it can be physically located at a military airport some miles away.

THE CONTROL TOWER AND ITS RESPONSIBILITIES

A control tower (Fig. 8-2) has four primary responsibilities:

- To separate and sequence aircraft transiting the area or in the traffic pattern
- To expedite arrivals and departures
- To control ground movements of aircraft and motorized vehicles
- To provide clearances as well as local weather and airport information to pilots, the last two primarily, but not exclusively, via the tape-recorded ATIS messages.

Fig. 8-2 *The Clearance Delivery position is in the foreground with ground controllers and local traffic controllers in the background.*

The basics of operating within the airport airspace are covered in Chap. 5. But a few additional points related particularly to Class D airports are in order.

- The tower has direct and sole control over only the traffic that is within the limits of its assigned airspace.
- Outside that airspace, the tower at a Class D airport may issue traffic advisories to aircraft with which it has been in contact, if its workload permits. That, however, is secondary to the controller's primary responsibility, which is to keep track of the types and N numbers of aircraft that have called in and to scan the skies within the area to sequence or separate landing, departing, and transiting traffic. Consequently, don't be lulled into a false sense of security just because you're in the vicinity of a Class D control tower. The VFR pilot's neverending responsibility is to keep both eyes open and be the best conflict resolver. That's true anywhere, but especially so near or around a tower-controlled airport where the volume of traffic is sufficient to warrant the very existence of that facility.
- The sole purpose of your first inbound radio call is to inform the controller of your presence, that you intend to enter Class D airspace and, if the tower is radar-equipped, to help identify your particular aircraft. So informed, the controller can now better plan the flow and sequencing of traffic into the airspace and the traffic pattern.

All Class B and C primary airport towers have the same radar display that appears on the Approach/Departure Control scopes. Called BRITE [or *bright radar tower equipment* (or the more advanced D-BRITE, the D standing for *digital*)], the equipment reproduces the displays received in the TRACON (Fig. 8-3). What appears, though, is a video compression transmitted to the tower by a phone line. If a Class D satellite tower is equipped with BRITE, as more and more are, it, too, is receiving its images via phone lines from the primary airport TRACON. (The BRITE acronym, by the way, also describes the purpose of the equipment, which is to produce images that can be easily seen in the bright environment of the tower cab.)

Despite its presence, however, not all tower controllers are radar-qualified. This doesn't mean that they have had no training and are unable to interpret what they see on the scope; it just says that they have not gone through the extensive FAA training as well as current approach control experience that is required to classify them as radar-certificated. Without that certification, the controller can only suggest that a pilot take certain actions beyond the 5-mile radius, if the radar image so indicates; but the controller cannot issue directives that would constitute an order or a command. Instead of saying, "Turn left zero three zero heading," it would be, "Suggest you turn left zero three zero heading."

CLASS C AIRSPACE: STRUCTURE, REQUIREMENTS, AND REGULATIONS

Class C airspaces are the fastest-growing addition to the controlled airspace system and are replacing the terminal radar service areas (TRSAs) throughout the country. The Class C concept was developed to provide more positive control of aircraft in the terminal area

Fig. 8-3 *The enhanced D-BRITE radar in the tower displays the same data as those on the Approach Control TRACON scopes.*

than was, or is, the case under the TRSA system. Pilot participation, meaning establishing radio contact with Approach Control and receiving traffic advisories, is optional in a TRSA. It's the pilot's choice, assuming the flight is VFR. In a Class C airspace, participation is mandatory.

Qualification criteria

To qualify as a Class C airspace, the airport must have an operating control tower served by radar Approach Control and the airport must meet at least one of the following criteria: 75,000 annual instrument operations at the primary airport; or 100,000 annual instrument operations at the primary and secondary airports in the terminal hub area; or 350,000 annual enplaned passengers at the primary airport.

As of the date of writing, 122 Class C airspaces exist. For those interested in the specific locations, check the current edition of the *Aeronautical Information Manual.*

Identifying Class C airspaces

Class C (or "Charlie") airspaces are easy to spot on the sectional, primarily because of the two solid magenta circles surrounding the primary airport. Figure 8-4 illustrates the design, with the circles that encompass the Jackson, Mississippi, International airport. Also, along with the usual frequency and basic runway information found in conjunction with the airport name, the sectional identifies the floors and ceilings of the airspace. In the Jackson example, $\frac{44}{\text{SFC}}$ means that the Class C controlled airspace—the airspace in which contact with ATC is mandatory—extends from the surface to 4400 feet AGL inside the inner circle. The $\frac{44}{17}$ (located at approximately the two o'clock position in the outer ring) indicates that the Class C airspace starts at 1700 feet AGL in that ring and rises to the same 4400-foot ceiling.

Another Class C–identifying source is the *Airport/Facility Directory,* as in Fig. 8-5. The fact that Jackson International is Class C is clearly established by the entry AIRSPACE: CLASS C. The *A/FD* also tells you what Approach or Departure frequency to use, depending on your location relative to the airport. As you can see in the ®APP/DEP CON entry, if your position or intended flight path is anywhere between 333° and 152° from the airport (generally north and east), you should contact Approach on the 123.9 frequency. Should your flight path be anywhere between 153° and 332°, the frequency is 125.25. When the tower and the Approach/Departure Control facility are closed, which they are from 0500 to 1200Z, Memphis Center handles the approaching and departing traffic on 132.5 (the next line down in the *A/FD*).

One other source for frequencies is the reverse side of the sectional's legend flap (Fig. 8-6). Here, you'll find some of, but not all, the same basic information.

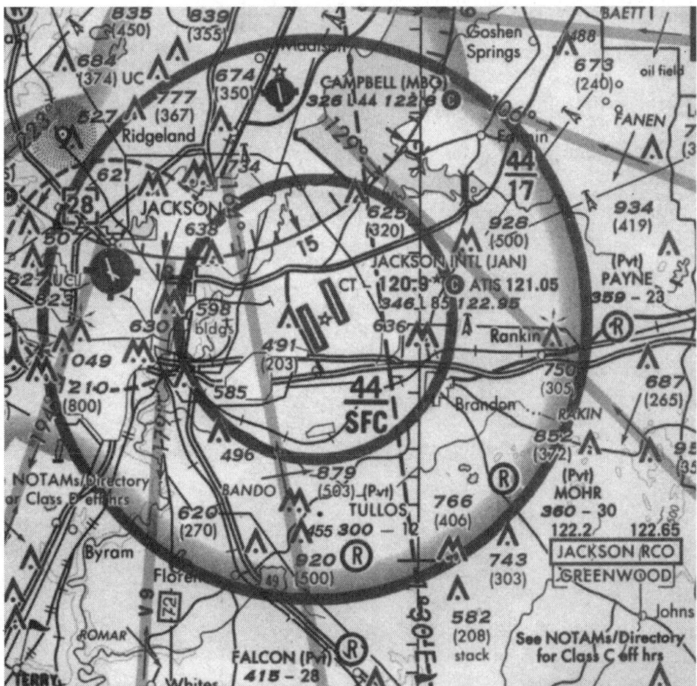

Fig. 8-4 *How the sectional depicts Class C airspaces.*

JACKSON INTL (JAN) 5 E UTC–6(–5DT) N32°18.67′ W90°04.55′ **MEMPHIS**
346 B S4 **FUEL** 100, JET A, OX 2 LRA ARFF Index C **H–4G, 5C, L–17D**
RWY 16R–34L: H8501X150 (ASPH–CONC–GRVD) S–130, D–165, DT–300 HIRL CL **IAP**
RWY 16R: REIL. VASI(V6L)—Upper GA 3.25° TCH 86.3′. Lower GA 3.0° TCH 52.4′. Trees. 0.4% up.
RWY 34L: MALSR. TDZL. Trees.
RWY 16L–34R: H8500X150 (ASPH–GRVD) S–75, D–200, DT–358 HIRL CL
RWY 16L: ALSF2. TDZL. Trees. **RWY 34R:** REIL. VASI(V4L)—GA 3.0° TCH 52′. 0.7% down.
AIRPORT REMARKS: Attended continuously. Heavy bird activity on and invof arpt. Ldg fee for non-commercial acft over 25,500 pounds, fee waived for larger non-scheduled acft with sufficient fuel purchase. Noise abatement procedures—acft over 12500 pounds on Rwy 16L and 16R climb rwy heading to 15.6 DME or as directed by ATC. When twr clsd ACTIVATE REIL Rwy 16R–120.7. U.S. Customs user fee arpt.
WEATHER DATA SOURCES: ASOS (601)932–2822. LLWAS.
COMMUNICATIONS: CTAF 120.9 **ATIS** 121.05 **UNICOM** 122.95
GREENWOOD FSS (GWO) TF 1–800–WX–BRIEF. NOTAM FILE JAN.
RCO 122.65 122.2 (GREENWOOD FSS) **RCO** 122.1R 112.6T (GREENWOOD FSS)
→ Ⓡ **APP/DEP CON** 123.9 (333°–152°) 125.25 (153°–332°)(1200–0500Z‡)
Ⓡ **MEMPHIS CENTER APP/DEP CON** 132.5 (0500–1200Z‡)
TOWER 120.9 (1200–0500Z‡) **GND CON** 121.7
→ **AIRSPACE: CLASS C** svc 1200–0500Z‡ ctc **APP CON** other times CLASS E.
RADIO AIDS TO NAVIGATION: NOTAM FILE JAN.
(H) VORTAC 112.6 JAN Chan 73 N32°30.45′ W90°10.06′ 153° 12.6 NM to fld. 360/05E.
ALLEN NDB (LOM) 365 JA N32°24.75′ W90°07.17′ 157° 6.5 NM to fld.
ILS 109.3 I–FRL Rwy 34L. (Unmonitored when twr closed)
ILS 110.5 I–JAN Rwy 16L. LOM ALLEN NDB. (Unmonitored when twr closed)
ASR (1200–0500Z‡)

Fig. 8-5 *The* A/FD *further identifies a Class C and its Approach Control frequencies.*

CLASS B, CLASS C, TRSA, AND SELECTED RADAR APPROACH CONTROL FREQUENCIES

FACILITY	FREQUENCIES	SERVICE AVAILABILITY
MEMPHIS CLASS B	125.8 338.3 (356°-175°) 119.1 291.6 (176°-355°)	CONTINUOUS
COLUMBUS AFB CLASS C	127.95 389.8 (090°-165°) 135.6 226.0 (165°-310°) 120.4 229.15 (310°-090°) O/T 127.1 269.4 ZME CNTR	0700-1900 MON-THU 0700-2100 FRI 1000-1700 SAT-SUN 0930-1700 HOL EXC CHRISTMAS & NEW YEARS DAY O/T CLASS G; E 700′ AGL & ABOVE
JACKSON CLASS C	123.9 317.7 (333°-152°) 125.25 319.2 (153°-332°) O/T 132.5 259.1 ZME CNTR	0600-2300
LITTLE ROCK CLASS C	135.4 353.6 (042°-221°) 119.5 306.2 (222°-041°)	CONTINUOUS
SHREVEPORT CLASS C	119.9 351.1 (153°-319°) 118.6 350.2 (320°-152°)	CONTINUOUS
FORT SMITH TRSA	125.4 393.0 (075°-255°) 120.9 228.4 (256°-074°) O/T 119.25 398.9 ZME CNTR	0530-2300
LONGVIEW TRSA	118.25 270.3 (EAST AT OR BELOW 4000′) 124.67 128.75 379.15 385.4 (WEST AT OR BELOW 5000′) 133.1 (AT OR ABOVE 4500′) O/T 135.1 269.2 ZFW CNTR	0600-2200
MONROE TRSA	126.9 (180°-359°) 118.15 (360°-179°) 388.0 O/T 135.1 346.25 ZFW CNTR	0545-2300
LITTLE ROCK AFB RADAR	119.5 306.2	CONTINUOUS
NAS MERIDIAN RADAR (MC CAIN)	119.2 374.9 (E) 120.5 269.6 (S) 120.95 269.6 (W) 314.8 (N) O/T 124.4 323.0 ZME CNTR	0700-2300
NOLF WILLIAMS RADAR	276.4	0700-2300

ZFW – Fort Worth, ZME – Memphis
O/T indicates other times

Fig. 8-6 *Another reference source for class identification is the reverse side of the sectional legend flap.*

The Class C airspace structure

The sectional outlines the circular plan view of Class C airspace, but there's more to it than that. Figure 8-7, a cross section, illustrates the typical lateral and vertical structure. Surrounding the primary airport is the *inner circle,* extending 5 nautical miles out from the airport and rising from the surface to approximately 4000 feet AGL. This might vary slightly, but it is the typical Class C ceiling.

Next comes the *outer circle,* with a 10-nautical-mile radius and a 1200-foot AGL floor. The floor, too, might vary slightly in altitude from Class C to Class C, but the outer circle's ceiling is the same as that for the inner circle.

Finally, the *outer area* is not depicted on any aeronautical chart, but it's there nonetheless. The perimeter of the area is generally circular, with a 20-nautical-mile radius from the primary airport. This dimension, however, is not entirely standard because individual facilities, in the interest of safety and local traffic count, have certain latitudes in defining the shape and size of the respective outer areas. Consequently, the limits can vary from a radius of 20 miles up to 30 or 40 miles, depending on the airport. Whatever its radius, the outer area still has the same common vertical limits of responsibility delegated to that particular facility, approximately 10,000 feet MSL.

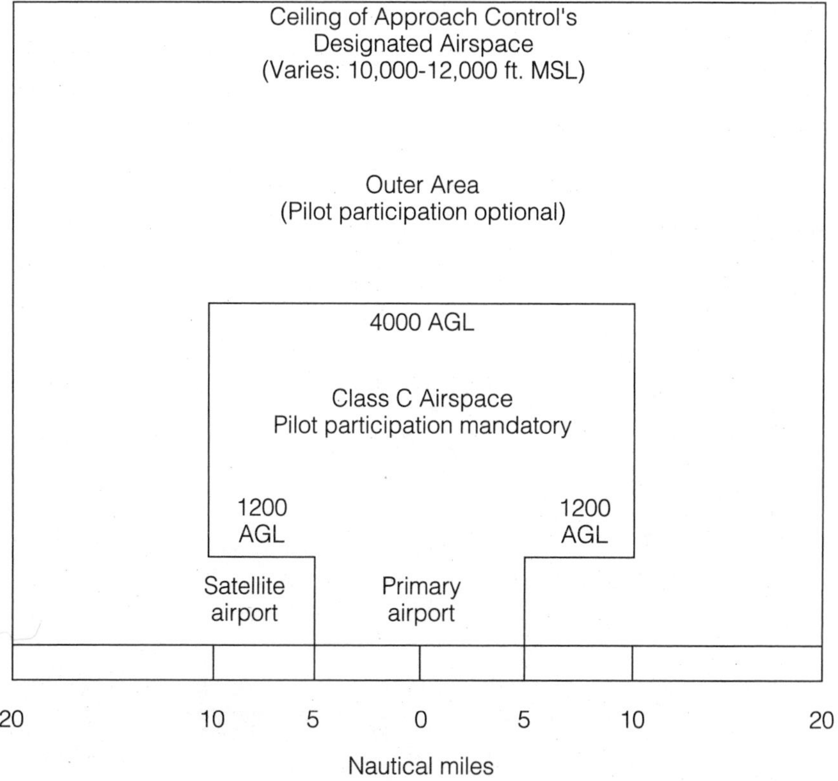

Fig. 8-7 *This drawing represents the basic structure of the Class C airspaces.*

Pilot qualifications and aircraft equipment

Class C airspaces have no minimum pilot requirements. From student on up, any pilot has access to this Class C airspace.

For equipment, a two-way radio capable of communicating with Approach/ Departure Control and the tower is required. An operable Mode C transponder is also required within the inner and outer circles (not the outer area) up to and including 10,000 feet MSL.

Operating regulations

To approach or depart a Class C airspace, the following regulations apply.

- When approaching a Class C airspace with intentions to land at any airport within the inner circle or to transit the airspace (lower than the 4000-foot ceiling), two-way radio communication with Approach Control must be established *before* you enter the outer circle—not the outer area. In the outer area, the pilot has the option of establishing contact for any traffic advisories. It's up to him or her. If contact is made, however, Approach Control has no option: It must provide the advisory service, whatever its workload might be inside the Class C airspace itself.
- While a literal "clearance" into a Class C airspace is not required, establishment of two-way radio communication is. To be more specific, if you call Approach and all you hear is "Stand by," you have not established two-way radio communication (by FAA's definition) and you may not enter the outer circle; that "Stand by" might have been addressed to another aircraft, unbeknownst to you. If, however, the controller responds with your aircraft N number "Cessna 1234, stand by," you have met the requirement and may proceed into the airspace. The mere fact that Approach specifically acknowledged your call sign is sufficient to allow you to enter the airspace, unless directed otherwise by the controller.
- Once you are in the airspace, Approach will issue instructions, vectors, or altitude changes. These should be acknowledged and followed unless doing so would place you in jeopardy or cause you to violate a VFR regulation. In such cases, you must advise the controller of the situation so that alternate instructions can be issued.
- Prior to your entering the inner circle, Approach will turn you over to the tower for final landing instructions and landing clearance.
- In departing the primary Class C airport, and after monitoring the current ATIS, the first step is to call Clearance Delivery (CD), which is usually located in the tower, next to the Ground Control position. At airports without CD, contact Ground Control. In either case, state your intentions and record the instructions you are given. For example:

You: Tallahassee Clearance, Cherokee Eight Five One Five November.
CD: Cherokee Eight Five One Five November, Tallahassee Clearance.
You: Clearance, Cherokee One Five November at Coastal Aviation with Hotel. VFR to Birmingham direct, requesting six thousand five hundred.
CD: Cherokee Eight Five One Five November, maintain four thousand. Departure frequency will be one two eight point seven. Squawk three three four two.
You: Roger, Cherokee Eight Five One Five November maintain four thousand, one two eight point seven, and three three four two.
CD: Readback correct, One Five November, contact Ground.
You: Will do. One Five November.

Next is the usual call to Ground Control and then the tower for takeoff clearance.

- If you are departing a satellite airport within the inner circle, contact the tower as soon as possible after takeoff and follow the normal traffic patterns.
- For departures, arrivals, or touch-and-gos at a satellite airport under the outer circle, if you plan to stay lower than the published outer circle floor and will not be entering the Class C airspace at any time, contact with Approach Control is unnecessary and shouldn't be made at all.

Services in the Class C airspace

Once two-way radio communication is established, Approach or Departure Control will give you vectors and approve altitude changes.

Within the 10-mile radius, Approach will

- Sequence all arriving traffic into the airspace
- Maintain standard separation between IFR aircraft of 1000 feet vertically and 3 miles horizontally
- Separate IFR and known VFR aircraft through traffic advisories or a 500-foot vertical separation
- Issue advisories and, when necessary, safety alerts to VFR aircraft

Relative to the last point, ATC, by the book, is not required to separate VFR aircraft from other VFR aircraft in a Class C airspace; however, in traffic-intense areas, controllers might provide the service out of a sense of obligation and to help prevent the possible later necessity of issuing traffic or safety alerts. Regardless, ATC will advise VFR pilots of the bearing (usually by the "clock" position: "Traffic at 2 o'clock"), the approximate distance, and the altitude of other traffic that might pose a potential problem.

A *safety alert* is issued when conflict between two aircraft appears imminent. The pilot to whom the alert is directed would be wise to follow ATC's instructions immediately: no arguing, no questioning, no delaying, unless you are aware of a safer alternative. An emergency is in the offing.

Can ATC refuse a pilot entry into the Class C airspace? Theoretically, no. In reality, though, controllers have occasionally been forced to deny entrance because of traffic saturation within the airspace and therefore have the prerogative of telling you, "Cessna 1234, remain outside the Class C (or Charlie) airspace and stand by." If you are told this, comply without argument. ATC is temporarily just too busy to accommodate any more activity.

Control compromise

Class C airport areas were designed to replace the TRSAs, in which pilot participation is strictly voluntary. The Class C area removes that option and thus increases the safety factor.

Has it met with popular acclaim? Not entirely. Pilots have been denied entry because of traffic saturation and ATC's resultant inability to sequence, separate, vector, and issue advisories. Early complaints have diminished, however, as pilots and controllers have mastered the system and polished local procedures. Perhaps it's not the ideal solution to traffic control in high-density areas, but it is certainly a better approach to safety than the looseness of the TRSA. In effect, Class C is a compromise, a balanced medium between the TRSA and the stricter controls of Class B.

CLASS B AIRSPACE: STRUCTURE, REQUIREMENTS, AND REGULATIONS

Now, and with a bit of history, let's look at those chunks of airspace that were subjects of considerable controversy during the latter years of the 1980s: terminal control areas (TCAs). The source of controversy was not so much the existence of the TCAs but rather their design and the related FAA pilot and equipment proposals. With at least four midair collisions within or near a TCA and an increasing number of reported near misses, the combined public and congressional pressure on the FAA to take action was considerable.

In response, the FAA issued Notice of Proposed Rulemaking 88-2, which contained some 40 proposed airspace and rule changes. As hearings on 88-2 progressed, several of the changes were dropped and others modified as the result of strong general aviation objections. The TCA resolution was thus the product of give-and-take by the FAA and those representing general aviation interests, particularly the Aircraft Owners and Pilots Association (AOPA).

Why TCAs existed is best summed up by quoting *FAA Handbook* 7400.2, issued July 11, 1988:

> The TCA program was developed to reduce the midair collision potential in the congested airspace surrounding an airport with high density air traffic by providing an area in which all aircraft will be subject to certain operating rules and equipment regulations. The TCA operating rules afford a level of protection that is appropriate for the large number of aircraft and people served by this type of airport. The TCA equipment requirements provide the air traffic control system with an increased capability to provide aircraft separation ser-

vice within the TCA. The criteria for considering a given terminal as a TCA candidate are based on factors which include the number of aircraft and people using the airspace, the traffic density, and the type or nature of operations being conducted.

Boiling down the factors used for TCA classification, the minimum criteria an airport must meet are at least 650,000 passengers enplaned annually, or the primary airport must have at least 150,000 annual instrument operations.

The current Class B airspaces

As of late 1998, the 31 cities and 35 airports listed in Table 8-1 are classified as Class B (Bravo) airspaces. The asterisks by certain locations indicate that special student VFR regulations exist, which I'll explain later in this chapter.

Identifying Class B airspace

If you refer to any sectional that has Bravo airspace, one of the first features that will catch your eye is a large blue-band rectangle or square surrounding the area—in this case (Fig. 8-8), the Seattle-Tacoma International Airport. The square represents the geographic area depicted on another chart, a *VFR terminal area chart* (TAC), which provides an enlarged and more detailed depiction of the area outlined by the square. Anyone nearing or intending to enter a Class B airspace should definitely have a current issue of that airport's TAC on board.

The Bravo airspace lies within the square and is easily spotted by the series of blue circles surrounding the primary airport. These might be exclusively circles, but more likely than not, there will be some irregularities, so structured to accommodate traffic at other nearby airports and/or IFR operations at the primary field.

Table 8-1

Atlanta*	Kansas City	Philadelphia
Baltimore	Las Vegas	Phoenix
Boston*	Los Angeles	Pittsburgh
Charlotte	Memphis	St. Louis
Chicago*	Miami*	Salt Lake City
Cleveland	Minneapolis	San Diego
Dallas/Ft. Worth*	Newark*	San Francisco*
Denver	New Orleans	Seattle
Detroit	New York: La Guardia*,	Tampa
Honolulu	John F. Kennedy*	Washington: Dulles, National*,
Houston	Orlando	and Andrews Air Force Base*

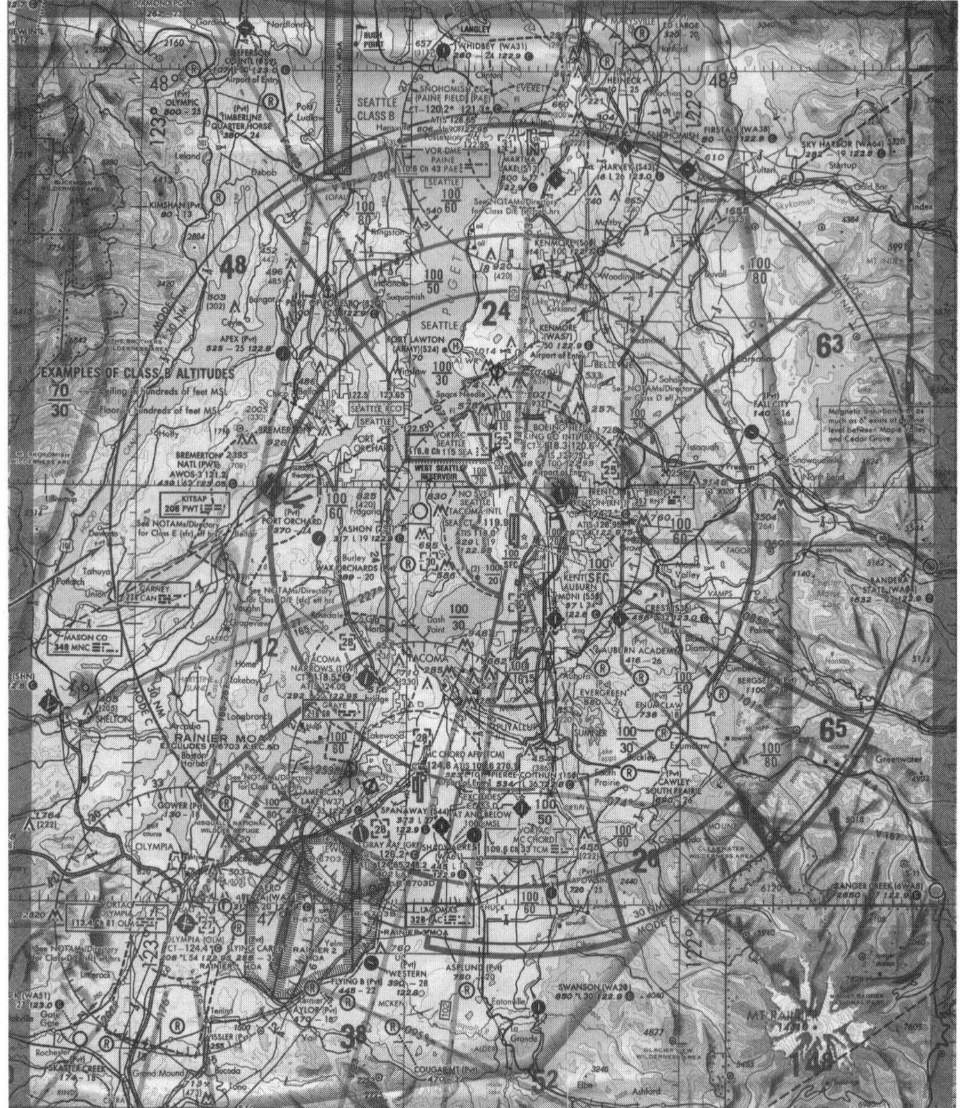

Fig. 8-8 *The large band-box helps identify a Class B airspace and also represents the area covered by the exploded and more detailed terminal area chart (TAC).*

The sectional has another identifying feature: Outside the blue square is a small rectangular box with the name of the terminal on the top line, plus recommendations that pilots use the VFR terminal area chart for "greater detail and clarity of information" (Fig. 8-9). And there is the always reliable *A/FD* as another source of data and reference.

So, identifying a Bravo airspace should be no problem. As with Class C, however, the sectional plan view does not give a clear picture of the Class B structure or configuration. The following might help those not familiar with that airspace.

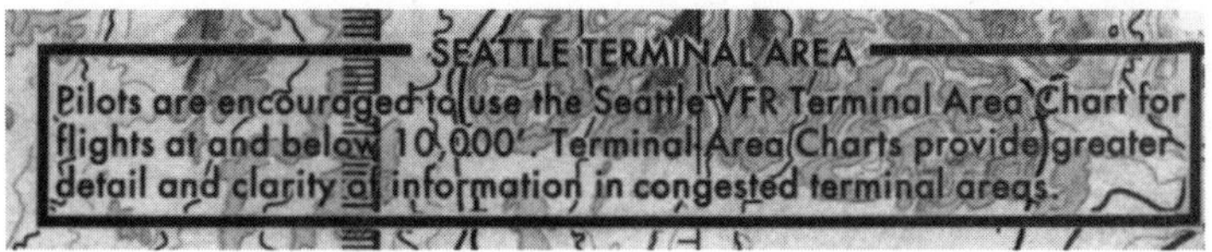

Fig. 8-9 *The small rectangular box near the band—in blue on the original—further identifies Class B.*

Class B airspace structure

The typical description of a Class B airspace is that it resembles an upside-down wedding cake, with the core surrounding the primary airport from the surface to the airspace's ceiling. The various levels, layers, or shelves (they're all synonymous) then extend laterally from the core at 3- to 10-nautical-mile increments (typically), with each layer having a prescribed altitude floor. All levels, however, rise to the same common ceiling of the particular airspace.

Figure 8-10 illustrates the basic structure. This Class B rises from the surface to 8000 feet (80/Surface) at the core. Moving up one level, the floor of the next-higher level is 2000 feet MSL with the same 8000-foot MSL ceiling ($\frac{80}{20}$). Farther out, the altitudes are from 3000 to 8000 feet ($\frac{80}{30}$), and so on. Thus, when operating below any of the floors, you're out of the airspace and out of any positive control by ATC (unless, of course, you happen to be within a satellite airport's Class C or D airspace). It's another story, though, within the Bravo airspace itself. Here is where the rules and regulations enter the picture.

Pilot requirements

To land or take off at the 13 busiest Class B airports (those identified by asterisks in Table 8-1), the pilot must have at least a private license. Student pilots, however, are allowed to enter the Class B airspace surrounding those airports and may land on and depart from the primary airport in all other Class B airspaces, *if* an authorized flight instructor has endorsed the student's logbook within the past 90 days. The endorsement must certify that operating instructions within the specific Class B airspace have been given and that, as the result of actual flight in the area, the student has demonstrated competency to make a safe solo flight in the Class B environment.

Equipment requirements

Unless otherwise authorized by ATC, the aircraft must be equipped with an operable VOR or *tactical air navigation* (TACAN) receiver, an operable two-way radio capable of communicating with ATC on the terminal frequencies, and an operable transponder with altitude-reporting capabilities (Mode C or Mode S).

Exceptions to these regulations are aircraft not originally certificated with an engine-driven electrical system, balloons, and gliders, as long as they remain outside any Class A, Class B, or Class C airspace and operate below the ceiling of the airspace area or 10,000 feet MSL, whichever is lower.

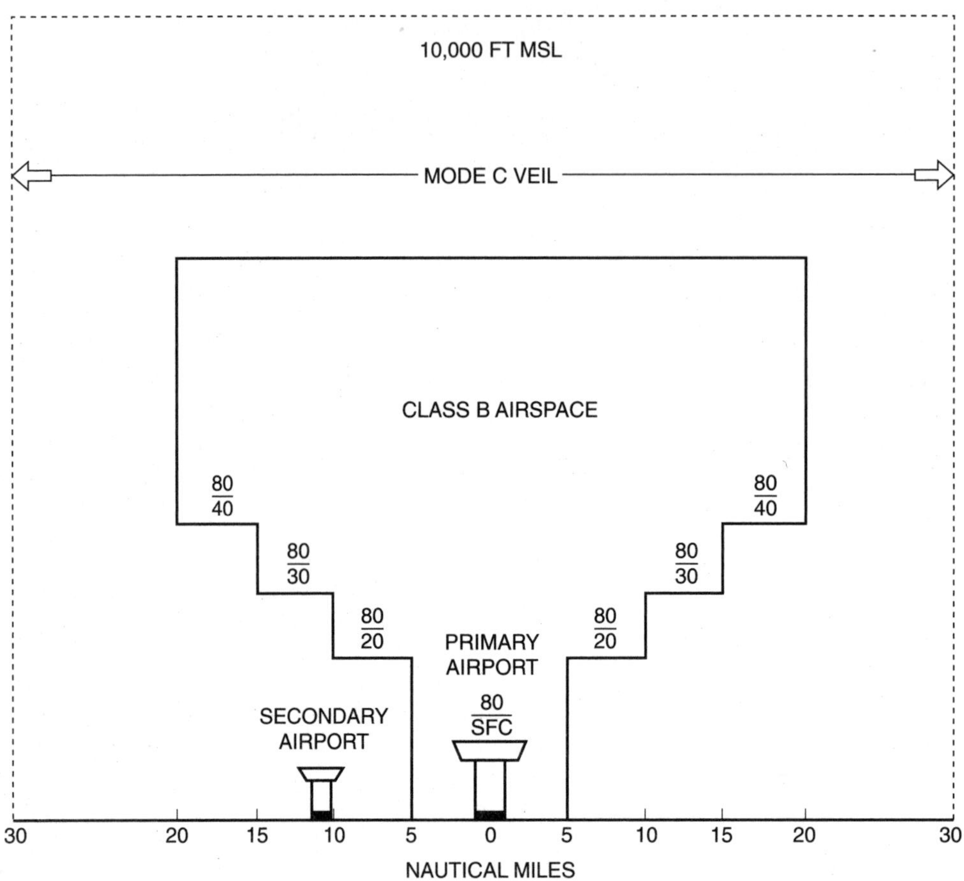

Fig. 8-10 *The structure of the basic Class B airspace is similar to this, but dimensions and configurations will vary considerably from one Class B to another.*

The Mode C veil

Another feature of this Class B airspace is the *Mode C veil.* If you check any sectional that has a Class B airport, such as the Seattle example in Fig. 8-8, you'll see a thin blue circle at the very outer extremes of the airspace. This represents the 30-nautical-mile "veil" that surrounds the primary airport (Fig. 8-10). The initial FAA regulation, which was effective back in July 1989, stipulated that all aircraft operating anywhere within that 30-mile radius had to have a Mode C transponder and that it had to be turned to the ALT position. Whether you were going into the actual Bravo airspace, were flying above its ceiling (but below 10,000 feet MSL), or were just shooting touch-and-gos at a grass strip 25 miles out from the core of the airspace, it made no difference. A turned-on Mode C was mandatory.

As you might imagine, this edict created a storm of protest, particularly from those aircraft owners or renters who operated out of the many small and uncontrolled airports near the outer fringe of the 30-mile circle. Reacting to the protests, the FAA issued Special Federal Aviation Regulation (SFAR) No. 62, which you can find either at the beginning or toward the end of FAR Part 91. This SFAR modified the regulation by excluding from the Mode C requirement aircraft that were based at or operated into or out of those so-called fringe airports. At the same time, in conjunction with Part 91.215, it also excluded balloons, gliders, and any aircraft "...not originally certificated with an engine-driven electrical system or which has not subsequently been certified with such a system installed...."

As part of the modification, however, the FAA stipulated that all non–Mode C aircraft were restricted to a 2-nautical-mile operating radius of the excluded airport or a 5-nautical-mile radius, if so directed by ATC. A second restriction stated that pilots wanting to leave the local airport area must do so by the most direct routing possible. *Direct,* in this case, means following as straight a line as possible out of the veil while avoiding natural obstacles, towns, or populated areas in the flight path that would cause pilots to violate the minimum safe altitudes stated in FAR 91.119. Said another way, once you go beyond the 2-nautical-mile airport radius, you must get out of the Mode C veil as rapidly as possible. There is no wandering around inside the veil or putting down at some other Mode C–excluded field that might be several miles away.

By the same token, an aircraft intending to land at one of these Mode C–excluded airports must enter the veil at a point as close to the airport as possible and proceed directly to it—again, without wandering or delaying.

There's one other piece of this SFAR No. 62: the maximum operating altitudes for non–Mode C aircraft in the veil area. Listed in the SFAR under the various Class B airports are those many smaller airports that are excluded from the Mode C requirement and the maximum AGL altitudes at which these aircraft can fly within the veil area. The altitudes vary from one Class B to another, but they are consistent within each. For example, the ceiling for all the veil airports around the Atlanta Class B airspace is 1500 feet AGL; at Boston, it's 2500 feet; at Houston, 1200 feet and so on. Across the country, the lowest ceiling is 1000 feet, and the highest is 2500 feet.

And still there is a bit more about SFAR No. 62. First, it really is a temporary ruling, because it was supposed to expire on December 30, 1993. In effect, it did expire officially, since nothing has been committed to writing to extend it. The Mode C exclusion still lives, though, and probably will remain alive but under a different SFAR number, name, FAR, or what-have-you. In fact, according to the FAA's Washington, D.C., office, a study of the subject is underway (as of early 1998) and a final ruling or decision should be forthcoming in the near future. (I'm not sure what *near future* means in this case, but I was given reasonable assurance that the exclusionary aspect of the SFAR would be continued.)

All told, approximately 300 of these are Mode C–excluded airports, so if you're planning a trip to one that is in the 30-mile radius, check the sectional first and then the *Aeronautical Information Manual. AIM* has a complete listing of the exclusions under the Bravo airspace in which the airport is located, along with the maximum operating altitude at that airport.

To summarize, and for reemphasis, the fact that an airport is exempt from the Mode C requirement does not mean that non–Mode C aircraft can operate inward toward the primary airport. They can land, take off, or practice touch-and-gos all day long, as long as they remain below the maximum altitude and stay within the 2- or 5-nautical-mile radius of the excluded airport. Otherwise, after takeoff, they must leave the veil as directly and expeditiously as possible. And the same principle applies to landing without Mode C: Enter the veil below the maximum SFAR No. 62 published altitude, proceed directly to the airport, join the traffic pattern, and land.

Yes, these regulations do limit the airspace for non–Mode C aircraft, especially near urban areas and high-density airports, but Mode C has a lot of advantages, not the least of which is the added safety it provides. Plus, it should keep pilots more alert to what they're doing and where they are.

Relative to that, if you accidentally or intentionally penetrate a Class B airspace without approval, you can be sure that someone on the ground knows it. Your position, combined with your Mode C altitude readout, gives you away. Oh, you might be able to outrun the radar coverage and get home unidentified, but the FAA is continually developing more sophisticated means of tracking airspace violators. And once you're caught, it could mean a license suspension, plus a black mark on your record. With Mode C in operation, though, you know you're probably being monitored, which alone ought to have a powerful effect on regulation abidance and attention to what you are doing.

Entering Class B airspace

If you want to land at a Class B primary airport or transit a portion of Bravo airspace to save time and fuel, one basic rule applies: You must be specifically and verbally cleared into the airspace by Approach Control before entering the airspace at any level.

Approach controllers stress this point again and again. What frequently happens is that the pilot calls Approach well outside the airspace. Approach responds. The pilot gives the aircraft position and makes his or her intentions known. Approach tells the pilot to squawk a certain transponder code and then to ident. The pilot squawks and idents. Approach comes back with "Radar contact." Now the problem: The pilot interprets "Radar contact" as approval to enter the Class B airspace—which isn't the case at all!

Perhaps a portion of the misunderstanding stems from *AIM,* where two definitions of radar contact appear in the Pilot/Controller Glossary, the second portion of which states:

> The term (radar contact) used to inform the controller that the aircraft is identified and approval is granted for the aircraft to enter the receiving controller's airspace.

This quote refers to a controller-to-controller communication, not controller-to-pilot. Pilots reading the definition might interpret it to mean that they are cleared into the airspace as soon as a controller calls them and announces "Radar contact." Not so. Until you distinctly hear "Cleared into the Class B (or Bravo) airspace," "Cleared to enter the Class B airspace," or "Cleared through the Class B airspace," you must remain outside that controlled area. Circle, slow down, do a 180, do whatever you have to do. Just don't go where you haven't been invited. It's illegal and can result in your being fined, grounded, and cited for the violation. The offense will also be on your record for insurance companies to see.

But forget the punishment for the moment. Whether intentional or inadvertent, violating the airspace is just plain dangerous. You're in a controlled traffic environment with high-speed turbine aircraft buzzing around you in arrival, transiting, or departure postures. It's Approach Control's job to see that all aircraft are properly separated; but if you barge in unannounced or without clearance, you could be the source of all sorts of traffic problems, up to, and potentially including, the dreaded midair.

Admittedly, though, willful violation of a Bravo airspace is rare. The primary cause is lack of knowledge or lack of preparation. Legally entering this area under VFR is no trick, if you've done the necessary homework, including answering at least these questions:

- Do I have at least a private pilot license? If not, and I'm flying solo as a student, have I received the proper Class B airspace training and logbook endorsement(s)?
- Do I have a VOR receiver that works?
- What are the Bravo lateral and vertical limits?
- How far out and at what checkpoint should I make the initial call to Approach Control?
- What are the radio frequencies for ATIS, Approach, Departure, tower, and Ground Control? And is my radio capable of using those frequencies?
- How should the initial call be worded? What should I say and in what sequence?
- What am I going to do if I'm not immediately cleared into the airspace?
- What will I do if I haven't understood an instruction?
- Have I familiarized myself with the airport layout, including the runways and the upwind, downwind, and base-leg headings for each runway?
- What action will I take if I can't get into the airspace at all? Will I have enough fuel to go around it or get to an alternate airport?
- Is my transponder working? Am I familiar with the terminology associated with its use? Has it been turned to the ALT position?

Don't wait until you can taste the icing on the proverbial Bravo cake. If you want to enter the airspace, give yourself plenty of time to make contact and receive the controller's instructions. Approach controllers recommend an absolute minimum of 10 miles from the airspace shelf you're planning to enter. Better still, make it 20 or 30 miles out. Approach's radar will still easily pick you up. Even at a relatively modest 110 knots of airspeed, it won't take you long to eat up those few miles.

How should this initial call go, and what could you expect to hear? Perhaps something like this:

You: Kansas City Approach, Cherokee Eight Five One Five November.
App: Cherokee Eight Five One Five November, Kansas City Approach, go ahead.
You: Approach, Cherokee Eight Five One Five November is over Lake Perry at five thousand five hundred, landing International with India.

App: Cherokee One Five November, squawk zero two six three and ident.
You: Roger, zero two six three. Cherokee One Five November. (Now push the Ident button just once.)

In a moment, Approach might come back with

App: Cherokee One Five November, radar contact.

Are you cleared into the Bravo airspace? Again, no. Wait until you hear

App: Cherokee One Five November, cleared into the Bravo airspace.

Included in this message might be instructions on headings to turn toward, altitude changes, or advisories of other aircraft—or these might come later. Whatever the case, from this point on, Approach Control will guide you into and within the Class B airspace until you near the tower controlled area. At that point, Approach will tell you to contact the tower for landing instructions.

Just one more thing: Do you have to make that first call to Approach before you enter the 30-mile Mode C veil? No. You're not in the Bravo airspace yet. As long as you have Mode C and it's switched to the ALT position, you're perfectly legal. Depending on your altitude, though, a call 30 miles or so out is about right because you could be as close as 10 miles (or maybe closer) to one of the higher Class B shelves—and those 10 miles can evaporate quickly before clearance into the airspace is approved. Give yourself plenty of time so that you won't have to involve yourself in aerial gyrations while you go through the contact, squawk, ident, and entrance approval procedures.

Departing a Class B airport

With only a couple of exceptions, departing a Class B primary airport is the reverse process and the same as leaving a Class C.

First, monitor ATIS.

Second, call clearance delivery, stating your intentions. You'll receive initial departure headings, altitude(s), squawk code, and Departure Control frequency.

Third, call Ground Control for taxi clearance.

Fourth, call the tower for takeoff permission.

Fifth, contact Departure when the tower so advises.

Sixth, follow Departure's instructions until you are clear of the airspace and Departure tells you to contact Center on such and such frequency or advises you that "radar service is terminated," that you are free to dial-in whatever frequency you wish, and to "squawk one two zero zero." Or the controller might say, "Squawk VFR," which means the same thing.

Alternately, you might hear this:

Dep: Cherokee One Five November, two seven miles north of International. Resume own navigation. Remain this frequency for advisories.

What's Departure telling you? First, that you've left the lateral or vertical limits of the Bravo airspace and are free to change headings or altitudes as you wish. Next, the controller is saying, without saying it, that you're still in Departure's airspace and will be for another 15 miles or so. The controller thus wants you to continue to monitor that frequency, to "stay with me," in the event that advisories of other traffic in your line of flight become necessary.

Finally, when you're clear of Departure's area of responsibility, if the controller hasn't automatically handed you off to Center, he or she will call you once more and tell you to change to whatever radio frequency you wish. It will be a short call, no more than this:

Dep: Cherokee One Five November, radar service terminated. Squawk one two zero zero. Frequency change approved. Good Day.

Now you can tune to another tower, a Flight Service Station, call Center to request VFR advisories, or, presumably, but not wisely, turn the radio off completely. The choice at this point is yours, as Departure will not provide traffic advisories once radar service is terminated.

Transiting a Class B airspace

The procedures for transiting a Class B airspace are the same as those for entering for landing. There's nothing new to be said, other than the fact that you will be with Approach or Departure Control the entire time.

Whether you'll receive transiting clearance will depend on the volume of traffic in the airspace at the time. Every controller I talked with, however, said he would gladly help a VFR pilot get through the area, workload permitting, but it might not be a straight line. For reasons of IFR Approach and Departure procedures and the runway(s) in use, you might have to be routed a few miles out of the way. Or you could be asked to change altitudes. Regardless of the deviations, however, your journey will be shorter than if you avoided the airspace altogether because of procedural uncertainty or fear of entering a territory presumably reserved for the "big" boys. If the airspace is crowded, Approach will tell you. Then circumnavigation may be your only choice. Otherwise, you'll get all the help you need. So saith those responsible for traffic control in this airspace.

Class B VFR routes

Despite—or maybe in tune with—those comments about transiting a Bravo airspace, there are a couple of alternatives at some, but not all, Class B airports. Where the alternatives do exist, they fall under the general heading of published VFR routes. As stated in *AIM,* "Published VFR Routes for transitioning (sic) around, under, and through complex Class B airspaces were developed through a number of FAA and industry initiatives." *AIM* goes on to say, "All of the following terms, i.e., 'VFR Flyway,' 'VFR Corridor,' 'Class B Airspace Transition Route,' and 'Terminal Area VFR Route,' have been used when referring to some of the different types of routes or airspace." As of the date of writing, the Bravo airports that offer one or more of these VFR routes are as follows:

Andrews Air Force Base (Washington, D.C.)
Atlanta
Baltimore
Charlotte
Dallas/Ft. Worth
Denver
Detroit
Dulles (Washington, D.C.)
Houston
Los Angeles
Miami
National Airport (Washington, D.C.)
O'Hare (Chicago)
Phoenix
St. Louis
San Diego
Seattle

By way of clarification, the following summarizes the basic features of the two more common routes and when ATC clearance is or is not required.

- *VFR flyways.* Again per *AIM,* a flyway is a general path for use by pilots planning flights into, out of, or near a complex terminal to avoid the immediate Class B airport airspace. This really means following paths that allow you to skirt the Bravo airport airspace that rises from the surface to its published ceiling—typically but not universally 8000 feet. These are not VFR pathways around the whole Class B airspace (you can do that any time without using flyways). Instead, they are routes to help VFR pilots avoid the areas of major traffic flows—meaning, of course, those surface-to-ceiling airspaces that surround the Bravo airports.

  Where these flyways exist, they are usually depicted on the reverse side of the terminal area chart (TAC) of the airport in question. Take Seattle, for example. Figure 8-11 illustrates the flyways—the bands on all sides of the terminal area with the altitude limitions, such as "Below 3000" and "Below 5000" (lower left). These bands appear in blue on the actual TAC, as does the statement of the purpose of the VFR flyways in Fig. 8-12. Clearance by ATC to enter a flyway is *not* required, but pilots should set their transponders on 1201 while on the flyway. Before using one of these shortcuts at a Bravo airport, check the local operating regulations. They can vary from one locale to another. Los Angeles, for instance, limits the airspeed to 140 knots, requires that navigation lights be on, and excludes all turbine-powered aircraft from the routes. Other airports could have different regulations, so know what's required before you venture forth.
- *Class B VFR transition routes.* (See Fig. 8-11 and note the double-pointed arrows that cross the airport area east to west.) These routes, which are depicted on the face of the TAC chart as well as the reverse side (but not on the sectional), make it possible for VFR aircraft to be cleared through the Class B airport airspace at certain airports. On both sides of the TAC, the routes appear as double-pointed arrows in magenta (Fig. 8-11 again). Their purpose, as *AIM* puts it, is this: "A Class B Airspace Transition Route is defined as a specific flight course depicted on a Terminal Area Chart (TAC) for transiting a specific Class B airspace. These routes include specific ATC-assigned altitudes, and pilots must obtain an ATC clearance prior to entering Class B airspace on this route." (*AIM* is quite "specific" here, isn't it?) Additional instructions (Fig. 8-13) are included on the TAC's reverse side, plus those in boxes at either end of the route (Fig. 8-11).

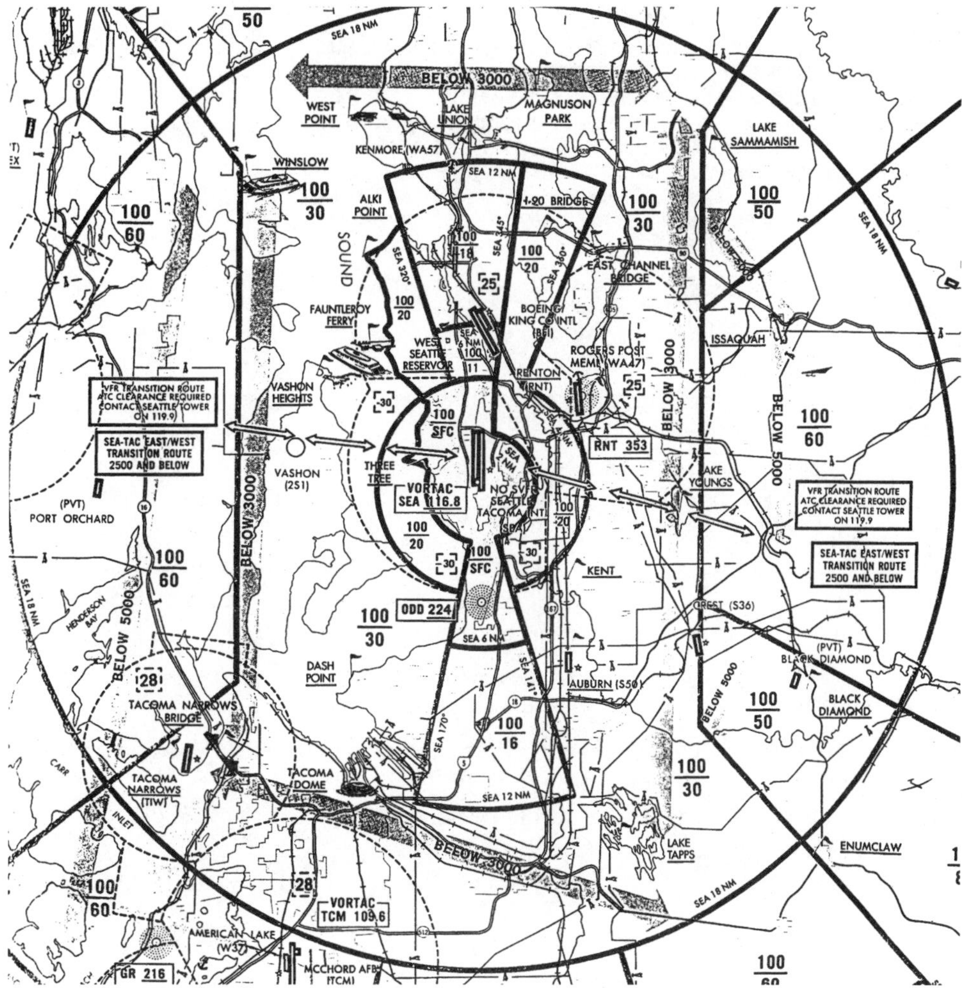

Fig. 8-11 *This chart illustrates the VFR flyways and transition routes in the Seattle Class B airspace.*

THIS CHART IDENTIFIES VFR FLYWAYS DESIGNED TO HELP VFR PILOTS AVOID MAJOR CONTROLLED TRAFFIC FLOWS. IT DEPICTS MULTIPLE VFR ROUTINGS THROUGHOUT THE SEATTLE AREA WHICH MAY BE USED AS ALTERNATES TO FLIGHT WITHIN THE ESTABLISHED CLASS B AIRSPACE. ITS GROUND REFERENCES PROVIDE A GUIDE FOR IMPROVED VISUAL NAVIGATION. THIS IS NOT INTENDED TO DISCOURAGE REQUESTS FOR VFR OPERATIONS WITHIN THE CLASS B AIRSPACE BUT IS DESIGNED SOLELY FOR INFORMATION AND PLANNING PURPOSES.

Fig. 8-12 *Another excerpt from the Seattle terminal area chart states the purpose of the VFR flyways.*

VFR TRANSITION ROUTES

THIS CHART ALSO IDENTIFIES VFR TRANSITION ROUTES IN THE SEATTLE CLASS B AIRSPACE. OPERATION ON THESE ROUTES REQUIRES ATC AUTHORIZATION FROM SEATTLE TOWER. UNTIL AUTHORIZATION IS RECEIVED, REMAIN OUTSIDE CLASS B AIRSPACE. DEPICTION OF THESE ROUTES IS TO ASSIST PILOTS IN POSITIONING THE AIRCRAFT IN AN AREA OUTSIDE THE CLASS B AIRSPACE WHERE ATC CLEARANCE CAN NORMALLY BE EXPECTED WITH MINIMAL OR NO DELAY. ON INITIAL CONTACT, ADVISE ATC OF POSITION, ALTITUDE, ROUTE NAME DESIRED, AND DIRECTION OF FLIGHT. REFER TO CURRENT SEATTLE VFR TERMINAL AREA CHART FOR USER REQUIREMENTS.

Fig. 8-13 *Additional instructions to those in* AIM *outline the operating regulations in VFR Class B transition routes.*

Note that this route takes the pilot directly over the Class B airport at 2500 feet or lower. The flyway, on the other hand, directs the pilot away from any part of the Bravo airspace.

Because of their rarity, or even nonexistence, I'm intentionally skipping a discussion of the uncontrolled VFR corridors and the terminal area VFR routes. In essence, a *corridor* is the equivalent of a hole, or series of holes, drilled in one or more levels of the Bravo airspace. No ATC clearance or communication with ATC is required. The terminal area routes, on the other hand, are based on reference to prominent surface features and/or electronic navigation aids. For anyone interested in more details, *AIM* has brief descriptions of both.

Remaining VFR

Whatever the reason for entering a Class B airspace, assuming you're VFR, you have the responsibility to adhere to VFR regulations. If clouds are around, Approach might give you vectors or altitude changes that would cause you to penetrate a cloud or cloud bank, all the while advising you to "remain VFR." If that happens, it's your responsibility to advise the controller accordingly. Yes, you're under ATC, but that doesn't authorize you to violate the VFR regulations.

Remember, though, that the standard VFR cloud separation of 500 feet below, 1000 above, and 2000 horizontally does not apply in the Class B airspace. Your only requirement is to remain clear of clouds, which, you recall, should reduce cloud avoidance altitude or direction changes and thus minimize disruptions to the flow of other traffic in the area. But do tell the controller immediately if a given instruction would cause you to violate that regulation. Your safety and the safety of others, plus your legality, could be at stake.

Related to the VFR issue is the possibility, in either Class B or Class C, that ATC will assign you a non-VFR altitude, perhaps 4000 feet going eastbound or 5500 feet westbound. That's ATC's prerogative while you're in one of the controlled airspaces; however, when you hear "Resume own navigation and altitudes. Maintain VFR," it means that you are to climb or descend to the appropriate VFR altitude.

Know before you go

Class B airspaces do scare off the ill-prepared or the unknowledgeable, which is understandable. If you're not ready to cope with the airspace, it's better to be scared off than to drive into the area, replete with unjustified self-confidence. The consequences, to put it mildly, could be serious.

Do pilots do this? Unfortunately, yes. In one example noted by an Approach controller, a Cessna 210 departed a satellite airport underneath, but not in, a Bravo airspace. The aircraft showed up on Approach's radar just east of the primary airport and well within the airspace. It had never contacted Approach and was not Mode C–equipped; thus, Approach had no idea at what altitude it was flying.

Meanwhile, the controller had vectored a descending Boeing 727 toward its downwind leg, and as the controller put it, "For some reason—I don't know why—I told the 727 to level off at 5000 feet, advising the pilot that I had traffic out there, wasn't talking to it, and didn't know its altitude. The 727 captain came back in a second, advising that the traffic was dead ahead at 4500 feet."

Intuition? Premonition? The controller didn't know. But the controller did know that if the 727 had been allowed to continue its descent, the likelihood of a 727-210 conflict was almost inevitable.

To track down the 210, the controller called the satellite airport tower, explained what had happened, and wanted to know the aircraft's N number. The tower had the information, and, by chance, the 210 pilot just then reestablished radio contact with the satellite tower. The end result was that the pilot of this errant aircraft had a few not so pleasant chats with FAA personnel.

Yes, some pilots do barge in where only the prepared should tread.

On the other hand, do controllers really want to play cops-and-robbers? Perhaps a few, but of those I interviewed and talked with, many of whom were pilots themselves, not one wanted to nail a pilot for a really minor infraction. Playing the bad guy is not in the makeup of most of those folks who are dedicated to serving the flying public, but with safety the overriding consideration.

Don't let these comments give the wrong impression. The FAA is very firm about violations. While the controller has the option of informally warning an offender of a minor violation, the decision to issue a written warning is up to supervision. If a supervisor who is either monitoring the position or is made aware of what happened and subsequently so concludes, the controller has no alternative but to write up, and thus formalize, the incident. The fact is: If you are guilty of an offense, be prepared for the consequences, minor or major.

I say again, though, that most controllers want to establish a collaborative relationship with the pilot population, while, in the process, hoping to bury any remnant of what at one time might have been a dictatorial, police-type reputation. Simply said, they are not sadists who enjoy hurting the very people they exist to serve.

THE TRSA—A FEW WORDS ABOUT THE TERMINAL RADAR SERVICE AREA

This element of the original terminal radar program is a peculiar mix of airspaces with some rather unique features.

1. The TRSA has never been a controlled airspace from a regulatory aspect.
2. It has no counterpart in the ICAO airspace system and is thus identified by a name rather than a letter.
3. Because of its level of IFR operations and passenger enplanements, the overall airspace lies between a Class C and a Class D, but in most cases, the airports themselves are Class D. If you look closely at Fig. 8-14, you'll see the segmented circle (blue on the sectional) surrounding the airport itself, thus identifying the airport and the 4.3-nautical-mile radius around it as a Class D.
4. The TRSA provides radar approach control service to IFR and VFR aircraft, but VFR traffic has the option of using or not using the service.
5. There are only a relatively few TRSAs around, and sooner or later all will probably either move up to a Class C or drop down to a Class D tower-only airport. In essence,

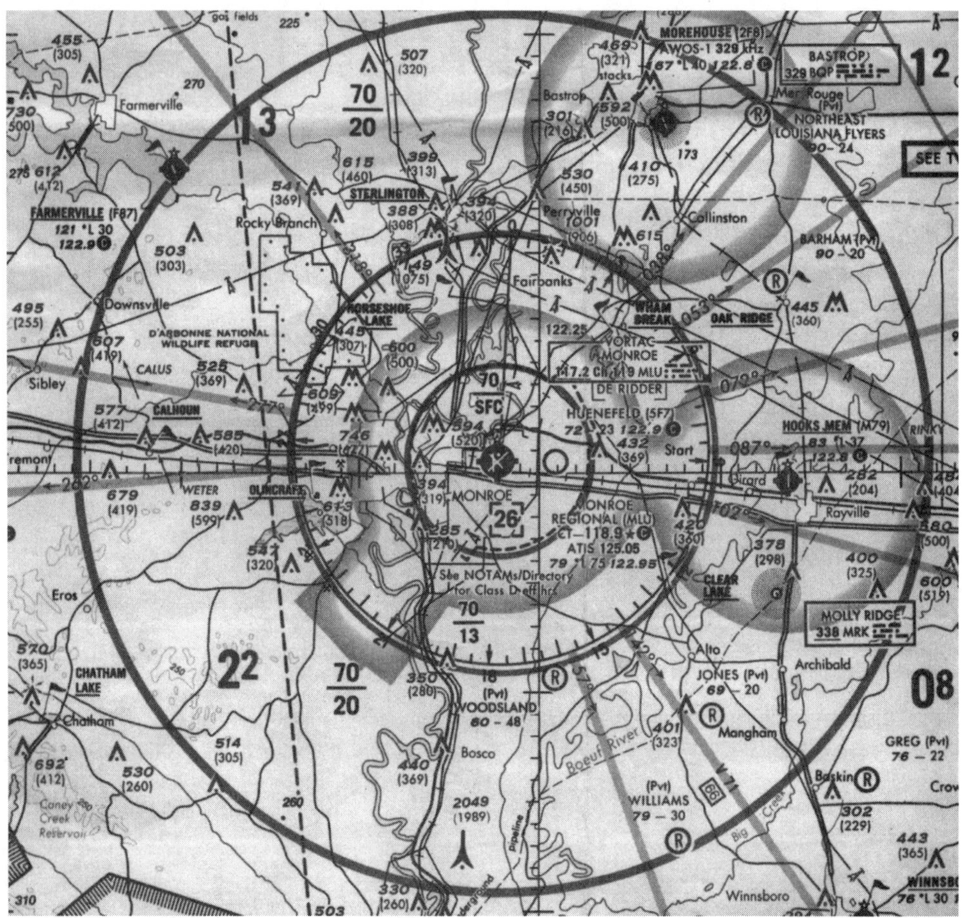

Fig. 8-14 *A typical TRSA resembles Class B in general appearance and has some physical characteristics of Class C, but its operating requirements really place it between Class C and Class D.*

you might view the TRSA as a Class D towered airport surrounded by circles or segments of partially controlled airspaces.

Despite their relative rarity and their peculiarities, however, I can't overlook their existence or the procedures involved in entering, departing, or transiting one of these neither-nor entities.

Identifying TRSAs

This is easy to do. They're spotted on the sectional chart by the black bands (they look almost gray) that surround the primary airport. The bands at the Monroe, Louisiana, TRSA (Fig. 8-14) reflect a perfect circle pattern, which is generally, but not necessarily, the typical design. Some TRSAs, for instance, have odd-shaped extensions for IFR aircraft protection; others have cutouts; still others have three or four bands with varying floor levels; and there are those that have only one perfectly circular ring or band. So design uniformity is not a TRSA trademark.

Note, too, in Fig. 8-14, the ceilings and floors of the rings: $\frac{70}{20}$ in the outermost ring and $\frac{70}{13}$ in the next ring. But then we come to the Class D airspace, again identified by the segmented circle and the segmented box enclosing the 26, indicating that the Class D airspace extends from the surface to 2600 feet MSL. Along with what the sectional tells you, more information about a TRSA is available in the *A/FD.* Figure 8-15 illustrates the Monroe Regional Airport data and, as per the arrow, how the type of airspace is identified.

TRSA services provided

First, an important point for VFR pilots: Specific clearance into a TRSA by Approach Control is not required. If, for whatever reason, you don't want to use the available radar services, you can refuse them in your initial call to Approach, or, if departing, to Ground Control, by merely stating, "Negative TRSA (pronounced "tersa") service." A question arises, however, as to why someone would not take advantage of the assistance ATC is ready to provide. Personally, I've always found it rather comforting to have help through a perhaps busy terminal environment. But should you choose to refuse it, just continue on your inbound course until you're within 10 miles or so of the airport Class D airspace and then contact the tower for landing instructions. Meanwhile, though, it would be smart to keep monitoring the Approach frequency to learn what you can about other traffic in the area, where it is, its altitude, and its intentions.

However, if you have decided that you do want the service, make that known in your initial call. For example, when arriving, and following the basic IPAI/DS, all you need to say is this:

> Monroe (or Regional) Approach, Cherokee One Four Six One Tango over Calhoun at five thousand five hundred, landing Monroe, squawking one two zero zero (or "squawking twelve" or "squawking VFR") with Echo. Request radar traffic information.

MONROE REGIONAL (MLU) 3 E UTC–6(–5DT) N32°30.65′ W92°02.26′ **MEMPHIS**
79 B S4 **FUEL** 100LL, JET A OX 1 ARFF Index C **H–4G, 5C, L–17C**
RWY 04–22: H7507X150 (ASPH–CONC–GRVD) S–75, D–170, DT–290 HIRL **IAP**
RWY 04: MALSR. **RWY 22:** MALSR. VASI(V4L)—GA 3.0° TCH 52′.
RWY 18–36: H5001X150 (CONC) S–60, D–75, DT–130
RWY 18: Trees. **RWY 36:** Trees.
RWY 14–32: H5000X150 (ASPH) S–75, D–170, DT–290 MIRL
RWY 14: VASI(V4L)—GA 3.0° TCH 70′. Thld dsplcd 301′. Trees. **RWY 32:** REIL. VASI(V4L)—GA 3.0° TCH 48′.
RUNWAY DECLARED DISTANCE INFORMATION

RWY 04:	TORA–7507	TODA–7507	ASDA–7507	LDA–7507
RWY 22:	TORA–7507	TODA–7507	ASDA–7507	LDA–7507
RWY 14:	TORA–5000	TODA–5000	ASDA–5000	LDA–4699
RWY 32:	TORA–5000	TODA–5000	ASDA–5000	LDA–5000
RWY 18:	TORA–5001	TODA–5001	ASDA–5001	LDA–5001
RWY 36:	TORA–5001	TODA–5001	ASDA–5001	LDA–5001

AIRPORT REMARKS: Attended continuously. Rwy 18–36 bumpy with vegetation growing thru cracks. Rwy 18–36 not avbl for air carrier ops with over 30 passenger seats. Taxiway A clsd to acft over 12,500 lbs E of Rwy 18 to Taxiway C. Taxiway E clsd to aircraft with wing span over 90′ East of Rwy 04–22. When twr closed HIRL Rwy 04–22 preset med ints. ALS Rwy 04 and Rwy 22 unmonitored. ACTIVATE ALS Rwy 04 and Rwy 22—CTAF. Rwy 04–22 NE 1500′ CONC wire combed; SW 6000′ grvd ASPH. NOTE: See Land and Hold Short Operations Section.
WEATHER DATA SOURCES: LLWAS.
COMMUNICATIONS: CTAF 118.9 **ATIS** 125.05 (1145–0500Z‡) **UNICOM** 122.95
DE RIDDER FSS (DRI) TF 1–800–WX–BRIEF. NOTAM FILE MLU.
RCO 122.25 (DE RIDDER FSS)
® **APP/DEP CON** 126.9 (180°–359°) 118.15 (360°–179°) (1145–0500Z‡)
® **FORT WORTH CENTER APP/DEP CON** 135.1 (0500–1145Z‡)
TOWER 118.9 (1145–0500Z‡) **GND CON** 121.9 **CLNC DEL** 121.65
AIRSPACE: CLASS D svc 1145–0500Z‡ other times CLASS E.
——► **TRSA** svc ctc **APP CON** within 25 NM below 7000′.
RADIO AIDS TO NAVIGATION: NOTAM FILE MLU.
(L) VORTACW 117.2 MLU Chan 119 N32°31.01′ W92°02.16′ at fld. 80/3E. **HIWAS.**
SABAR NDB (LOM) 219 ML N32°27.25′ W92°06.25′ 042° 4.8 NM to fld. Unmonitored when tower closed.
ILS 109.5 I–MLU Rwy 04. LOM SABAR NDB Unmonitored when tower closed.
ILS 109.5 I–MZR Rwy 22. Unmonitored when tower closed.
ASR (1145–0500Z‡)

Fig. 8-15 *Further identification and information about a TRSA is, as always, in the* A/FD.

Approach will now provide the TRSA services until you near the control tower's airspace, at which point Approach will tell you to contact the tower on its assigned frequency. From then on, the tower controller takes over until you're safely down and clear of the runway. Ground Control enters the picture at that point for taxi clearance to wherever you want to park.

And when you're departing, the call goes like this:

> Monroe Clearance, Cherokee One Four Six One Tango at Legacy Aviation, VFR west to Shreveport via Victor 94 at four thousand five hundred with Echo. Request radar traffic information.

Once you are at or just beyond the TRSA's outer limits, Departure will normally, but not always, hand you off to Center for flight following and will advise you accordingly.

That's all there is to it. If you don't want the TRSA service, merely substitute the word *negative* for *request.*

Thus, when you are departing, the sequence of contacts or calls is the same as that in a Class B or C:

1. ATIS
2. Clearance Delivery
3. Ground Control
4. Tower
5. Departure Control
6. Center (if handed off or you initiate the request for en route traffic advisories)

The TRSA service is designed to provide separation between all IFR and all participating VFR aircraft. VFR aircraft will be separated from other VFR/IFRs by 500 feet vertically, or by visual separation, or by target resolution, meaning that space is maintained on the radar screen between targets when the broadband radar system is used. In other words, there is "green between" the targets on the screen.

AIM, under the heading of "Terminal Radar Services for VFR Aircraft," has considerably more details on the subject than are given in this brief overview. Consequently, should you be planning to fly into a TRSA, you would do well to consult that resource for further details.

CONCLUSION

The intent of this chapter has been to outline the principles and operating requirements in the Charlie and Bravo airspaces. Some aspects of importance in understanding the air traffic control system have intentionally, but temporarily, been omitted, such as how the Approach/Departure Control operation functions, its coordination with the tower cab and Center, or a nontechnical overview of the radar and computer equipment that make the system function. Subsequent chapters will fill the gaps.

Is knowledge of the terminal areas absolutely essential? No, not if, as a VFR pilot, you stay clear of the Class B, C, and D airspaces; otherwise, it is essential. Too many of us avoid these controlled areas because of uncertainty and probably at least a modicum of fear. But then there are those who don't know what they don't know. With unbridled cockiness or, even worse, dangerous ignorance, they drive onward into forbidden territory unannounced; they mess up the radio communications; they ask too many questions that could have been answered with proper preflight preparations; they fail to admit that they didn't understand an instruction; they forget to turn on their transponder; they don't have Mode C in a Class B environment but still take up airtime trying to get into the airspace on a routine, nonemergency flight—and the offenses could go on.

If we plead guilty to any of the above, maybe the fault is the quality of instruction we received. The cause, though, is secondary. It's what we do or don't do that matters. Flying in and around these terminal areas requires no unusual level of brilliance or even experience, but it does demand knowledge coupled with practice. The combination is likely to result in a level of piloting skill that permits us to sally forth safely and with justified confidence in whatever airspace environment we might find ourselves.

9
Terminal Radar Approach and Departure Control facilities

PICTURE ANY MAJOR TERMINAL—SAY, AN ATLANTA, A CHICAGO, OR New York's Kennedy Airport—with only the basic glass-enclosed room, or cab, that sits atop the control tower structure. Then picture the scene if three or four controllers in that cab were solely responsible for separating and sequencing all the arriving, departing, and transiting traffic within a 35- to 45-mile radius of the airport. Conservatively stated, the scene at best would be chaotic.

Enter, then, the role of Approach and Departure Control—the function that does the separating, sequencing, vectoring, and advising of all aircraft within Class B and C airspaces, except for the approximately 5-mile radius of airspace surrounding the primary airport and any satellite fields in the area. Approach Control (for simplicity's sake, I'll refer to the function as Approach), with its computers and radar equipment, is the bridge between the outside world and the tower for all arriving and departing aircraft. In essence, it does what no busy tower could possible do all by itself with any degree of order or safety.

WHERE IS THE FACILITY LOCATED AND WHO OPERATES IT?

First, despite the basic sameness of the radar service, the overall approach and departure function has five different names or titles, depending on which government agency or service has the operating responsibility. More specifically, their names, their acronyms, and the responsible agencies are as follows:

- Terminal Radar Approach Control (TRACON), FAA
- Radar Approach Control (RAPCON), FAA/Air Force
- Radar Air Traffic Control Facility (RATCF), Navy/FAA
- Army Radar Approach Control (ARAC), Army
- Air Traffic Control Tower (ATCT), only the towers to which Approach Control authority has been delegated

As to the physical location of the facilities (by that, I mean where the facility is located on the airport itself), five possibilities exist:

- It's located in the control tower structure but in a darkened room on a floor somewhere below the tower cab itself.
- It could be separate from the tower structure, but is still on the airport property and provides approach service to the airport as though it were located in the tower building.
- The function is not physically on the airport but rather at a larger nearby terminal.
- The service might be provided by the ARTCC in whose area the airport is located.
- It could be provided by an ARTCC down to the minimum altitude at which its radar can capture the image of the aircraft. Lower than that altitude, the controller uses manual, nonradar procedures to separate and sequence IFR traffic.

With these five possibilities, how do you know what airports have what? The *Airport/Facility Directory* is the best determining source (Figs. 9-1 through 9-5).

Do the TRACON controllers have any view of the outside world as they fulfill their responsibilities? No. Their job is to control all traffic in their airspace (beyond the roughly 5-mile radius around the airport itself) by radar and radar alone. The room, or work area, is dark, with only the radarscopes and lighted computer buttons providing most of the illumination.

QUESTIONS AND ANSWERS

Now for more details. What follows are a few questions asked of various Approach Control specialists, primarily at the Kansas City Class B and the Wichita Class C airspace facilities. In considering their responses, keep in mind that while basic FAA control procedures apply everywhere, there might well be certain local variations from facility to facility, depending upon the size, traffic volume, and airspace complexity of an individual location. Recognizing that minor differences can exist, the controllers' responses to the questions will hopefully clarify some issues that VFR, and perhaps IFR, pilots might have wondered about.

SANTA BARBARA MUNI (SBA) 7 W UTC–8(–7DT) N34°25.57′ W119°50.42′ **LOS ANGELES**
10 B S4 **FUEL** 100LL, JET A OX 1, 2, 3, 4 TPA—See Remarks LRA ARFF Index C **H–2A, L–3B**
RWY 07–25: H6052X150 (ASPH–PFC) S–110, D–160, DT–245 HIRL **IAP**
RWY 07: MALSR. Tree. Rgt tfc. **RWY 25:** REIL. VASI(V4L)—GA 3.0° TCH 46′. Thld dsplcd 314′. Fence.
RWY 15R–33L: H4183X100 (ASPH) S–48, D–63, DT–100 MIRL
RWY 15R: REIL. Tree. **RWY 33L:** Road. Rgt tfc.
RWY 15L–33R: H4179X75 (ASPH) S–35, D–41, DT–63
RWY 15L: Thld dsplcd 217′. Tree. **RWY 33R:** Rgt tfc.
AIRPORT REMARKS: Attended 1330–0600Z‡. Fee for fuel after hours call 805–964–6733 or 967–5608. Numerous flocks of birds on and in vicinity of arpt. Arpt has noise abatement procedures ctc arpt manager 805–967–7111. Due to limited ramp space at the airline terminal non–scheduled transport category acft with more than 30 seats are required to ctc arpt manager 24 hour PPR to arrival. TPA—1000(990) small acft, 1500(1490) large acft. Pure jet touch/go or low approaches prohibited. When twr clsd ACTIVATE MIRL Rwy 15R–33L CTAF. NOTE: See Land and Hold Short Operations Section.
WEATHER DATA SOURCES: LAWRS.
COMMUNICATIONS: CTAF 119.7 **ATIS** 132.65 (805) 967–0283 (1400–0700Z‡) **UNICOM** 122.95
HAWTHORNE FSS (HHR) TF 1–800–WX–BRIEF. NOTAM FILE SBA.
→ Ⓡ **APP/DEP CON** 125.4 (330°–150°) 120.55 (151°–329°) (1400–0700Z‡)
→ Ⓡ **L.A. CENTER APP/DEP CON** 119.05 (0700–1400Z‡)
TOWER 119.7 (1400–0700Z‡) **CLNC DEL** 132.9 **GND CON** 121.7
AIRSPACE: CLASS C svc 1400–0700Z‡ ctc **APP CON** other times CLASS E.
RADIO AIDS TO NAVIGATION: NOTAM FILE HHR. VHF/DF ctc FSS.
SAN MARCUS (H) VORTAC 114.9 RZS Chan 96 N34°30.57′ W119°46.26′ 201° 6.1 NM to fld. 3620/14E. **HIWAS.**
GAVIOTA (L) VORTACW 113.8 GVO Chan 85 N34°31.88′ W120°05.47′ 101° 13.9 NM to fld. 2620/16E.
ILS/DME 110.3 I–SBA Chan 40 Rwy 07. Unmonitored when twr clsd.

Fig. 9-1 *The symbol ® means that the Santa Barbara Approach/Departure Control facility is located on the airport. When closed, Los Angeles Center Approach/Departure Control provides the service.*

PANAMA CITY–BAY CO INTL (PFN) 3 NW UTC–6(–5DT) N30°12.73′ W85°40.97′ **NEW ORLEANS**
21 B S4 **FUEL** 100LL, JET A OX 1, 2 LRA ARFF Index B **H–5D, L–18F, 19A**
RWY 14–32: H6308X150 (ASPH–GRVD) S–100, D–174, DT–300 HIRL **IAP**
RWY 14: MALSR. **RWY 32:** REIL. VASI(V4L)—GA 3.0° TCH 50′. Trees.
RWY 05–23: H4884X150 (ASPH) S–40, D–70, DT–120 MIRL
RWY 05: VASI(V4L). Trees. **RWY 23:** VASI(V4L)—GA 3.0° TCH 39′. Trees.
AIRPORT REMARKS: Attended continuously. Banner towing below 500′ adjacent to rwys and coastline. ARFF equipment and personnel meet FAR 139 index C, call (904) 769–4791/6033. Extensive Helicopter operations from ramp. Acft arriving/departing S.E.–N.W. use caution due to intensive military jets transiting arpt tfc area 1500′ and above on apch to Tyndall AFB. ACTIVATE HIRL Rwy 14–32; MIRL Rwy 05–23; MALSR Rwy 14; REIL Rwy 32 and taxiway lgts—CTAF. Flight Notification Service (ADCUS) avbl. NOTE: See Land and Hold Short Operations Section.
WEATHER DATA SOURCES: LAWRS.
COMMUNICATIONS: CTAF 120.5 **ATIS** 128.3 (1200–0400Z‡) **UNICOM** 122.95
GAINESVILLE FSS (GNV) TF 1–800–WX–BRIEF. NOTAM FILE PFN.
RCO 122.1R 114.3T (GAINESVILLE FSS)
→ Ⓡ **TYNDALL APP/DEP CON** 119.1 (blo 5000′) 119.75 (above 5000′) (1300–0500Z‡)
→ **JAX CENTER APP/DEP CON** 124.77 (0500–1300Z‡)
TOWER 120.5 FCT (1200–0400Z‡) **GND CON** 121.6
AIRSPACE: CLASS D svc 1200–0400Z‡ other times CLASS G.
RADIO AIDS TO NAVIGATION: NOTAM FILE PFN.
(L) VORTAC 114.3 PFN Chan 90 N30°12.98′ W85°40.86′ at fld. 10/00W.
LYNNE NDB (LOM) 278 PF N30°19.60′ W85°46.94′ 143° 8.6 NM to fld.
ILS 110.5 I–PFN Rwy 14. BC unusable. LOM LYNNE NDB. (ILS unmonitored when twr closed).

Fig. 9-2 *This is an example of a RAPCON, where Tyndall Air Force Base provides service to the civilian Panama City–Bay County airport.*

FULTON CO ARPT–BROWN FLD (FTY) 6 W UTC–5(–4DT) N33°46.75′ W84°31.28′ **ATLANTA**
841 B S4 **FUEL** 100LL, JET A, OX 1, 2, 3, 4 LRA **H–4H, 6F, L–20E, A**
RWY 08–26: H5796X100 (ASPH–GRVD) S–105, D–121, DT–198 HIRL **IAP**
RWY 08: MALSR. Trees. **RWY 26:** REIL. VASI(V4L)—GA 3.0° TCH 52′. Trees. Rgt tfc.
RWY 14–32: H4158X100 (ASPH) S–30 MIRL
RWY 14: REIL. VASI(V2L)—GA 4.0° TCH 52′. Trees. **RWY 32:** REIL. Thld dsplcd 200′. Towers.
RWY 09–27: H2801X60 (ASPH) S–35, D–45, DT–72
RWY 09: Trees. **RWY 27:** Trees. Rgt tfc.
AIRPORT REMARKS: Attended continuously. Rwy 32 has three lgtd twr on centerline 32 ft AGL (873 ft MSL) 650 ft from thld. When twr clsd ACTIVATE MALSR Rwy 08—CTAF; HIRL Rwy 08–26 preset step 3 ints only. Flocks of birds on and invof arpt during dalgt hrs. Rwy 14–32 CLOSED 0200–1100Z‡ indef. Noise sensitive area all quadrants; no run ups authorized on any ramp. Flight Notification Service (ADCUS) avbl. NOTE: See Land and Hold Short Operations Section.
WEATHER DATA SOURCES: LAWRS.
COMMUNICATIONS: CTAF 118.5 **ATIS** 120.175 (0800–0759Z‡) **UNICOM** 122.95
MACON FSS (MCN) TF 1–800–WX–BRIEF. NOTAM FILE FTY.
ATLANTA RCO 122.6 122.2 (MACON FSS)
→ Ⓡ **ATLANTA APP/DEP CON** 121.0
COUNTY TOWER 118.5 120.7 (0800–0759Z‡) **GND CON** 121.7 **CLNC DEL** 123.7
AIRSPACE: CLASS D svc 0800–0759Z‡ other times CLASS E.
RADIO AIDS TO NAVIGATION: NOTAM FILE PDK.
PEACHTREE (L) VOR/DME 116.6 PDK Chan 113 N33°52.54′ W84°17.93′ 245° 12.5 NM to fld. 970/02W.
FLANC NDB (MHW/LOM) 344 FT N33°45.74′ W84°38.34′ 082° 6 NM to fld. NOTAM FILE FTY.
NDB unusable byd 12 NM.
ILS 109.1 I–FTY Rwy 08. LOM FLANC NDB. (G.S. unusable when twr not operating). LOC unusable byd 15 NM blo 3500 ft MSL.

Fig. 9-3 *The Atlanta TRACON provides radar Approach/Departure service to the Fulton County airport, which is about 15 miles from Atlanta's Hartsfield Airport.*

Q. I understand that towers are rated by levels—level 1 the least busy, up to level 5, the busiest. What determines these levels?
A. *It's based on counts of all traffic handled—VFR, IFR, and satellite activity, whether landing, taking off, or transiting our area. We're* (Kansas City) *currently a level 4 with a minimum of at least 60 handlings per hour. A level 5 must handle at least 100 per hour, and a level 3 is in the 40 range.*

Q. Approximately how many miles out from the airport does Approach's area of responsibility extend?
A. *About 55 miles, which is well beyond the limits of the actual Class B airspace, of course. That doesn't mean that a VFR aircraft, for example, is under our control out that far, but our radar coverage is that extensive.*

Q. You're working an IFR aircraft for a landing. At what point do you turn the aircraft over to the tower for landing clearance?
A. *It can vary, but certainly no later than the final approach fix (FAF).*

Q. I'm VFR approaching a Class B airspace for landing and have been with Center for flight following. Will Center now hand me off to Approach without my requesting it?
A. *Very possibly, but it's not automatic. Just be prepared to introduce yourself to Approach for the first time in case there is no handoff and Center has terminated radar coverage, telling you to contact Approach, change to the advisory frequency, or whatever.*

WILLIAMSPORT REGIONAL (IPT) 4 E UTC–5(–4DT) N41°14.52′ W76°55.31′ **NEW YORK**
529 B S4 **FUEL** 100LL, JET A OX 1 ARFF Index A **H–3I, 6I, L–24G**
RWY 09–27: H6449X150 (ASPH–GRVD) S–65, D–100, DT–190 HIRL **IAP**
RWY 09: REIL. VASI(V4L)—GA 3.0°TCH 58′. (Unmonitored). Trees. **RWY 27:** MALSR. Railroad. Rgt tfc.
RWY 12–30: H4280X150 (ASPH) S–200, D–200, DT–400 MIRL
RWY 12: Trees. **RWY 30:** Brush. Rgt tfc.
RWY 15–33: H3502X100 (ASPH) S–13
RWY 15: Thld dsplcd 1175′. Trees. **RWY 33:** Brush. Rgt tfc.
AIRPORT REMARKS: Attended 1100–0400Z‡. Fuel and svcs available 1100–0400Z‡ Mon–Fri; 1100–0300Z‡ Sat–Sun and holidays; after hours call 717–323–1717. Arpt CLOSED to ultralight and banner towing ops. Rwy 15–33 CLOSED to acft with seating capacity in excess of 30 passenger seats. Twy J CLOSED to acft with wing span over 78 ft. PPR 12 hours for unscheduled air carrier ops with more than 30 passenger seats 0500–1100Z‡ call arpt manager 717–368–2444 or 717–368–2446. Weather report not avbl 0500–1100Z‡. Rwy 9, VASI skewed 10°to N of Rwy 9 centerline & originating 1050 ft inboard of landing threshold. Deer and birds on and invof arpt especially apch end Rwy 27. When twr closed ACTIVATE MALSR Rwy 27, HIRL Rwy 09–27, REIL Rwy 09 and twy lgts—CTAF; MIRL Rwy 12–30 off. For landside access from apron when twr clsd ctc IPT AFSS 717–368–1545 or frequency 122.65/122.2. Rwy 15–33 cracked with weeds growing through cracks. Ldg fee. NOTE: See Land and Hold Short Operations Section.
WEATHER DATA SOURCES: ASOS (717) 368–3420.
COMMUNICATIONS: CTAF 119.1 **UNICOM** 122.95
WILLIAMSPORT FSS (IPT) on arpt. 122.65 122.2 122.1R. TF 1–800–WX–BRIEF. NOTAM FILE IPT.
RCO 122.1R 114.4T (WILLIAMSPORT FSS)
→® **NEW YORK CENTER APP/DEP CON** 124.9
TOWER 119.1 FCT (1130–0330Z‡) **GND CON** 121.9
AIRSPACE: CLASS D svc 1130–0330Z‡ other times CLASS E.
RADIO AIDS TO NAVIGATION: NOTAM FILE IPT. VHF/DF ctc WILLIAMSPORT FSS
(L) VOR/DME 114.4 FQM Chan 91 N41°20.31′ W76°46.49′ 238° 8.8 NM to fld. 2090/09W.
PICTURE ROCKS NDB (MHW) 344 PIX N41°16.61′ W76°42.61′ 267° 9.8 NM to fld.
ILS 110.1 I–IPT RWY 27. GS unusable blo 650′. LOC unusable 1 NM to AER abv 2200 ft.
COMM/NAVAID REMARKS: VHF/DF unusable 150°–200° byd 20 NM blo 5000′.
• •
HELIPAD H1: H125X160 (CONC)
HELIPORT REMARKS: Helipad H1 located adjacent to Twy 'J'.

Fig. 9-4 *The New York Center Approach/Departure Control provides radar service to Williamsport, PA, through New York's remoted radar facilities.*

HAYS MUNI (HYS) 3 SE UTC–6(–5DT) N38°50.70′ W99°16.44′ **WICHITA**
1998 B S4 **FUEL** 100LL, JET A ARFF Index Ltd. **H–2E, L–6G**
RWY 16–34: H6300X100 (ASPH) S–28, D–48, DT–86 MIRL **IAP**
RWY 16: REIL. VASI(V4L)—GA 3.0° TCH 38′. P-lines. **RWY 34:** MALSR. VASI(V4L)—GA 3.0° TCH 27′.
AIRPORT REMARKS: Attended dalgt hrs. After hrs for fuel call number posted. Arpt CLOSED to air carrier ops with more than 30 passenger seats except 24 hrs PPR call arpt manager 913–628–7370. Ultralight activity on and invof arpt. ACTIVATE MIRL Rwy 16–34, VASI Rwy 16 and Rwy 34, REIL Rwy 16 and MALSR Rwy 34—CTAF.
WEATHER DATA SOURCES: AWOS–3 125.525 (785) 625–3562.
COMMUNICATIONS: CTAF/UNICOM 122.8
WICHITA FSS (ICT) TF 1–800–WX–BRIEF. NOTAM FILE HYS.
RCO 122.3 (WICHITA FSS)
→ **KANSAS CITY CENTER APP/DEP CON** 124.4
RADIO AIDS TO NAVIGATION: NOTAM FILE HYS.
(L) VORTACW 110.4 HYS Chan 41 N38°50.86′ W99°16.61′ at fld. 2020/10E. **HIWAS.**
DME unusable 220°–030° byd 35 NM blo 3700′
VOR unusable 220°–030° byd 35 NM blo 4100′ 030°–220° byd 35 NM blo 3500′
NETTE NDB (LOM) 374 HY N38°46.16′ W99°15.09′ 339 4 7 NM to fld.
ILS 111.5 I–HYS Rwy 34. LOM NETTE NDB (LOC only)

Fig. 9-5 *The Hays, Kansas, airport is beyond the Kansas City Center's radar coverage, but the Center can provide that service down to about 4000 feet AGL. From there on, the handling is by "manual," or nonradar, methods. The absence of the ® indicates this type of service.*

Q. How frequently do you have to reject a VFR request to transit the Bravo airspace?
A. *I don't know how frequently, but the only time we reject a VFR request is when our traffic volume requires it.*

Q. On average, how many controllers—tower and Approach—do you have on duty at one time?
A. *Usually 10 or 11, plus two supervisors. In the tower, there's one each assigned to Clearance Delivery, Ground Control, local control, and the cab coordinator position. The rest are downstairs in Approach Control.*

Q. Is there any way a pilot can determine what frequency to use to establish initial contact with Approach, assuming, of course, that there's been no handoff or previous contact with a Center?
A. *Yes. Check the frequencies published in the* A/FD *or on the back of the sectional chart's legend flap. What frequency to use depends on the airport and the direction of flight. Coming into the airspace from the east, you'd probably contact Approach on one frequency, another frequency if coming from the west, and maybe yet a third if from the south. If, by chance, the one you chose isn't the right one, Approach will so advise you.*

Q. Do you have any advance information on a VFR flight plan aircraft that would be entering your airspace?
A. *Not unless the pilot has been receiving traffic advisories from Center and had been handed off to Approach for transiting or landing purposes. We'd know about that aircraft because we had accepted the handoff. Otherwise, we have no prior information. IFR, of course, is a different matter.*

Q. For VFR traffic transiting the airspace, do you have a preferred altitude?
A. *At some terminals, there are preferred, or perhaps required, VFR flyways or transition routes, but that's not universally true. Much depends on the runways in use, the flow of IFR traffic, and IFR traffic at satellite airports for which Approach is responsible.*

Q. Another question on transiting the airspace: I'm coming in VFR from the east and want to go through the airspace to the west. I've been monitoring the east frequency for several miles, and there seems to be little traffic or activity. When I make my first call and request clearance to the west, the request is denied "because of workload." How can that be? The controller obviously isn't that busy.
A. *No, (the controller) might not be, but what you're not likely to know is the volume of activity the west controller is handling. At the time of your call, he could be too busy with IFR traffic to accommodate a VFR transit. The east controller knows what's going on and would have to refuse your entry request.*

Comment: Another factor to consider is that the controller might be engaged in several off-frequency activities, such as landline coordination with nearby VFR towers, Center sectors, or other Approach positions; he or she might be in the process of generating VFR or IFR flight strips or perhaps be involved in any number of functions of which the pilot could not be aware. So silence on the air should not imply that the controller is sitting there with nothing to do. As a Wichita Approach controller put it, "Actual time talking on the frequency is not at all indicative of a controller's workload—though I completely understand that that is about the only method a pilot has to try to judge (the controller's workload)."

Q. In another vein, I'm practicing instrument approaches to a satellite airport in your airspace. Is the controller I'm talking to also handling the primary airport traffic?
A. *It's unlikely. Usually there is a satellite controller who is responsible for just the satellite operations, including practice approaches as well as bona fide IFR traffic.*

Q. The controllers are assigned to specific geographic sectors, right?
A. *Right. Again, however, the volume of traffic at a terminal can make a difference, as do the runways in use. At this location, we have three sectors: east and west, north and south, and satellite. The last covers eight airports in our area, including three with VFR towers, one that's a part-time military tower, and four that are uncontrolled.*

Q. I have departed either the primary airport or one of the satellites, VFR, and have received advisories from Approach. I request a handoff to Center for en route advisories. What do you do when I make the request?
A. *You've already told us your route of flight, and we know what position, or sector, at Center handles IFR and VFR traffic in that geographic area. It's then just a matter of activating what we call an "override" phone that connects us directly with that sector controller. We'll ask if he can handle a VFR flight. His workload permitting, he'll say yes, so we'll give him your aircraft type, N number, present position, altitude, first point of landing, and squawk. Meanwhile, he's manually filling out a VFR flight strip on you. Once the information has been relayed, we'll tell you to contact Center on such and such frequency. All you do now is get on the air, identify yourself with aircraft type and N number, verify your present altitude, if climbing, and the desired altitude; or if you've reached your cruising altitude, merely verify what it is. The call is simple:* "(Blank) Center, Cherokee Eight Five One Five November is with you at five thousand, climbing to seven thousand five hundred." *Don't say any more. Center already has the other pertinent information.*

Q. I imagine it's the same for arrivals when Center hands me off to you folks.
A. *Exactly the same.*

Q. What if Center is too busy to give me advisories?
A. *The sector controller will tell me, I'll tell you, advise you that radar service is terminated, ask you to squawk 1200, and bid you good day. You're on your own now to see and avoid.*

Q. What if I'm VFR and intend to land at the primary airport in a Bravo airspace, whether I've been using Center or not. Can you refuse to clear me into the airspace?

A. *Only if the weather is below VFR minimums or if local conditions make it impossible for us to handle any VFR operations. Otherwise, assuming you meet the pilot and equipment qualifications, I'll clear you, separate you from IFR traffic, advise you of other possible VFR traffic, and vector you to the airport. There could be a clearance delay, though, if the departing or arriving IFR traffic were heavy.*

Q. What if I want to go through a portion of the airspace and land at a satellite that is under but not in the Class B airspace? Would you still clear me and give me the normal services?
A. *That's strictly a matter of workload. If I can, I will. Otherwise, stay under Class B and contact the tower at the satellite. If it's an uncontrolled field, self-announce your position and intentions 10 to 15 miles out.*

Q. On a cross-country trip, using Center for advisories, my route takes me near an Approach Control airport. Maybe it's a Class B or C, but I'm going to go around or above the airport, regardless of what it is, and I'm not going to land there. Why, then, does Center tell me to contact Approach? I might be 30 miles away from the primary airport.
A. *Because you'll be entering that Approach Control's airspace, and it's now Approach's responsibility, not Center's, to give you advisories. Again, though, if Approach is too busy, the sector controller might not be able to accept the handoff. Center will then tell you that radar service is terminated and to squawk 1200. If you want advisories down the road, you'll have to reestablish contact with Center.*

Q. Are these handoffs also handled by override phones?
A. *For VFRs, yes. On an IFR flight plan, however, everything is computerized, and the transfer of control is more or less automatic. That's not the best use of the term, but it's reasonably descriptive of what happens.*

Q. Speaking of *automatic,* or *automated,* I've heard a lot about something called a *slewball.* Explain it to me, would you?
A. *First, what you're referring to is called a trackball today and looks a little like a computer mouse, except that it doesn't have the left and right pushbuttons, or clickers. Instead, picture a tennis ball with all but the top 10 percent sliced off and discarded. That remaining 10 percent is then a rounded movable dome set in a casing that generally resembles the computer mouse. Then picture a video game or a computer monitor where you can move a pointer, an arrow, or a symbol to a certain position by manipulating a control of some sort. The trackball is the control we manipulate, and the symbol in our unit is simply a letter, such as a W for a west controller, E for east, C for center, H for handoff, and so on. When we want to make some computerized change to an identified aircraft in the area, we move the trackball until the letter is placed on the radarscope symbol of that aircraft. Then, by punching certain computer buttons, we can change the aircraft transponder code, initiate a handoff to Center, or do anything else we wish that involves the computer.*

Q. How does this sort of handoff go?

A. *Like this—but keep in mind we're talking only about IFR handoffs. VFRs are done by phone. Let's say an aircraft is departing the airspace to the northeast. Our scope shows the aircraft N number, its altitude, and ground speed. The E indicates that the east controller is handling the aircraft. This constitutes the data block. Now to the handoff process itself.*

Four sectors at our Center handle all departures, arrivals, and transits within our immediate area. These are positions 40, 42, 46, and 48 in the Center complex. Position 40 handles the northeast sector, which our controllers automatically know. When the aircraft nears the outer limits of our airspace, the east controller moves the trackball E up to the aircraft's symbol, hits the C for Center button, and then the Enter button on the computer console. As he does this, the entire data block appears and blinks on Sector 40's radarscope. When that controller accepts, or "buys," the handoff by punching a computer button on his console, the data block in Approach blinks, and the E changes to a C. After the C appears, we then call the pilot and advise, "Cherokee Eight Five One Five November, contact (Blank) Center on 125.25 (or whatever the frequency might be). Good day." *We'll keep One Five November on our scope, though, until he actually crosses the line into Center's airspace.*

That's all there is to it. It's an automatic handoff, assuming Sector 40 accepts it; if the controller can't do so immediately, we will have to hold the aircraft in our airspace. No IFR aircraft can go from one controlled airspace to another without the approval of the receiving sector or facility.

Q. A question about those things called *flight strips.* Would you decode this one for me (Fig. 9-6)?

A. *Sure. The aircraft N number is obvious, as is the type, a PA-28. For those unfamiliar with it, one of a series of letters follows the slash to indicate the type or types of avionic equipment aboard the aircraft. In this case, the A means that One Five November has a DME and a transponder with altitude-reporting capabilities. The 613 is merely the computer identification number. Moving over a column, 4626 is the transponder code given the pilot to squawk. P1620 indicates the proposed departure time, and 40 is the requested 4000-foot altitude. MCI is the departure point, and TOPEK is the "gate" through which the aircraft will be vectored out of our airspace. The balance indicates the route of flight to its termination at MKC.*

N8515N	4626	MCI	+TOPEK+			
PA28/A	P1620		MCI MKC V4 TOP STJ MKC			
613	40					

Fig. 9-6 *This computer-generated IFR flight strip originated at an FSS and was automatically sent to the Center computer, which then transmitted it to Approach Control 30 minutes before the planned 1620 UTC departure.*

Q. A second question, then: Who originates these strips? How do they end up in Approach?
A. *They start at a Flight Service Station. When the pilot files an IFR flight plan, the FSS enters the information in its computer. That computer then "talks" to the central core, or host computer, in the Center, which interprets the data, processes the flight strip, and sends it to the appropriate Approach Control facility. Approach receives the printed strip from its computer 30 minutes before the proposed departure time. That time is valid for 2 hours, unless the pilot is delayed and contacts Approach, the tower, or at an uncontrolled airport, the Flight Service Station to request an updated departure.*
Q. Is there anything like this for a VFR flight plan?
A. *No. A VFR flight plan is just between the FSS at which it was filed and the FSS in whose area the terminating airport is located.*

Q. I'm flying IFR and want to land at an airport in your airspace that has, let's say, a VOR but only a VFR tower—that is, it has no radar, no BRITE. I've heard many pilots complain that it often takes a lot of time for Approach to set them up and turn them over to the tower for final landing clearance. Now here's a satellite field without much traffic, but the delays often seem unnecessarily long. Why?
A. *That's the disadvantage of a strictly VFR tower. Before we can let you pass the outer marker on an instrument approach, we must know that the aircraft ahead of you is actually on the ground. So to space things properly, we have to have a 6-mile separation between aircraft, rather than the normal 3 miles where the tower has BRITE radar. You're right. A lot of pilots do complain about the delays, but they might not understand that we must have the spacing so that the VFR tower can give us a downtime of the first aircraft before we can switch the next aircraft in line to the tower frequency—and we must make that switch before the second aircraft reaches the outer marker.*

Q. So it's a matter of maintaining the proper spacing until you get that downtime.
A. *That's exactly what it is.*

Comment: The Wichita controller added these paraphrased comments: "While that explanation is correct, there are also many other situations." He goes on to cite cases of multiple airports in the vicinity with overlapping airspaces; the type, nature (as an emergency), and volume of traffic within one or more of those areas; the release of an IFR departure in the area and its potential effect on both landing and departing aircraft; the number of final approach courses in the airspace and the number of courses that cross other final and departure courses. He mentioned additional complicating factors, but combined with the Kansas City controller, these comments seemed to answer my "Why?" question rather effectively.

Q. Do Approach controllers ever work the tower?
A. *Yes, if they have been tower-certificated. Here, we rotate. We can do that because we're all tower- and radar-certificated. That's not true everywhere, though. Many tower controllers have not gone through the radar training and certification process, so they're limited to strictly tower duty.*

Q. Which do you think is the more stressful, tower or Approach?
A. *I'd say Approach. You're working a lot more traffic in a relatively confined airspace. Because of the volume, you have to be constantly alert to where the traffic is, whether it's following your instructions, the proximity of one aircraft to another, and so on. The same is true in the tower, but to a lesser extent. Yes, if I had to choose, I'd say there is more pressure in Approach. Being able to work both positions, though, varies the job and makes it a lot more interesting.*

CONCLUSION

Those were some of the questions asked to get a better feel of what goes on behind the scenes. Coupled with the observations and comments of various controllers cited in the last chapter, their responses here did shed further light on how things work in those dark and windowless facilities.

Suffice it to say, the Approach/Departure Control function is an essential element in the whole ATC system, regulating the safe and efficient flow of traffic in and around our busiest airports. As I said at the start of this chapter, chaos would indeed reign were it not for this vital link in the ATC chain.

10
Flight Service Stations

IT'S TIME TO LEAVE THE ENVIRONMENT OF THE IMMEDIATE AIRPORT and venture into the out-country. Two facilities enter the picture: Flight Service Stations (FSSs) and Air Route Traffic Control Centers, so let's look first at Flight Service because of the role it plays in planning and embarking on a cross-country excursion of any duration.

THE FSS ROLES IN THE AIR TRAFFIC SYSTEM

The FAA states that three major components comprise the air traffic control system: en route air traffic control, terminal air traffic control, and Flight Service Stations. If you are considering the basic flight-related components, the FAA is correct. Literally, though, it's incorrect. Flight Service Stations are an essential element of the air traffic system, but they do not "control" traffic in any way. If the FSS role could be reduced to three principal functions, they would probably be to *inform, advise,* and *search.*

To inform

A given FSS has a wealth of data immediately available to help the IFR or VFR pilot intelligently plan a flight. Everything is there: local, en route, and destination weather, winds and temperatures aloft, icing, cloud levels, visibilities, forecasted conditions, outlooks, NOTAMs, military operations, etc.

To advise

Here is where the FSS is not a controlling agency. It can neither authorize nor deny any pilot the right to take off, or a VFR pilot to operate in IFR conditions or enter an active military operations area. It can suggest a course of action, such as, "VFR is not recommended," but that's all. It's the pilot's decision to go or not go. With the experience the FSS specialist has, however, coupled with the data available, it behooves a pilot to heed the specialist's counsel. There are enough pilots who didn't and who aren't around today to regret their indiscretion.

To search

This is a role with which many of us are perhaps not thoroughly familiar. I'll review the sequence of events later, but let's just say for now that when a pilot on a VFR flight plan fails to close out a flight plan within 30 minutes of the estimated arrival, the FSS takes the first steps to locate the aircraft. No, no one from a Flight Service Station literally goes out and searches for the missing plane, but its people do initiate and participate in what could be an exhaustive as well as expensive operation.

To put a little meat on these somewhat bare bones, then, the services that make up the FSS's three functions could be summarized in this way:

- Accepting and closing flight plans
- Conducting preflight weather briefings
- Communicating with VFR pilots en route
- Assisting pilots in distress
- Disseminating weather information
- Publicizing NOTAMs
- Working with search-and-rescue units in locating missing aircraft
- Monitoring air navigation radio aids

FSS CONSOLIDATION

Back in 1985, there were 294 FSSs across the country. In 1988, the number had dropped to around 200, while currently (1998) there are only 61 to serve the 50 states. The cutback over the years was the result of just one step in an extensive equipment modernization program designed to upgrade all the ATC facilities. In the case of the FSSs, the plan was to consolidate the nearly 300 stations into 61 highly sophisticated *Automated Flight Service Stations* (AFSSs). The plan was realized by the middle 1990s, and the locations of most of the current AFSSs are depicted in Fig. 10-1. (A few additional installations have been added since this charting was issued by the FAA, but I have not been able to locate an updated version.)

This move, of course, originally met with considerable opposition from the general aviation population. Alaskan pilots were particularly vocal, along with those in the lower 48 states where local weather characteristics were such that on-site, not remote, FSSs were considered essential. As the result of heavy lobbying by, among others, the Aircraft

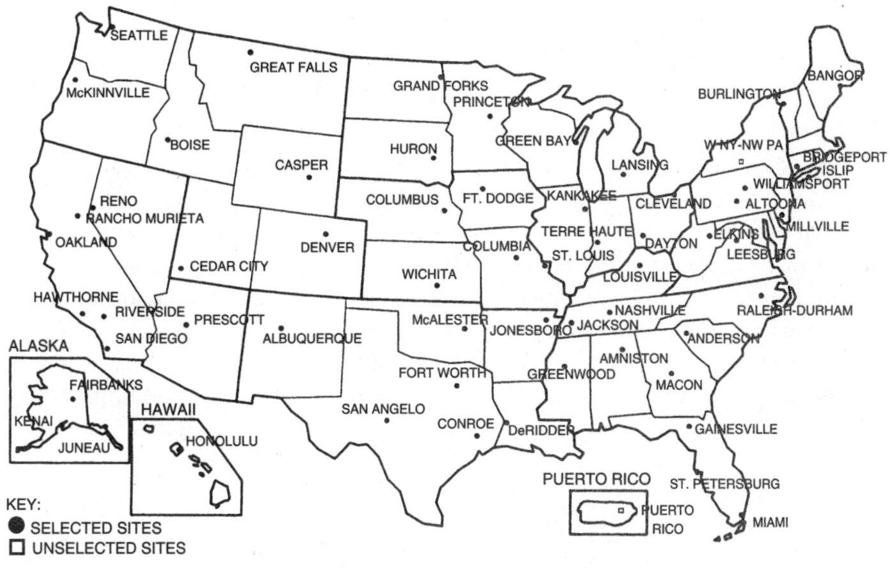

Fig. 10-1 *Locations of the 61 FSSs.*

Owners and Pilots Association (AOPA), the FAA reexamined several of the proposed closings and concluded that 31 should remain open because they were located in "significant weather areas." These were called *Auxiliary Flight Service Stations,* or XFSSs. According to the FAA's Air Traffic Operations Office in Washington, D.C., however, no XFSSs remain, except for about 13 in Alaska. Meanwhile, the AFSS count remains at 61 (barring the temporary closing of the St. Louis facility because of a damaging flood a couple of years ago).

Consolidation does have some drawbacks, most notably, the loss of in-person briefings, except at those airports where an AFSS is physically on the property. (Let's refer to it simply as an FSS from here on.) Nothing can replace the advantages of seeing for oneself the radar screens, charts, tables, and so on and discussing conditions face-to-face with a specialist.

On the opposite side, however, the pluses are many:

- Greatly improved automation and computer capabilities
- Faster flight plan filing
- More complete and more real-time weather data
- With the *Model 1* or Model 2 full-capacity (M1FC) computer, instant weather reports of conditions 25 miles either side of an extended cross-country route, such as between New York and St. Louis
- Color radar graphics, similar to but more detailed than those used in TV weather broadcasts

- Automatic radar warnings of approaching significant weather
- Fewer FSS specialists, with resultant lowered personnel costs

The minuses are thus few and the pluses many. Still, although greatly diminishing in volume, there have been complaints. With the telephone the only means for most of us to talk to a FSS, busy signals and waiting times have been sources of pilot irritation; of course, the wait time depends upon the weather conditions and the pilots requesting a briefing. When everything is socked in, all the briefers are naturally busy. But then in good weather or bad, there are those pilots who offer disorganized information and/or aren't prepared for the sequence of data they will be given. These folks obviously tie up the lines and cause excessive, as well as unnecessary, delays to other callers.

All in all, according to most pilots, the scales tip in favor of the pluses. Once you are in contact with a specialist, the briefings are faster and more complete, flight plan filing is almost instantaneous, and many more automated services are available through pilot menu accessing.

A TYPICAL FSS: POSITIONS AND STAFFING

The Columbia, Missouri, FSS is typical of the majority of consolidated stations. Some are smaller, others larger, but this facility ranks ninth in activity and is equipped with all the automated hardware available today. To get an idea of its layout, which, again, is representative, a floor plan (Fig. 10-2) and a photograph (Fig. 10-3) might help. The positions available for staffing are

13 Briefing
3 Flight watch
3 In-flight
1 NOTAM update
2 DATA (to correctly phrase arriving data for computer input)
1 Broadcast [*Hazardous In-Flight Weather Advisory Service* (HIWAS) and *Transcribed Information Briefing Service* (TIBS)]. TIBS is the acronym replacing *Pilot Automatic Telephone Weather Answering Service* (PATWAS).
1 Supervisory

The current personnel headcount at Columbia is 60:

44 Specialists
6 Supervisors
1 Quality assurance specialist
1 Area manager
1 Chief
1 Administrative assistant
1 Secretary

The typical daytime staffing, depending, of course, on need, is one in-flight specialist, five to nine briefers, and one to two flight watch specialists, or roughly, about 10 specialists, plus staff, on duty at the same time. That doesn't sound like a lot of people,

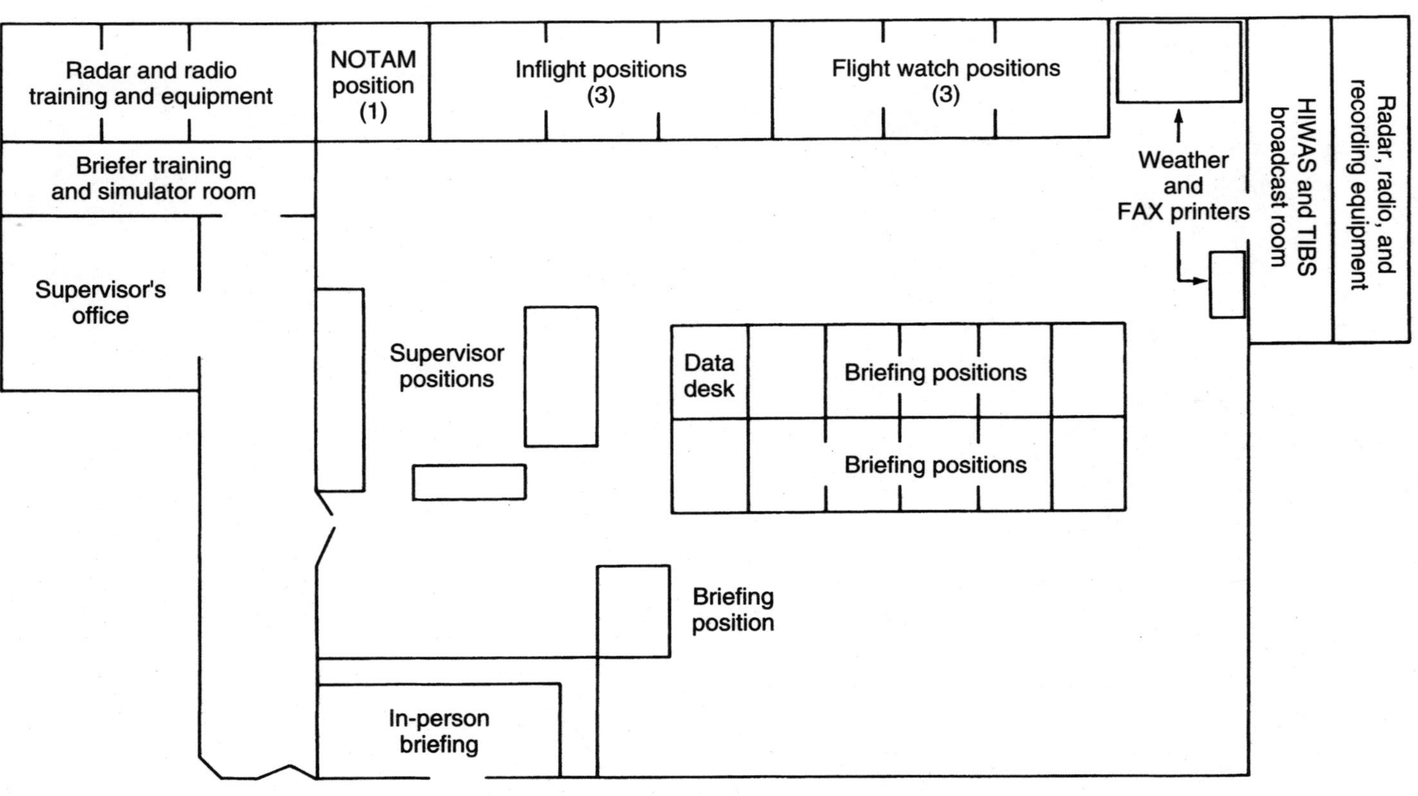

Fig. 10-2 *The functions and positions in the Columbia, Missouri, FSS.*

Fig. 10-3 *Some of the typical briefing positions.*

especially considering that the FSS is currently responsible for all of Missouri and one very aviation-active county in Kansas. However, I've been in a number of older FSSs that have only a relatively small area of responsibility, and a staffing of 7 to 10 specialists and supervisors was not unusual. Automation, plus sophisticated computerization, makes the difference.

ROAMING THROUGH THE FSS

With the general layout in mind, let's walk through the FSS, again remembering that what is seen is typical of almost all FSSs. Also, during this tour, suggestions will be offered for pilots using the various services.

NOTAM desk

The specialist at this desk is responsible for recording and updating all NOTAMs and entering them in the computer so that they are available to the briefers. While it is a momentary digression from the subject at hand, a few words about NOTAMs are pertinent at this point because of their importance to the pilot.

The *Aeronautical Information Manual* defines a NOTAM as "time-critical aeronautical information which is of either a temporary nature or not sufficiently known in advance to permit publication on aeronautical charts or in other operational publications." *AIM* then goes on to say that the "...aeronautical information...could affect a pilot's decision to make a flight. It (the NOTAM) includes such information as airport or primary runway closures, changes in the status of navigational aids, ILSs, radar service availability, and other information essential to planned en route, terminal, or landing operations."

Accordingly, and depending on their source and importance, NOTAMs fall into one of three categories: *Flight Data Center* (FDC) NOTAMs, NOTAM Ds (distant), or NOTAM Ls (local).

An important point to keep in mind is that conditions reported in an FDC or NOTAM D that are expected to exist for an extended period are included in the next biweekly issue of the *Notices to Airmen* publication (NTAP). Once published, those NOTAMs are not volunteered during weather briefings. Consequently, if a pilot has not had access to the latest NTAP, it's his or her responsibility to ask if any 2-week-old or longer NOTAMs exist that would affect the planned flight.

FDC NOTAMs

The National Flight Data Center (FDC) in Washington issues FDC NOTAMs, which are regulatory in nature. Most amend standard instrument approaches, designate restricted airspace, or alter the airway structure. They are transmitted nationwide to all FSSs, and the FSSs maintain a file of current, unpublished NOTAMs that affect the airspace within 400 nautical miles of their facility. FDC NOTAMs more than 400 miles from the FSS or NOTAMs that have already been published are given to the pilot only on request.

NOTAM Ds

All navigational facilities that are part of the National Airspace System receive NOTAM Ds, which communicate changes to the published status of airspace obstructions or components of the airspace system, such as radio or TV tower lighting outages, runway closures and commissionings, navigational aids out of service, or other system operational deviations. NOTAM Ds generally have potential concern to a wide pilot population and are thus given distant dissemination. Current (nonpublished) NOTAM Ds are sent by the weather computer network, are compiled and retransmitted every hour, and are appended to the weather of the affected station until published in the NTAP.

To illustrate how a NOTAM D is initiated, assume that an airport runway is to be closed for resurfacing. The airport manager so advises its area FSS, at which point the NOTAM desk prepares the NOTAM and enters it in the computer. The information then goes to the U.S. NOTAM Service office in Washington, which transmits the final, possibly slightly edited NOTAM to the Weather Message Switching Center (WMSC) in Atlanta. At this point, the WMSC appends the NOTAM information to each hourly weather report for dissemination to all FSSs, public-use airports, seaplane bases, and heliports that are listed in the *Airport/Facilities Directory.*

NOTAM Ls

Local NOTAMs are usually of interest to relatively few pilots and are thus reported to and retained by each FSS for only the facilities within its own geographic area of responsibility. The Ls include such information as taxiway closures, repair crews near or crossing a runway, rotating beacon outages, or airport lighting aid outages that don't affect instrument approaches.

While this is only a brief summary, its intent, in part, is to alert pilots to the importance of asking the briefer if any NOTAMs exist that might affect a planned flight. NOTAMs that have not yet been published and are still valid will be volunteered. Otherwise, as I said, the responsibility falls on the pilot to initiate the request, assuming the pilot hasn't had access to the biweekly publication.

It's at the NOTAM desk, then, where the recording, updating, and necessary editing occur and where the NOTAMs are entered in the computer for briefing purposes.

In-flight

You reach the *in-flight specialist* when you contact the FSS by radio to open, amend, or close a flight plan; request a weather update; file a flight plan while en route (not a recommended procedure); or make a position report.

Figure 10-4 shows a series of lights, 48 in all. While there are some duplications, each light represents a radio frequency on which you can call the in-flight specialist. Including the few duplications (those where two radio outlets use the same frequency but are geographically miles apart), this panel could handle up to 48 frequencies.

The main issue here is that when you call in, the light representing the frequency you're using blinks, but it blinks only while you're talking. The instant you release the microphone button, the blinking stops. Perhaps the specialist heard your call, but if otherwise occupied and unable to see the blinking, he or she has no way of knowing which frequency to reply on. So you get no response.

The point is this, a point that specialists stressed to me time after time: When you call, state the frequency you're using and your actual, or approximate, geographic location.

For example, you're at or over St. Joseph, Missouri, about 140 miles northwest of Columbia. The St. Joseph remote communications outlet (RCO) frequency to the FSS is 122.3, but Sedalia, Missouri, 45 miles west of Columbia, also has a 122.3 RCO. If you call in and merely say, "Columbia Radio, Cherokee Eight Five One Five November," the specialist, who might be talking to another aircraft, is unlikely to spot the blinking light and will have no way of knowing what frequency you're on.

Next time you call, "Columbia Radio, Cherokee Eight Five One Five November, on 122.3." That's more helpful, but are you at St. Joseph or Sedalia? The specialist still can't tell, if the blinking light went unnoticed.

One more time you call, "Columbia Radio, Cherokee Eight Five One Five November, on 122.3 at Saint Joe." Now, even if the light was missed, the specialist knows which transmitter to activate to acknowledge your call.

The format, then, is "(Blank) Radio" (always "Radio," not "Flight Service," in these calls), aircraft type, N number, frequency that you're calling on (which might be a VOR, so mention the VOR by name as well), and location. Now you'll get a response.

I said a moment ago that you could file a flight plan while en route by contacting the in-flight position. That's true, but again, it's not a recommended procedure. It takes up airtime and possibly blocks out others who are trying to get a call through.

As an example, while observing the one Columbia in-flight specialist on duty at the time, I noted at least 10 minutes was spent briefing an airborne pilot who then wanted

Fig. 10-4 *This is the bank of 48 frequency lights that the in-flight position must monitor.*

to file an IFR flight plan. Both requests were thoughtless and most likely unnecessary. These were details the pilot should have handled on the ground. Meanwhile, the specialist wasn't available to respond to other calls that were coming in.

Another point worth noting: You're on a VFR cross-country with or without a filed flight plan. And you have or haven't been in contact with a Center for en route traffic advisories. Whatever the combination, you'd like to be sure that someone down there knows where you are and has an immediately retrievable record of your call. So you get on the air to the nearest FSS and make a brief position report upon acknowledgment of your call: "Jonesboro Radio, Cherokee Eight Five One Five November position report. Over Walnut Ridge at 1510, VFR to Tupelo."

Now, if a problem arises and you go down before having time to dial 7700 or contact another facility, the search for you that the FSS initiates will be limited to the territory between Walnut Ridge and Tupelo. That one position report could be the lifesaver, should you end up in Farmer Brown's cow pasture.

Being in contact with a Center as you cruise along is an excellent practice, but Center exists primarily for IFR operations and is not designed to keep an en route progress check of VFR aircraft. The FSS does, however, maintain flight-following records, if you periodically call in. Like insurance, you might never need it, but that one call is a small price to pay for the additional "insurance coverage" that it provides.

Flight watch

The next positions are *flight watch,* often referred to as EFAS, the En route Flight Advisory Service. You're cruising down an airway and would like an updated, detailed report on the weather ahead. If you've been getting advisories from Center, contact the controller with whom you've been talking and advise that you're temporarily leaving the assigned frequency to call flight watch (Fig. 10-5). (That, by the way, is a procedure always to keep in mind. Never leave one facility to go to another without informing the first facility, which might have a need to reach you.)

With Center advised, tune to 122.0, the common low-altitude flight watch frequency across the country and address the call to the ARTCC responsible for the area in which you are flying, not the FSS. Because you're transmitting on the 122.0 frequency, you'll still be contacting the FSS facility, despite the oral address. Following your aircraft identification number, also include the name of the VOR closest to your present position. This the specialist needs to know in order to select the most appropriate transmitter/receiver outlet for communications coverage. For example, to reach the Macon (Georgia) flight watch, with the ARTCC located in Atlanta: "Atlanta Flight Watch, Cherokee Eight One Five One November, Albany VOR."

If you're not sure which FSS or Center is responsible for the area you're in, just address the call to "Flight Watch," again indicating the VOR station you are near, such as "Flight watch, Cherokee Eight Five One Five November, Durango VOR." Once contact has been established, go ahead with your message.

Not all FSSs provide EFAS. Those that do are shown on the inside back cover of the *A/FD*. In the North Central *A/FD*, for example, although there are several other FSSs, only Columbia, Missouri (COU), and Princeton, Minnesota (PNM), offer the service through their various remote outlets (Fig. 10-6).

Fig. 10-5 *The flight watch position is equipped with charts, video images, and related data to help the specialist provide in-flight pilots with the most up-to-date weather reports.*

ENROUTE FLIGHT ADVISORY SERVICE (EFAS)

Radio Call: Flight Watch-Freq. 122.0

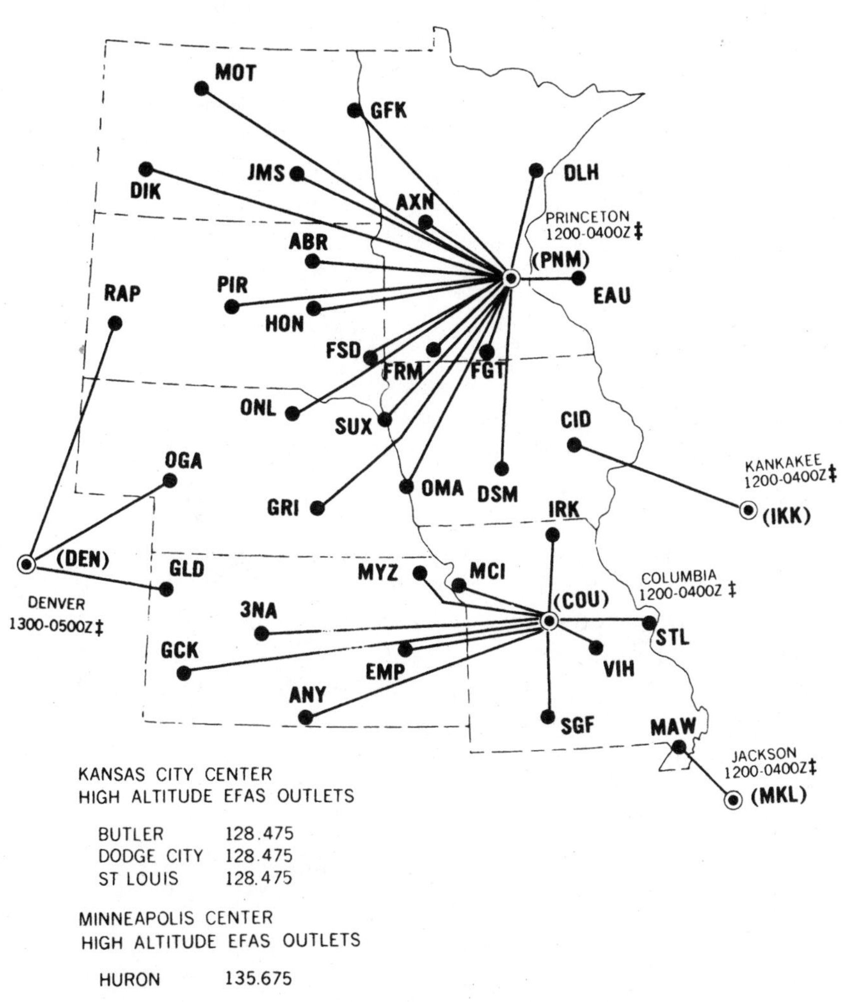

◉ FLIGHT WATCH CONTROL STATION (FWCS)

● COMMUNICATION OUTLETS

Fig. 10-6 *The inside back cover of the appropriate* A/FD *indicates the FSSs that provide flight watch service.*

Keep in mind that EFAS means *en route* flight advisories. It is thus designed to communicate weather conditions after departure climb-out and before the descent for landing, although immediate destination conditions will be provided on request. Also, you should be flying between 5000 feet AGL and 17,500 feet MSL. Between 18,000 and 45,000 feet MSL, EFAS can be contacted on discrete frequencies established for each ARTCC area.

Perhaps a question has already come to mind. If FSS has an in-flight position, why call flight watch, or vice versa? For one, in-flight has responsibilities other than just reporting weather, and the weather information available is not as complete or detailed as flight watch's. Weather is a flight watch specialist's sole responsibility, with no responsibility for flight plans, position reports, or the like. Flight watch is thus much more likely to be available for the specific weather-related information you want. Also, the specialist is more thoroughly trained in meteorology than the in-flight positions and is thus better equipped to read, interpret, and determine potential weather conditions. In-flight can certainly be of help, but flight watch is the FSS's primary source for short-range and real-time weather.

Pilot reports (PIREPs)

Something else is important: While flight watch gives weather information, it also wants to know what is actually happening right now where you are. If all is calm and routine, that's one thing; but if conditions, forecast or not, are such that they might pose problems for other pilots, the EFAS specialist wants to know.

What I'm talking about, of course, are pilot reports (PIREPs). Charts, radar graphics, maps, and so forth are essential, but nothing can replace first-hand descriptions of actual now-conditions that a pilot is experiencing. Just as flight watch will give us PIREPs it has received, it asks that pilots volunteer them, when necessary. One of this specialist's principal duties is to serve as a collection point for the exchange of PIREPs with other en route aircraft. Of course, a PIREP can be given to any ground facility with which you may be communicating: Center, Approach, tower, or the FSS in-flight position; however, en route, flight watch is the primary contact.

Once received, and depending upon the nature of the conditions reported, PIREPs are used by

- Air traffic control towers to expedite the flow of traffic in the airport vicinity and for the avoidance of hazardous weather
- Air Route Traffic Control Centers to expedite en route traffic flow, for favorable altitude determination, and to communicate hazardous weather information to en route aircraft
- FSSs for briefings, in-flight advisories, and weather avoidance information to en route aircraft
- The National Weather Service to amend or verify aviation forecasts; to issue, when necessary, advisories; and for meteorological studies and research

A PIREP is thus not just a casual communication. Depending upon what is reported, it could be critical to the well-being of others.

Of primary concern to ground facilities are reports of these weather phenomena:

- Icing: trace, light, moderate, severe
- Turbulence: light, moderate, severe, extreme
- Clear air turbulence: light, moderate, severe, extreme
- Thunderstorms
- Wind shear: loss or gain of altitude and/or airspeed experienced
- Clouds: bases, tops, layers
- Flight visibility or restrictions: haze, smoke, dust
- Precipitation
- Actual wind direction and speed, and temperature aloft

Be sure to report the conditions, particularly icing and turbulence, in accordance with *AIM*'s definitions as summarized in Tables 10-1 and 10-2. For example, turbulence

Table 10-1. The various intensities of turbulence and how they are described.

Turbulence Reporting Criteria Table

Intensity	Aircraft Reaction	Reaction Inside Aircraft	Reporting Term–Definition
Light	Turbulence that momentarily causes slight, erratic changes in altitude and/or attitude (pitch, roll, yaw). Report as **Light Turbulence;** [1] or Turbulence that causes slight, rapid and somewhat rhythmic bumpiness without appreciable changes in altitude or attitude. Report as **Light Chop.**	Occupants may feel a slight strain against seat belts or shoulder straps. Unsecured objects may be displaced slightly. Food service may be conducted and little or no difficulty is encountered in walking.	Occasional–Less than $^1/_3$ of the time. Intermittent–$^1/_3$ to $^2/_3$. Continuous–More than $^2/_3$.
Moderate	Turbulence that is similar to Light Turbulence but of greater intensity. Changes in altitude and/or attitude occur but the aircraft remains in positive control at all times. It usually causes variations in indicated airspeed. Report as **Moderate Turbulence;** [1] or Turbulence that is similar to Light Chop but of greater intensity. It causes rapid bumps or jolts without appreciable changes in aircraft altitude or attitude. Report as **Moderate Chop.** [1]	Occupants feel definite strains against seat belts or shoulder straps. Unsecured objects are dislodged. Food service and walking are difficult.	NOTE 1. Pilots should report location(s), time (UTC), intensity, whether in or near clouds, altitude, type of aircraft and, when applicable, duration of turbulence. 2. Duration may be based on time between two locations or over a single location. All locations should be readily identifiable.
Severe	Turbulence that causes large, abrupt changes in altitude and/or attitude. It usually causes large variations in indicated airspeed. Aircraft may be momentarily out of control. Report as **Severe Turbulence.** [1]	Occupants are forced violently against seat belts or shoulder straps. Unsecured objects are tossed about. Food service and walking are impossible.	EXAMPLES: a. Over Omaha. 1232Z, Moderate Turbulence, in cloud, Flight Level 310, B707.
Extreme	Turbulence in which the aircraft is violently tossed about and is practically impossible to control. It may cause structural damage. Report as **Extreme Turbulence.** [1]		b. From 50 miles south of Albuquerque to 30 miles north of Phoenix, 1210Z to 1250Z, occasional Moderate Chop, Flight Level 330, DC8.

[1] High level turbulence (normally above 15,000 feet ASL) not associated with cumuliform cloudiness, including thunderstorms, should be reported as CAT (clean air turbulence) preceded by the appropriate intensity, or light or moderate chop.

Table 10-2. The icing conditions that describe the four degrees of accumulation.

---

1. ***Trace:*** Ice becomes perceptible. Rate of accumulation is slightly greater than the rate of sublimation. It is not hazardous even though deicing/anti-icing equipment is not utilized unless encountered for an extended period of time (over 1 hour).

2. ***Light:*** The rate of accumulation may create a problem if flight is prolonged in this environment (over 1 hour). Occasional use of deicing/anti-icing equipment removes/prevents accumulation. It does not present a problem if the deicing/anti-icing equipment is used.

3. ***Moderate:*** The rate of accumulation is such that even short encounters become potentially hazardous and use of deicing/anti-icing equipment or flight diversion is necessary.

4. ***Severe:*** The rate of accumulation is such that deicing/anti-icing equipment fails to reduce or control the hazard. Immediate flight diversion is necessary.

EXAMPLE–
PILOT REPORT: GIVE AIRCRAFT IDENTIFICATION, LOCATION, TIME (UTC), INTENSITY OF TYPE, ALTITUDE/FL, AIRCRAFT TYPE, INDICATED AIR SPEED (IAS), AND OUTSIDE AIR TEMPERATURE (OAT).

NOTE–
1 RIME ICE: ROUGH, MILKY, OPAQUE ICE FORMED BY THE INSTANTANEOUS FREEZING OF SMALL SUPERCOOLED WATER

in a Cessna 152 might seem severe but, by definition, is only moderate or light. Misuse of terms because of unfamiliarity with them could mislead others to whom the PIREP is relayed.

When you submit a PIREP, of course it depends on what conditions you are reporting. If it's a routine PIREP reporting moderate turbulence (per the Table 10-1 description) in basically clear air, you'd go through the first six elements of the PIREP element code chart (Table 10-3), perhaps also element 7, if pertinent, and then skip to element 11, turbulence. As an example, after you establish contact with the Princeton, Minnesota, EFAS, the call would go like this:

> PIREP. About 60 west of Grand Forks VOR on Victor 430 at 1845 UTC. Eight thousand five hundred. Cherokee 180. Scattered clouds. Continuous moderate turbulence last 40 miles. Cherokee One Five November.

If any portion of the PIREP needs clarification, flight watch or the ground facility you have contacted will ask the necessary questions. Once your report is in, it will be organized and coded for transmission to other weather circuits.

Table 10-3.
The sequence in which a PIREP should be submitted and the contents of the report, as applicable to the current conditions.

PIREP ELEMENT CODE CHART

	PIREP ELEMENT	PIREP CODE	CONTENTS
1.	3–letter station identifier	XXX	Nearest weather reporting location to the reported phenomenon.
2.	Report type	UA or UUA	Routine or Urgent PIREP
3.	Location	/OV	In relation to a VOR
4.	Time	/TM	Coordinated Universal Time
5.	Altitude	/FL	Essential for turbulence and icing reports
6.	Type Aircraft	/TP	Essential for turbulence and icing reports
7.	Sky cover	/SK	Cloud height and coverage (sky clear, few, scattered, broken, or overcast)
8.	Weather	/WX	Flight visibility, precipitation, restrictions to visibility, etc.
9.	Temperature	/TA	Degrees Celsius
10.	Wind	/WV	Direction in degrees true north and speed in knots
11.	Turbulence	/TB	See AIM paragraph 7–1–20
12.	Icing	/IC	See AIM paragraph 7–1–19
13.	Remarks	/RM	For reporting elements not included or to clarify previously reported items

Briefing and the flight plan

The next part of our tour looks at briefing. The briefing positions are located in the center of the room (Fig. 10-3). Here are the people you talk to when you telephone the FSS. Each position is equipped with a computer screen, keyboard, and radar display (Fig. 10-7), which puts a wealth of data at the specialist's fingertips, including local conditions where you are, en route and destination weather, ceilings, visibility, winds and temperatures aloft, icing information, forecasts, PIREPs, NOTAMs—just about anything you could want to plan a flight.

At this point, a few words are in order regarding preparation before you call the FSS and the sequence of information you can expect to receive.

First, there is the matter of preparation. Many specialists have commented on the lack of information pilots initially supply and/or the disorganization of the information. The briefer, or specialist, will give you what you ask for but can't read your mind. If you're in Albuquerque and want the weather in Salt Lake City, that's what you'll get, but no more, unless you request it.

Quite obviously, then, the first thing to do before you pick up the phone is to plot the flight and then complete the FAA flight plan form (Fig. 10-8). Once you have the briefer on the line, state your qualifications (as student, private, commercial) and whether you are instrument-rated. From that point on, read off the information you have entered in boxes 1 through 10 on the FAA flight plan form:

Fig. 10-7 *Another view of a typical briefing position.*

1. Type of flight—VFR or IFR
2. Aircraft N number
3. Aircraft type and special equipment, which means the alphabetical identification of the avionics you have on board, the most common of which are the following (if you have GPS or flight management systems on board, see *AIM* for better identification):

   A DME, transponder with altitude encoding
   B DME, transponder with no altitude encoding
   C RNAV, transponder with no altitude encoding
   D DME, no transponder
   R RNAV, transponder with altitude encoding
   T Transponder with no altitude encoding
   U Transponder with altitude encoding
   W RNAV, no transponder
   X No transponder

   Example: If a Piper Cherokee 180 had a DME and a transponder with altitude encoding, the entry in box 3 would be PA-180/A.
4. True airspeed
5. Departure point

6. Proposed departure time [UTC (Zulu) time, not local time]
7. Intended cruising altitude
8. Route of flight
9. Destination, or first stopping point if the intended ground time will exceed 1 hour
10. Estimated time en route

After box 10, tell the specialist what type of briefing you want: *standard, abbreviated,* or *outlook.* A standard briefing is just what it says. The specialist will give you all the data pertinent to your route of flight and proposed altitude. If you've had a standard briefing and a couple of hours later want an update, ask for the abbreviated. The outlook should be requested when your departure is 6 hours or more from the briefing; however, in this case, be sure to call back, tell the briefer you've received the outlook, and then request the full standard.

Assuming you've asked for a standard briefing, the specialist will give you the information in this sequence:

1. Adverse weather conditions.
2. A synopsis of existing fronts and other weather systems along your line of flight. If conditions are obviously unfavorable, based on 1. and 2., it is at this point that the

Form Approved: OMB No. 2120-0026

U.S. DEPARTMENT OF TRANSPORTATION
FEDERAL AVIATION ADMINISTRATION

FLIGHT PLAN

(FAA USE ONLY) □ PILOT BRIEFING □ VNR
□ STOPOVER

TIME STARTED | SPECIALIST INITIALS

1. TYPE	2. AIRCRAFT IDENTIFICATION	3. AIRCRAFT TYPE/ SPECIAL EQUIPMENT	4. TRUE AIRSPEED	5. DEPARTURE POINT	6. DEPARTURE TIME		7. CRUISING ALTITUDE
					PROPOSED (Z)	ACTUAL (Z)	
VFR							
IFR							
DVFR			KTS				

8. ROUTE OF FLIGHT

9. DESTINATION (Name of airport and city)	10. EST. TIME ENROUTE		11. REMARKS
	HOURS	MINUTES	

12. FUEL ON BOARD		13. ALTERNATE AIRPORT(S)	14. PILOT'S NAME, ADDRESS & TELEPHONE NUMBER & AIRCRAFT HOME BASE	15. NUMBER ABOARD
HOURS	MINUTES		17. DESTINATION CONTACT/TELEPHONE (OPTIONAL)	

16. COLOR OF AIRCRAFT

CIVIL AIRCRAFT PILOTS. FAR Part 91 requires you file an IFR flight plan to operate under instrument flight rules in controlled airspace. Failure to file could result in a civil penalty not to exceed $1,000 for each violation (Section 901 of the Federal Aviation Act of 1958, as amended). Filing of a VFR flight plan is recommended as a good operating practice. See also Part 99 for requirements concerning DVFR flight plans.

FAA Form 7233-1 (8-82) CLOSE VFR FLIGHT PLAN WITH ____________ FSS ON ARRIVAL

Fig. 10-8 *The information to give the briefer at the outset of the call is simple—boxes 1 through 10 on the FAA flight plan form—then stop. The briefing will begin at this point.*

briefer will probably state, "VFR is not recommended." Otherwise, or if you still want more information, the briefing will continue.

3. A summary of current weather along the route of flight, based on surface observations, radar observations, and PIREPs.
4. A summary of forecast en route weather.
5. Detailed forecast destination weather.
6. A summary of forecast winds at your proposed altitude range and, if requested, temperature information.
7. Unpublished NOTAMs that could affect your flight, if requested.
8. Additional information you request, such as active MOAs or MTRs in your line of flight, or published NOTAMs.

As a suggestion, before you call a FSS, put these main headings on a piece of paper, leaving space between each for notes:

1. Adverse weather
2. Synopsis (along route of flight)
3. Current en route weather
4. Forecast en route weather
5. Forecast destination weather
6. Winds and temperature (at proposed altitude)
7. NOTAMs
8. Other: MOAs, MTRs, published NOTAMs, and the like

Now you'll know what's coming and in what order—you just fill in the blanks.

Filing the flight plan

Before the days of FSS consolidation, the typical practice was to get the briefing, hang up the phone, replot the flight as necessary based on the briefing, and then call back to file the flight plan. There was, and perhaps still is, an element of logic to that in the nonautomated FSSs.

It's a different story, however, today. As you're giving the briefer the data you have entered in boxes 1 through 10 on the flight plan form, the briefer is entering those data into the computer. After box 10, the weather is reported in the sequence I've just outlined. Once any questions you might have had have been answered, the briefer will ask for the balance of the flight plan form information, boxes 11 through 17.

At this point, assuming that the weather will have no material effect on your route of flight or will require extensive replanning, ask the briefer to file the flight plan, which, in effect, has already been done because it's in the computer.

Here is something to keep in mind: While you provide the data on the flight plan form, speak slowly enough and clearly enough that, as one FSS manager put it, "the specialist typing the information can absorb and digest it." Doing as the manager suggests saves time, especially if the specialist doesn't have to ask you to repeat data that could not be understood or that you transmitted too rapidly.

Afterward, and based on the briefing, do whatever replotting is necessary. If your en route or estimated arrival times are going to change to any measurable degree, just correct the filed times when you radio the FSS to open the flight plan. Thus you save another telephone call and possibly a wait, and you won't be duplicating information that the original briefer had already entered in the computer.

Another means of filing a flight plan offered by the FSSs is *fast file.* When you make the initial telephone contact, a recording will read off the menus of service available, including fast file, and the subsequent number to dial. When you do so, all that's necessary is to give the data in the exact sequence of the flight plan form. Everything is recorded and stored in the FSS's computer, ready for reference when you make the radio call opening the flight plan.

A suggestion made by the McAlester, Oklahoma, FSS is worth noting. In essence, the comment was that fast file is heavily used in areas with large volumes of traffic and when the FSS is very busy. In areas of less traffic or on less busy days, the preferred method is to establish contact with a specialist who copies the flight plan directly, asks questions that might need to be asked, and determines where the caller can be reached over the next few minutes if a discrepancy of some sort is discovered.

To go back to what I said earlier, the FSS is not a controlling agency. If the briefer observes that "VFR is not recommended," the decision to go or not go is yours; however, the fact that the recommendation was made is recorded as part of the briefing, just in case....The briefer has made the recommendation; but if you want to fly in the face of knowledgeable advice, well, it's your neck.

As somewhat of an aside, when you or I receive a briefing or file a flight plan, we're not competing with the air carriers. Almost all airlines have their own weather sources and dispatchers, and their flight plans are filed directly with the originating Center. Even more, flight plans for daily scheduled flights are stored in Center's computer and retrieved prior to the scheduled flight departure. In essence, then, the service I've been discussing is for general aviation IFR and VFR operations; so let's use it.

Closing the flight plan

Failure to close a flight plan after landing is one of the more common and costly pilot oversights. Admittedly, it's an easy thing to forget. You're tired after a few hours in the air; friends, family, or business associates are waiting for you; you're in a hurry to get one of the last rental cars; you're a student and your instructor is anxious to hear how things went on your first cross-country; you just want to get the airplane tied down or hangared so you can get home. Whatever the case, you forget that final responsibility. The last line on the flight plan form says, in capital letters, CLOSE VFR FLIGHT PLAN WITH__________________FSS ON ARRIVAL.

To minimize the chance for oversight, immediately radio the nearest FSS, if it's possible to reach it on the ground, when you come to a halt on the ramp. Otherwise, make a mental note to pick up a phone as soon as you're in the terminal or FBO's shop, and simply dial the nationwide number: 1-800-WX BRIEF. Don't let outside interferences distract you. The results could be costly.

What happens when a flight plan is not closed

The following is the sequence of events when you file a flight plan but don't close it out:

1. Upon departure, you radio the appropriate FSS to open your flight plan; let's call the first FSS "Alpha."
2. The in-flight specialist sends the flight plan to the FSS that is responsible for the area of your destination airport; let's call the second FSS "Bravo." All that is transmitted is your aircraft type, N number, destination, and ETA.
3. You land at your destination, or some other airport, and fail to close out the flight plan with any FSS.
4. Thirty minutes after your ETA, the computer in FSS Bravo flashes the flight plan data sent by Alpha, indicating you are overdue and haven't closed the flight plan.
5. FSS Bravo sends a query to FSS Alpha to determine if you actually departed or were delayed.
6. FSS Alpha calls your departure airport to verify your actual departure.
7. Because you did depart, FSS Alpha so notifies Bravo and sends to Bravo the balance of your flight plan information: route of flight, fuel on board, number of passengers, your name and address.
8. Bravo calls the tower or FBO and your intended destination to see if you landed.
9. If so, and your aircraft is located, that is the end of the search. Let's assume, however, that you landed at a different airport than originally intended, or that neither you nor your plane can be located at your planned destination. The search then goes on.
10. One hour after your ETA, FSS Bravo initiates an *information requested* (INREQ). This goes to all FAA facilities along your route of flight, including Centers and towers to determine if any facility has heard from you. If one has, the search can be focused on the territory between your last reporting point and destination. A copy of the INREQ is also usually sent to the applicable search-and-rescue unit, alerting it to the possibility of a downed aircraft.
11. If there has been no recorded or immediately available evidence of any en route contact, all FSSs along the route of flight begin telephoning every airport 50 miles either side of the route.
12. If these actions draw a blank, $1^1/_2$ hours after your ETA, an *alert notice* (ALNOT) is sent to every FAA facility along your route.
13. Each facility does further checking, such as playing back tapes to find any record of radio contact with you. The search-and-rescue unit also alerts the Civil Air Patrol. The Air Force might enter the investigation, contacting family or business associates to determine if they have heard from you or if you had indicated any possible route deviation before departing. All FSSs in the area broadcast over the

VORs each hour that an aircraft has been lost and asks pilots to monitor 121.5 (the emergency frequency) for an activated emergency locator transmitter (ELT).

14. The physical search begins.

See what problems can be caused by a simple oversight? In one case, hardly exceptional, an FSS made more than 100 telephone calls to airports along a pilot's route before the pilot was located safely at an airport other than the planned destination. The pilot's only excuse? He forgot!

All this only emphasizes the value of making periodic position reports to an FSS. If you should have a problem, the search can then be narrowed to the area between the last reporting point and your destination.

Today's aircraft are dependable, but things do go wrong. How much better to keep people down there informed of your progress than to fly merrily along and perhaps flounder for hours in an obscure cornfield while others are searching thousands of square miles for a small speck on the ground. And don't disregard the expense of a search—justified or not—in both time and money.

Filing to the first stop

You've got a 6-hour journey ahead of you, but you plan to make a pit stop about midway. Should you file a flight plan to the final destination or to the midpoint airport? The answer is rather apparent: If you're going to be on the ground 1 hour or more at that airport, file to the next point of landing, no matter how many legs the trip might have.

Say you leave Point A at 1200 local, planning to stop briefly at Point B, but you file to your destination, Point C, with an ETA of 1800 local. Thirty minutes out, the prop grinds down to windmilling status, you hit a furrow in the forced landing, and you end up on your back. It's now 1230, but it will be 1830 before the FSS at Point C even starts asking questions about you. The more intensive wheels of inquiry won't begin to roll until 1900 local. That might mean 6 $^1/_2$ hours trapped upside down in a bent airplane before a search even starts to get serious.

If you had filed to the midway point, Point B, with a 1500 ETA, the search would have started at 1530, a full 3 hours earlier. Also, the search efforts would be limited to the area between Points A and B, further enhancing the chances of rescue and survival.

Caution and wisdom do contribute to pilot longevity.

Transcribed services

The next stop on the tour of the FSS is a small room where two transcribed services are recorded. One is *Hazardous In-flight Weather Advisory Service* (HIWAS), and the other is *Transcribed Information Briefing Service* (TIBS).

HIWAS

This service is a continuous broadcast over those VOR navigation aids so indicated by a small square in the lower right corner of the VOR identification box (Fig. 10-9). Included in the broadcasts, as pertinent, are *severe weather alerts* (AWWs), *airman's meteorological information* (AIRMETs), *significant meteorological information* (SIGMETs),

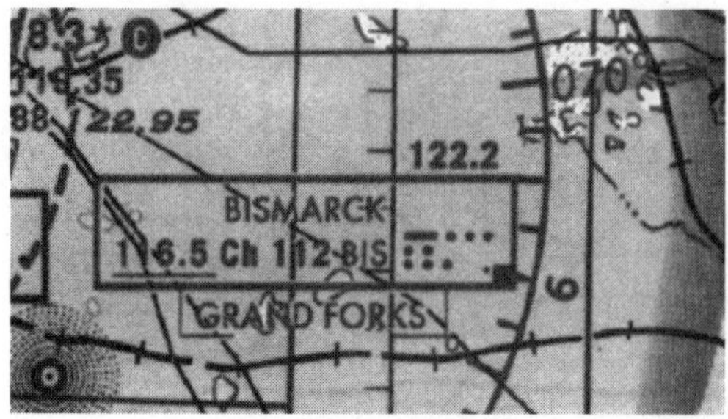

Fig. 10-9 *The small square in the lower right corner identifies the VORs that transmit HIWAS.*

convective sigmets (WSTs), *urgent pilot reports* (UUAs), *area forecasts* (FAs), and *Center weather advisories* (CWAs). If no weather advisories have been issued, an hourly statement to that effect is recorded and broadcast over the selected VORs.

The HIWAS is provided 24 hours per day, and the FSS completes the recording of the applicable data within 15 minutes after receipt. The actual broadcast message includes

- Statement of introduction
- Summary of the reported conditions (AWW, SIGMET, AIRMET)
- Recommendations to contact the FSS for further details
- Request for PIREPs

Example:

> HIWAS FOR JACKSONVILLE CENTER AREA AND PORTIONS OF ATLANTA AND MIAMI CENTER AREAS RECORDED AT ONE FIVE THREE ZERO ZULU. CONVECTIVE SIGMET ONE SEVEN ECHO. FROM FIVE ZERO SOUTH OF ST. PETERSBURG TO THREE ZERO SOUTH OF COLUMBUS, LINE OF THUNDERSTORMS THREE FIVE MILES WIDE MOVING EAST AT ONE FIVE KNOTS. MAXIMUM TOPS FOUR SEVEN THOUSAND. ISOLATED THUNDERSTORMS OBSERVED ON WEATHER RADAR VICINITY OF CRESTVIEW. IFR CONDITIONS ARE REPORTED AT VALDOSTA AND JACKSONVILLE. CONTACT FLIGHT WATCH OR FLIGHT SERVICE FOR ADDITIONAL DETAILS. PILOT REPORTS ARE REQUESTED.

In addition, Centers and airport traffic control towers alert pilots to the existence of a HIWAS condition on all except the emergency frequency, 121.5. A typical Center alert is shorter:

> ATTENTION ALL AIRCRAFT: MONITOR HIWAS OR CONTACT A FLIGHT SERVICE STATION ON FREQUENCY __________ MEGAHERTZ OR __________ MEGAHERTZ FOR NEW CONVECTIVE SIGMET (NUMBER) INFORMATION.

TIBS

This FSS service is similar to what has been known as *Pilots' Automatic Telephone Weather Answering Service* (PATWAS), but covers many more geographic areas.

To be more specific, once you have reached the FSS and listened to the recorded menu of services available, dial 201, which is the universal number to access TIBS. Another recording then tells you what subsequent 200-series number to dial for the desired information. Those numbers range from 202 to 224, although not all numbers might be currently in use. You'll then hear a transcript of the meteorological conditions within a 50-mile radius of the location you have selected. For example, at the Columbia FSS, by dialing the following numbers, except 202, 203, 211, 214, and 215, the weather data at the selected cities, locations will be summarized:

202 Weather synopsis
203 Thunderstorm activity
206 Springfield
207 Joplin
204 Columbia
208 Cape Girardeau
205 Kansas City
209 St. Louis
210 Kirksville
211 Winds aloft
214 ATC delays
215 How to get a quality briefing

Under the PATWAS system, the caller was limited to the conditions within a 50-nautical-mile radius of the FSS location. TIBS, however, offers a much wider range of locations, plus other pertinent data, simply by dialing the applicable numbers.

Despite the benefits of TIBS, it should not be a substitute for a standard briefing. Everything might be fine at departure and destination points, but what about the in-between weather? TIBS won't really tell you that. What about VORs that might be out, runway construction at the en route airports, or active MOAs on the route of flight? TIBS provides area weather information and can be helpful in arriving at a go/no-go decision. If things look good, fine. But get the other details from a briefing specialist.

In-person briefing

The final stop on the FSS tour is the *in-person briefing* position (Fig. 10-10). Here the pilot can see firsthand the weather radar displays, the computerized forecasts, winds aloft printouts, and all the information the telephone briefer provides. This type of briefing can be more instructive, particularly when conditions are marginal or questionable. It's sometimes difficult to visualize things over the telephone. Unfortunately, this advantage is being lost with consolidation, except for those operating where a FSS is located. Here is something to consider: When you plot a cross-country flight with overnight stops, and

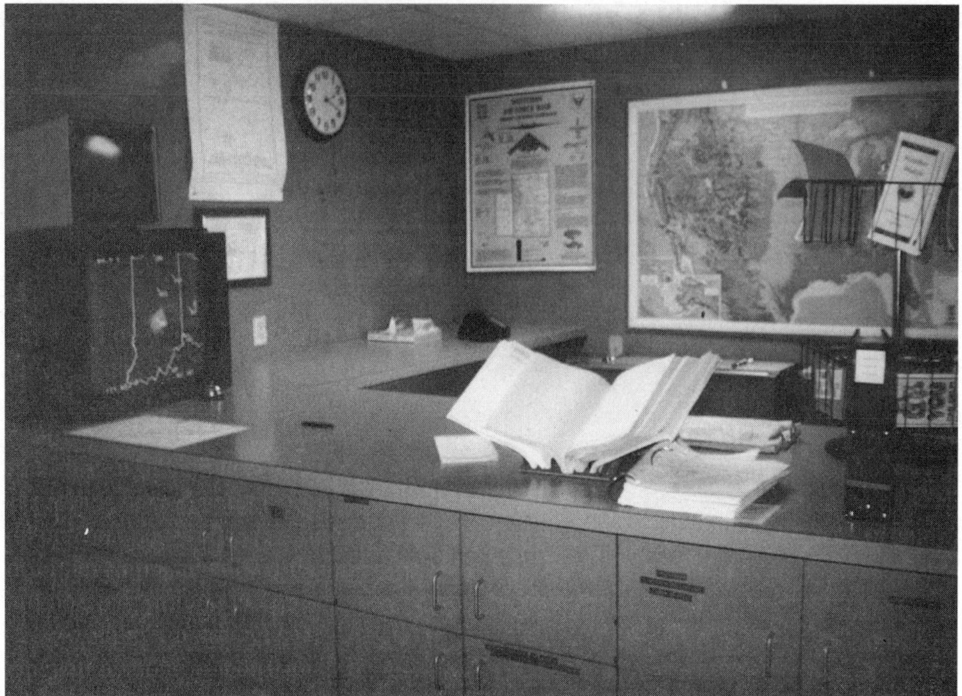

Fig. 10-10 *The in-person briefing position.*

if it is practical to do so, perhaps you should plan to land at an airport with a FSS. You'd then be able to enjoy the benefits of an in-person briefing and flight plan filing prior to departure the next day.

INSURANCE AND THE FSS

If one word could sum up the value of Flight Service to the VFR pilot, it would probably be *insurance.* Indeed, the services available are optional. You don't have to get a briefing, file a flight plan, make periodic position reports, get weather updates from flight watch, offer PIREPs, and—except for FAA test purposes—know anything about Flight Service, what it does, or what it offers.

But that seems more than a little shortsighted. Here's a facility with a wealth of information at its disposal and one that could literally be a lifesaver in an emergency. There are those among us, however, who don't know what services are available or how to use them. And there are those who consider themselves above the need for briefings, filing a flight plan, and the rest. Perhaps, just perhaps, this chapter might persuade the nonusers that taking advantage of Flight Service is simply common sense.

11
Air Route Traffic Control Center

WE'VE LEFT THE IMMEDIATE AIRPORT VICINITY AND STARTED HEADing toward a distant destination—well, it might not be "distant," but it's a cross-country excursion of some sort—and we have at our disposal one more FAA facility to help us along the way: the Air Route Traffic Control Center (ARTCC).

In one respect, "at our disposal" is somewhat of a misstatement, because Center exists primarily for IFR, not VFR, operations. Its first responsibility is to control IFR flight plan aircraft, ensure proper separation, monitor the aircraft's fix-to-fix and point-to-point progress, issue advisories, and sequence the aircraft into the terminal environment. Thus, in marginal weather conditions or when the volume of IFR traffic is heavy, Center might have no time to provide services to pilots operating VFR. Those are considered to be additional services and are at the discretion of the individual controller, depending on the workload.

Barring such situations, Center can play an important role in enhancing the safety of VFR flight by providing a variety of assistance: advising us of other traffic in our vicinity, alerting us if we should inadvertently (or perhaps carelessly) venture into an active MOA, offering vectors around potentially severe weather conditions, or helping us in an emergency.

Unfortunately, though, many VFR pilots are reluctant to request the services that are available. The reasons are varied: the belief that Center is only for the big boys who drive the widebodies or the high-time IFR pros; lack of knowledge of what Center does and how it functions; fear of being a nuisance to controllers who have enough to do without worrying about a Cessna 152 or Cherokee 140; uncertainty of how to communicate with the facility; reluctance to get on the air and perhaps display ignorance, make mistakes, or sound sort of stupid.

Whatever the case, whatever the cause, it's too bad, because Center not only will help but wants to help the VFR pilot whenever its workload permits. Controllers across the country have so stated, and the FAA encourages that help. Accordingly, a review of what a Center is, what it does, and how the VFR pilot can avail himself of the available service might help diminish some of this pilot reluctance—if such reluctance exists.

CENTER LOCATIONS AND AIRSPACE RESPONSIBILITIES

Twenty Centers blanket the continental United States, plus one each in Alaska, San Juan, Honolulu, and Guam. Those within the 48 states are listed in Table 11-1, while Figure 11-1 depicts all 24 Centers and the airspace for which each is responsible. As the figure indicates, any given Center has a fair piece of airspace to control, the typical Center being responsible for approximately 100,000 square miles or more. To service such an expanse, the geography is first divided into *areas,* and each area then subdivided into *sectors,* with one controller and perhaps an assistant controller usually handling a sector.

A logical question is how a Center, physically located perhaps several hundred miles from an aircraft, can maintain radio contact and radar coverage. The answer, of course, is through many remote air-ground radio outlets and a fewer number of remote radar antennas that are connected to the Center via microwave links and landlines. The microwave signal is essentially the primary radar carrier, while landlines serve as backups in the event of a microwave outage.

Figure 11-2 illustrates the Kansas City Center airspace and the various sector boundaries, as well as the radio frequencies in the sectors. From left to right, the extreme western limit just touches the southeastern corner of Colorado, and the eastern limit reaches

Table 11-1 The Air Route Traffic Control Centers in the continental United States.

Albuquerque	Houston	Minneapolis
Atlanta	Indianapolis	New York
Boston	Jacksonville	Oakland
Chicago	Kansas City	Salt Lake City
Cleveland	Los Angeles	Seattle
Denver	Memphis	Washington, D.C.
Fort Worth	Miami	

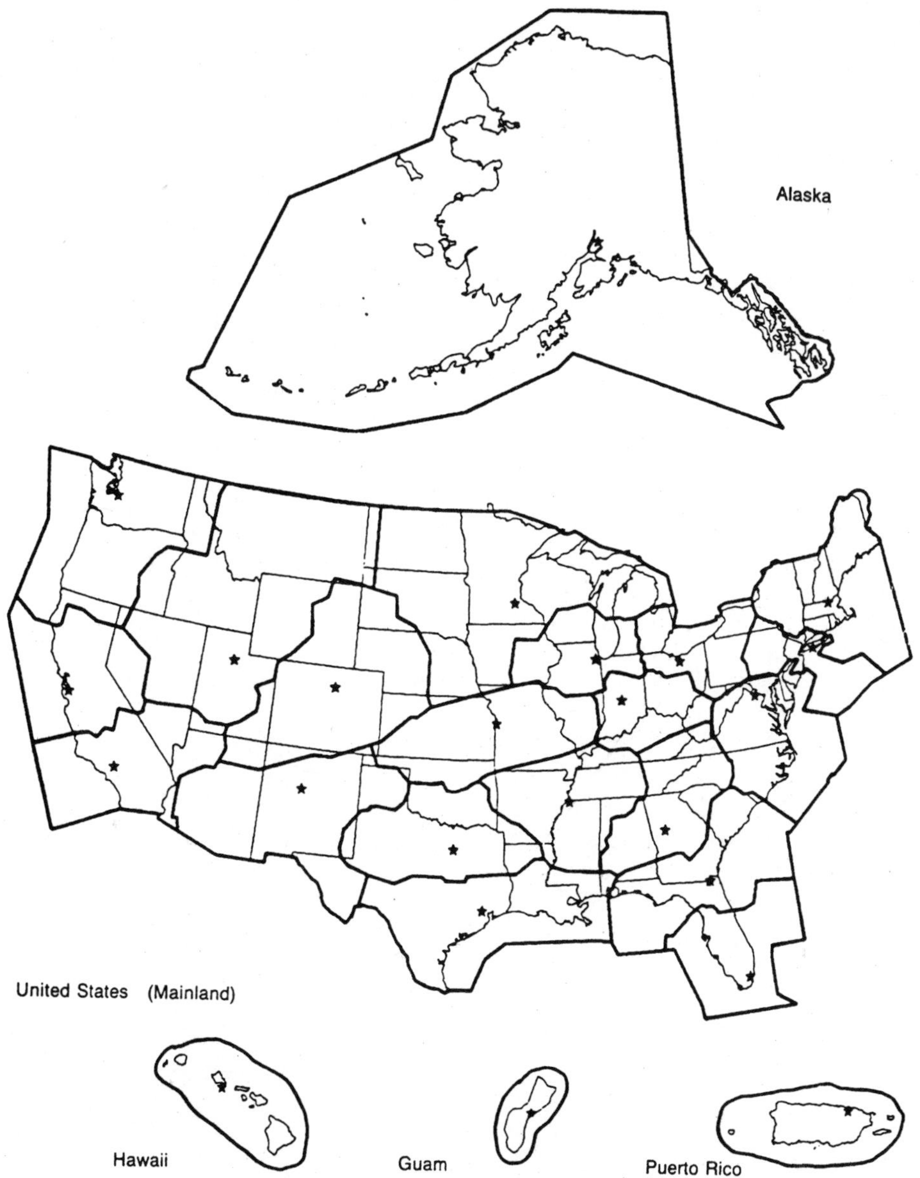

Fig. 11-1 *The locations of the 24 Centers and the general geographic areas for which each is responsible.*

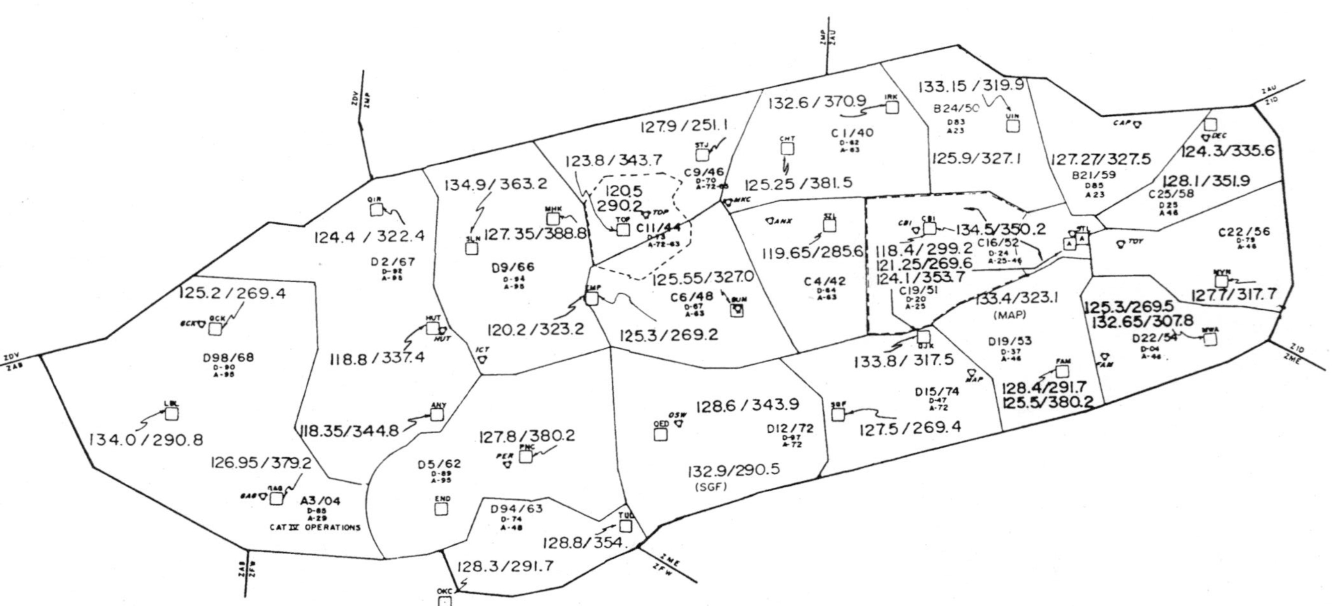

Fig. 11-2 *The sectors and respective frequencies within Kansas City Center's airspace. The squares identify remote communications outlets, and the triangles are VOR locations.*

almost to Indiana. The square boxes designate the *remote communications air/ground* (RCAG) locations and their radio frequencies.

Figure 11-2 also illustrates the changing of frequencies as you move across the airspace. Going from sector to sector means that you're leaving one controller's area and entering that of another. As this occurs, the first controller will call you and advise you to change from the current frequency to the one monitored by the next controller. This is the *handoff* process, which is very similar to the steps Approach takes when it transfers the monitoring of an aircraft from the terminal area to a Center. The only major difference is that this handoff is between facilities, while the other is between sector controllers, separated, perhaps, by only a few feet. (Handoffs are subsequently described in detail in this chapter, along with brief examples of the correct communication procedures.)

Figure 11-2 illustrates something else: You'll note that several of the sectors have two or more frequencies back to Center. As the aircraft moves out of the range of one, the controller will tell the pilot "Change to my frequency, 134.9" or "Contact me now on 134.9." This simply means that the pilot will be talking to the same controller but on another frequency. The key to what's happening is the use of *my* or *me.* Be alert to that, because it will have some effect on what you say when you make the change and reestablish radio contact.

HOW A CENTER IS ORGANIZED

Not all Centers are identical in physical layout, but the Kansas City Center (actually located in Olathe, Kansas, about 20 miles southwest of Kansas City) is typical in terms of size, staffing, and layout. Figure 11-3, which requires a bit of explanation, is a drawing of the facility's overall design, while Fig. 11-4 illustrates just one of the sector positions.

At the left and outside the boxed-in areas (Fig. 11-3), you'll see the letters A to D. These identify the four rows of controller positions and their related radar, radio, and telephone equipment. The rows are then divided into geographic airspace areas, arbitrarily designated here as Flint Hills, Trails, Ozark, Prairie, and Rivers/Gateway.

The next breakdown is the division of the areas into sectors, with each sector responsible for the control of high (HI) altitude or low (LO) altitude traffic. For ease of reference, Fig. 11-3 is an enlargement of the Trails area and its various sectors. Either above or below the position symbols is the coding for these sectors, such as SLN-HI (Salina High) and MKC-HI (Kansas City High). These are the sectors in Trails that handle flight operations from 24,000 up to 60,000 feet MSL. Meanwhile, the low-altitude operations (up through FL23,000 feet) are the responsibility of the sectors identified as IRK-LO (Kirksville), ANX-LO (Napolean, a VOR), BUM-LO (Butler), STJ-LO (St. Joseph), and FOE-LO (Forbes Air Force Base—low, 5000 feet and below). In small print, again, either above or below the position, you'll see the VORs in the sector, in this case, MKC, MCM (Macon, MO), and IRK in the IRK-LO sector. The encircled numbers (40, 42, 48, 46, etc.) identify the locations of the sector radarscopes, which are also called PVDs, or *planned visual displays.*

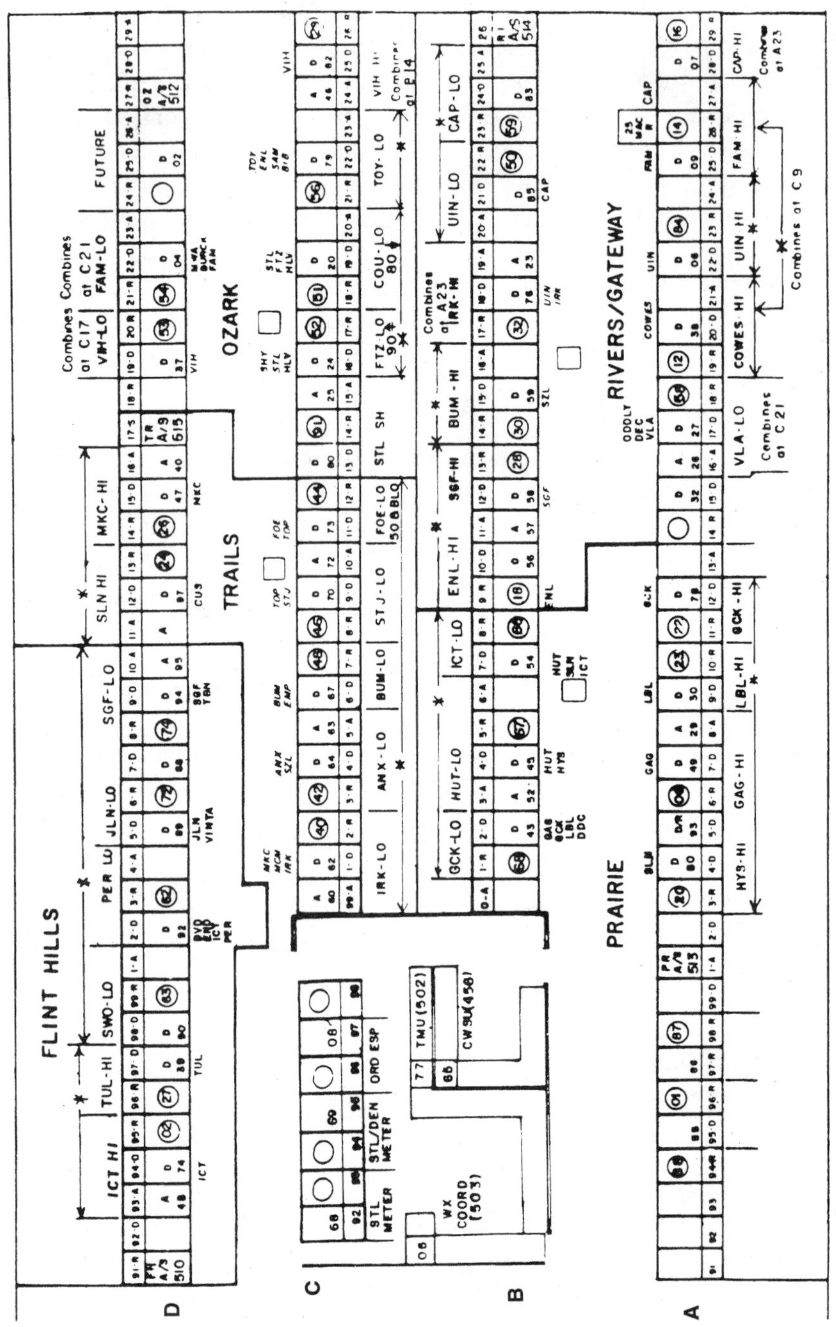

Fig. 11-3 *The floor plan of the Kansas City Center is typical of others throughout the country.*

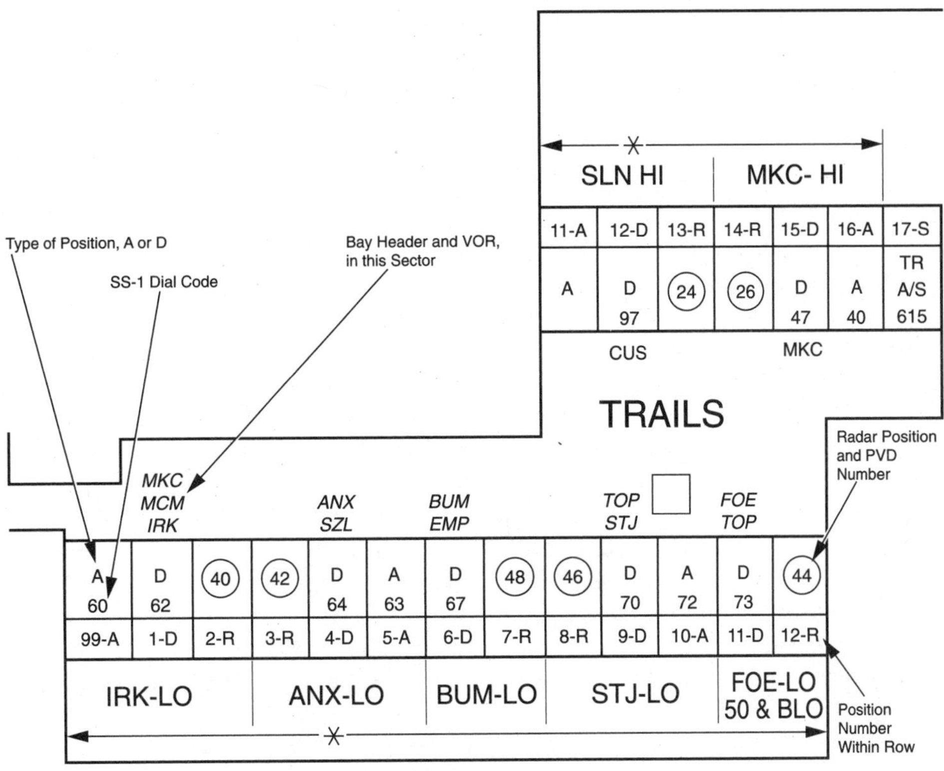

Fig. 11-4 *An enlargement of the Trails area and its sectors.*

Adjacent to the PVD numbers are the letters A and D. What the A originally stood for is apparently lost in history, at least in the Kansas City ARTCC, but today it is commonly called the *A side,* to which new employees (meaning those who have completed the initial screening and training at the FAA's Oklahoma City Academy and are called *developmentals*) are assigned. It's not unusual, however, to find fully qualified and experienced personnel—personnel who have reached what is called the "full performance level," or FPL—working the position. Whatever the case, the A side is primarily responsible for removing the computerized flight strips from the printers and hand-delivering the strips to the appropriate sector controller. Additionally, for example, if a Flight Service Station wanted to correct or update a filed flight plan, the FSS would call the A side's telephone dial-code (such as 60, in the IRK-LO sector) and the A side would manually amend the flight plan data. His or her job is thus rather clerical in nature, but these tasks, basic as they may be, are essential to the FPL who is manning the PVD and to the smooth control of traffic about to enter the FPL's sector.

The letter D, in Fig. 11-5, represents the data, or D-side, position and also refers to the "developmental," still in a training capacity and not yet a qualified FPL. As with the A side, however, an FPL could be working this position, depending on staffing needs or staffing limitations. In either case, the D-side person is responsible for much of the paperwork, communicating information to the PVD FPL; racking, revising, or updating flight strips; handling landline phone calls; assisting in emergencies; and generally serving as the right hand to the FPL who is actually on the radio at a PVD and controlling sector traffic.

As part of the training process and when the workload permits, the developmental puts on a headset and observes as the FPL communicates with his or her sector traffic. Depending on his level of training, the developmental also could sit at the position and actually control the sector traffic, *but* (and it's an important *but*) he or she does so only under the eyes and ears of an instructor or an FPL.

On the other hand, the developmental may have reached the stage of training and competency that enables him or her to function as a *manual,* or *nonradar,* controller. At that skill level, the developmental is qualified to handle IFR traffic in nonradar situations, such as an IFR aircraft that is preparing to land at a distant Class E or G airport and has descended to an altitude below Center's radar coverage. In cases like this, the only way to separate and control the aircraft in IMC weather is by radio, by following a strict set of procedures, and then by trusting in the pilot's flying skills and ability to follow instructions. Otherwise, it is not until the stage of radar certification is reached and the developmental is classified as an FPL that he or she mans the radar position free of immediate supervision or in-person monitoring. I should point out, however, that, regardless of the individual's level of experience, every radio communication is taped for whatever future need it might serve. So in a sense, even the most knowledgeable and long-tenured FPL can never escape some sort of moment-by-moment performance monitoring.

To round out the makeup of a sector, you'll note that either above or beneath the sector's PVD is a number and then the letter R, such as 2-R in the IRK-LO sector or 13-R in SLN-HI. The number is simply the position number within the row, and the R, quite logically, identifies the radar position.

The *selective signaling (SS-1) dial code* in Fig. 11-4 is the direct-line number that a controller or outside facility, such as Approach, would use to reach a specific sector and its A or D specialist. In the illustration, to contact the A or D in Sector 40, the caller would merely dial 60 or 62, respectively, and be directly connected to the position.

Position numbers in the row are identified 99-A and 1-D. For maintenance or a telephone outage, the problem would be reported as at Position 99-A or 1-D.

Finally, the horizontal line with the asterisk defines the sectors that are combined during the midnight shift when traffic is at its ebb (Figs. 11-3 and 11-4).

One other set of functions not yet mentioned are those to the left between Rows B and C in Fig. 11-3. STL METER, STL/DEN METER, and ORD ESP (ESP means *en route spacing*) are computerized displays of all aircraft currently within the Center's area of responsibility that are going to land at St. Louis, Denver, and O'Hare. Rather than allowing 20 or 30 planes to deluge a given terminal airspace at the same time, an orderly flow of arriving traffic is established by *metering.*

Based on terminal weather conditions, runways in use, or other local factors, the maximum number of arrivals per hour that the airport can accommodate is established. The Center computer then assigns each inbound flight a specific time by which it is to arrive over a given fix that is located well outside the terminal's Approach Control airspace. If the aircraft fails to arrive at the fix within 2 minutes before to 2 minutes after that assigned time, or if it doesn't appear that it will, the sector controller handling the flight will instruct the pilot to speed up, slow down, or take any other action necessary to slot the aircraft into the planned arrival pattern.

The metered displays of the aircraft for which that controller is responsible also appear on the controller's sector PVD, but only those aircraft. The controller is thus expected to take unilateral action to maintain the precise time schedule of flights into the terminal area.

In the case of O'Hare, the Chicago Center handles that traffic, but Kansas City tries to ensure the proper en route spacing of ORD-bound aircraft in its airspace so that there won't be an unnecessary buildup once the traffic is handed over to Chicago. The same principle applies to traffic going into Denver.

Overall coordination is the responsibility of the *traffic management unit* (TMU). These specialists are constantly monitoring the meters to ensure that the computer-generated spacing and timing are being met. When discrepancies occur, it's up to the TMU, through the sector controllers, to ensure compliance with the designed arrival flow.

The other function in this complex is the *center weather service unit* (CWSU). The planned visual displays at the controllers' positions in a Center are all computer-generated; thus, from a weather point of view, what the controller sees on the scope is only a series of lines, some close-set, others more widely separated, superimposed with an H (heavy) to identify thunderstorm intensity. Unlike the terminal ARTS II or III radar that produces a much more realistic image of the weather, these lines alone are really of minimal help in guiding a pilot around or through conditions that might exist out there.

The CWSU, however, has a real radar picture of the weather, with the various degrees of thunderstorm activity in color. Using this and other available data, the CWSU briefs the controller supervisors twice a day on what's happening and what to expect. Then, if severe weather or turbulence develops between briefings, the CWSU issues a typed *general information* (GI) message that goes to all position printers, alerting controllers to current disturbances, where they are, and the degree of reported intensity.

That's the overall physical organization of a typical Center, a small portion of which is illustrated in Fig. 11-5. Other Centers might have different layouts, but the functions are the same, and basically so is the hardware. I say *basically* because advances are coming rapidly, and not all Centers receive the same new equipment at the same time.

USING CENTER'S SERVICES

What happens when we contact a Center for advisories, and why is it to the VFR pilot's advantage to utilize the services available? Let's review a few of the procedures to follow, as well as certain controller recommendations, particularly for VFR pilots.

Determining the correct Center frequency

Alternatives for obtaining ARTCC frequencies are offered because it's not always easy to determine the correct frequency for the area you're in. The *A/FD* and en route

Fig. 11-5 *As much as a darkened room will permit, this picture illustrates the elements that make up a sector suite in a typical Air Route Traffic Control Center.*

low-altitude charts give a general idea, but as the Kansas City Center sector-frequency chart illustrated (Fig. 11-2), a given sector could have several frequencies. Furthermore, how many of us have a sector-frequency chart on board? It's not something routinely distributed to the public. These alternatives, however, are available:

- If you've filed a flight plan, ask the FSS specialist what the frequency is for your initial route of flight.
- If you forget or didn't ask the FSS, get the frequency from Clearance Delivery, Ground Control, or the tower.
- If departing a Class C or Class B airspace and you are not handed off to Center, ask Departure Control.
- If you're en route and want to establish contact with Center for the first time, merely radio the nearest FSS, giving your aircraft identification, position, and altitude, and then make the request.

Calling Center for advisories

Assume there has been no handoff from Approach or another Center. You decide en route that you want traffic advisories, so you get on the mike and call a Center for the first time.

A point that controllers continually stress is this: Do nothing more than establish contact in that initial call. Don't volunteer any information other than the aircraft type and N number, such as: "Kansas City Center, Cherokee Eight Five One Five November." (Period!)

The reason for this is that the controller might be talking with an aircraft on another frequency and wouldn't hear your call or could be momentarily involved in other matters. Once the call is heard, though, the controller's probable first action would be to glance at the flight strips to see if there is one with your N number—which wouldn't be the case if you're VFR and this is your first contact with Center.

In the past, the procedure at this point was for the controller to begin hand writing a VFR strip. Now, however, the controller originates a computer flight strip and begins keying it in as soon as your call has been acknowledged and you start supplying the essential information. While talking or listening to you, the controller will be

1. Requesting a transponder code from the computer
2. Identifying your aircraft on radar
3. Typing in "VP" (meaning VFR flight plan), aircraft type, first landing point, and aircraft call sign

The processed flight strip will then look just like an IFR strip, except that it will be identified VFR.

Keep in mind what is happening on the ground and the need to speak clearly. The dialogue after your initial call would go like this:

Ctr: Cherokee Eight Five One Five November, Kansas City Center. Go ahead.
You: Center, Cherokee Eight Five One Five November is over Butler at seven thousand five hundred, VFR to West Memphis. Request advisories.
Ctr: Cherokee One Five November, Roger. Squawk one seven zero one and ident.
You: Roger, one seven zero one. Cherokee One Five November.
Ctr: Cherokee One Five November, radar contact. Altimeter two niner three five.
You: Two niner three five. Cherokee One Five November.

From here on, Center will advise you of traffic that is or might be in your line of flight:

Ctr: Cherokee One Five November, traffic nine o'clock, three miles, a Cessna 172, altitude seven thousand five hundred.
You: Negative contact. Looking. Cherokee One Five November.

If, in a couple of minutes, you do spot the 172, tell Center:

You: Center, Cherokee One Five November has the traffic.
Ctr: Cherokee One Five November, Roger. Thank you.

Controllers like such information. It's one less thing they have to worry about.

Another reason for first establishing contact and waiting for the call to be acknowledged is that some pilots get on the mike and ramble on and on with unnecessary trivia, including the fact that they've got the family dog in the rear seat. As the trivia flows, the controller has two IFR aircraft on a merging pattern, both at the same altitude. Watching them come closer and closer, he feels his blood pressure rise, but the controller is helpless to do anything about the impending crisis. The rambler has the frequency tied up.

Also, when you request advisories, give Center only your next point of landing, not necessarily your final destination. If you're on the first leg of a four-leg flight, where you're ultimately going is useless information to the controller. Where you're going to land first is what matters.

It's the old admonition, again: Know what you need to say, say it, and get off the mike.

A word about frequencies

Perhaps you've experienced this: You've been using a Center for advisories, or were merely eavesdropping. You hear the controller call another aircraft, but you hear no response.

The controller might have as many as six frequencies to work with. You're talking on one, but a second pilot is transmitting on another. The controller's transmissions, however, go out on all frequencies assigned to that position.

IFR versus VFR flight strips

While controllers originate the VFR flight strips, IFRs are a different matter. When an IFR flight plan has been filed, the FSS computer sends the basic information to the Center computer, where it is automatically stored until 30 minutes before the planned departure. The computer then *spits out* (as controllers term it) the data on a flight strip. The A side tears off the strip, takes it to the appropriate sector controller position, inserts it in a plasticlike holder, and places the holder on a slanted rack, along with the other IFR and VFR strips (Figs. 11-6 and 11-7). Now when the aircraft is handed off from Approach, from sector to sector, or Center to Center, the controller responsible has the pertinent flight data right there (Fig. 11-8). Figure 11-9 is an example of an actual IFR strip, decoded in Table 11-2.

ARTCC radar system

Unlike Approach Control, which has the ARTS II or III radar that produces target symbols as well as alphanumeric data, Centers use the *National Airspace System Stage A,* or the Planned Visual Display we've already mentioned. With ARTS II or III, as you'll remember from Chap. 7, two systems function in unison: primary and secondary radar, or broadband and narrowband. It's the combination of the two that produces a particular aircraft symbol, depending on whether it is just a primary target without an operating transponder, one with Mode 3/A, one with Mode C, and the like.

The Center's en route NAS Stage A relies on just the narrowband radar. In this system, the signal goes out and hits the target, and then the "reply" is processed through the

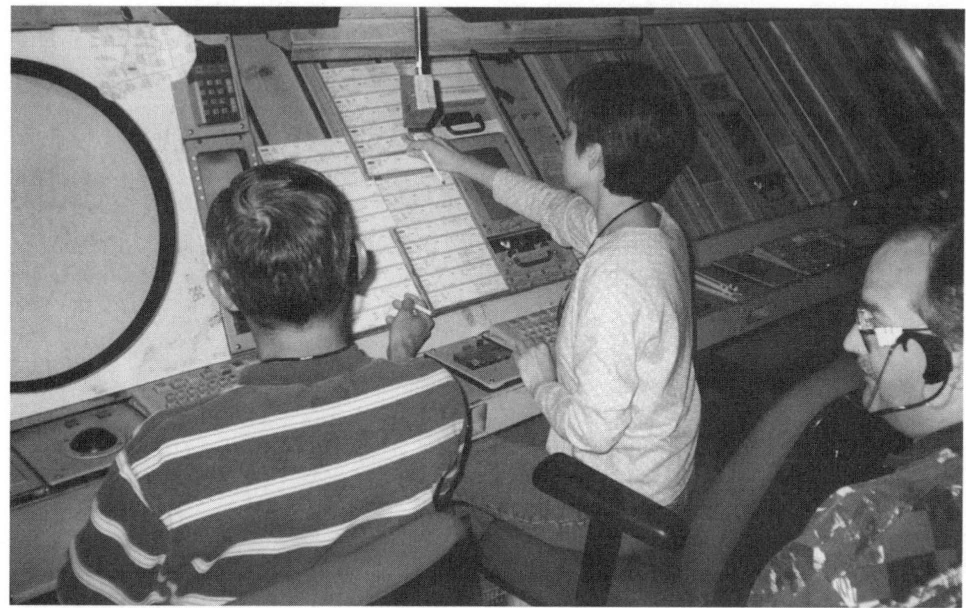

Fig. 11-6 *A typical controller's position in a Center, with the PVD and the flight strip racks.*

Fig. 11-7 *The IFR flight strips for yet-to-depart aircraft are on the left. Those en route are on the right.*

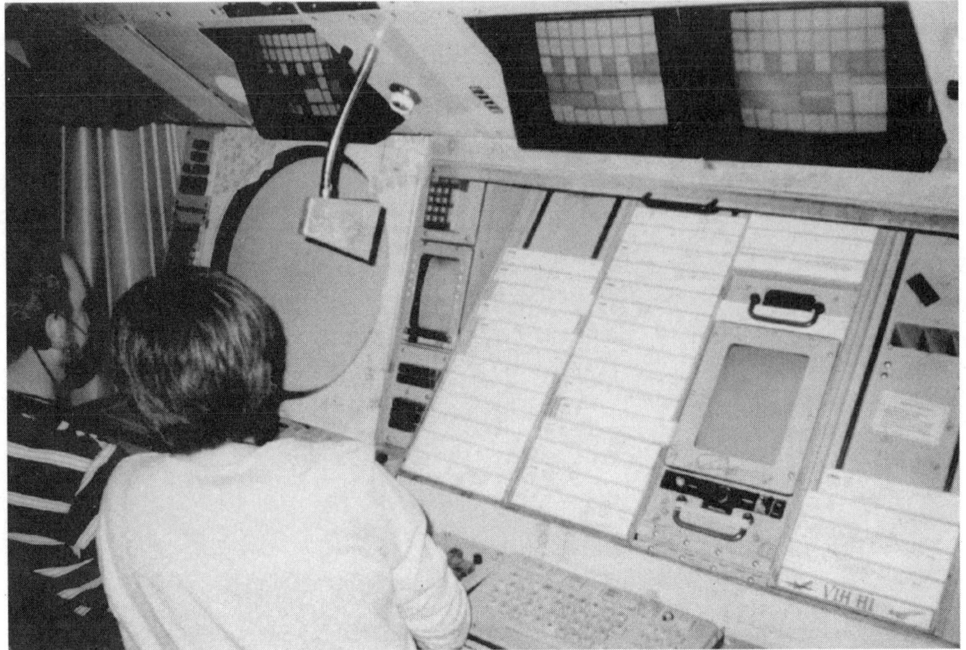

Fig. 11-8 *The controller has the racked strips immediately available as needed.*

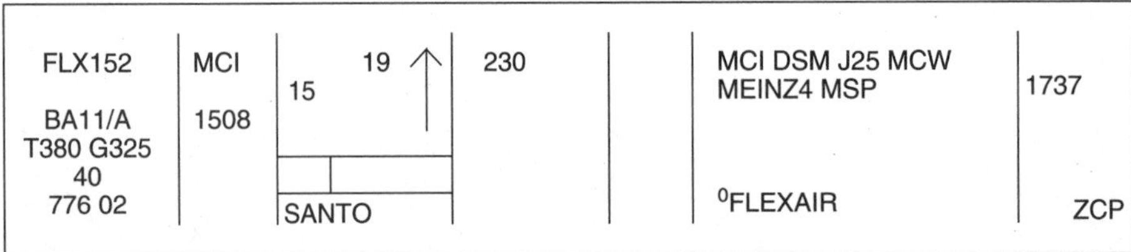

FLX152 BA11/A T380 G325 40 776 02	MCI 1508	15 19 ↑ SANTO	230		MCI DSM J25 MCW MEINZ4 MSP ⁰FLEXAIR	1737 ZCP

Fig. 11-9 *The only noncomputerized entry on this IFR strip is the penciled-in up arrow identifying the departing aircraft.*

computer, which produces only a digital alphanumeric readout of the pertinent aircraft data. As Fig. 11-10 illustrates, there are no ARTS III-type symbols and no weather depictions, other than lines or solid areas, with the superimposed H indicating areas of heavy precipitation.

The Stage A radar does, however, produce various computer-generated images. These are briefly illustrated and described in Fig. 11-10, under the four main headings of Target Symbols, Position Symbols, Data Block Information, and Other Symbols.

Relative to the data block information in Fig. 11-10, note the possible variables from number 10 through number 25 that could be displayed. Of those, only the data in numbers 10, 11, and 12 (the starred items) constitute a full data block. The other alphanumerics

Table 11-2 Figure 11-9 decoded.

FLX152	FlexAir Flight 152
BA11/A	Type of aircraft, BAC111, equipped with DME and Mode C transponder
T380	True airspeed of 380 knots
G325	Ground speed of 325 knots
40	Sector 40
776	Computer identification number
02	The second strip for this flight
MCI	Departed Kansas City International
1508	Departure time (UTC)
15 19	Time aircraft should be over the SANTO fix (1519 UTC)
230	Assigned altitude: flight level 230 (approximately 23,000 feet)
MCI DSM J25 MCW MEINZ4 MSP	Route of flight from MCI to Minneapolis
°FLEXAIR	The call sign when the flight has an unusual three-letter designation, such as FLX
1737	Transponder code
ZCP	Minneapolis Center, the facility receiving the handoff from Kansas City Center

(Note: ZMP is the normal code for Minneapolis Center, but ZCP is the computer coding.)

convey additional information about the target when or if any condition listed between numbers 13 and 25 exists or materializes. For example, the assigned transponder code might have been 2345, but the pilot entered 2435 (number 17 in Fig. 11-10 at about the four o'clock position). Or the aircraft was assigned an altitude of 14,000 feet but is 300 feet above that altitude at 14,300 (number 18, Fig. 11-10 at the seven o'clock position). Or the pilot has radio failure and is squawking the RDOF (radio failure) 7600 code (number 23 at the twelve o'clock position, Fig. 11-10).

Figure 11-11 illustrates what basic data blocks would look like for an IFR and a VFR aircraft being tracked on Center's radar system. The IFR operation, when decoded, is explained in Table 11-3.

The VFR data block is basically the same, except that VFR 55 identifies the aircraft as VFR and cruising at 5500 feet.

That, briefly, is the NAS Stage A system used in the various ARTCCs. Again, it differs from ARTS in that its symbols are computerized, while the ARTS images are generated by the combination of primary and secondary radar.

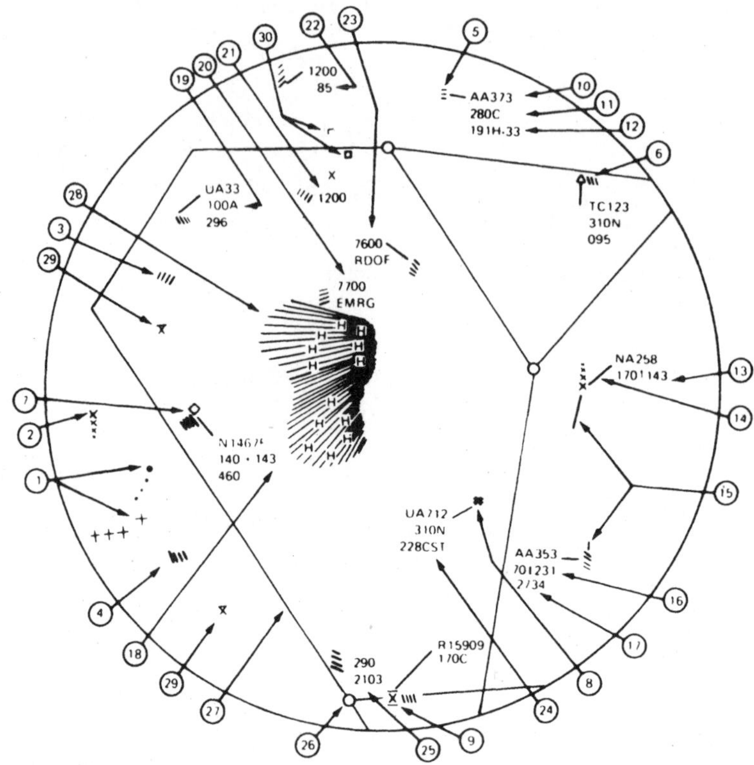

Target Symbols

1 Uncorrelated primary radar target + ●

2 *Correlated primary radar target X

3 Uncorrelated beacon target /

4 Correlated beacon target \

5 Identing beacon target ≡

(*Correlated means the association of radar data with the computer projected track of an identified aircraft)

Position Symbols

6 Free track (No flight plan tracking) △

7 Flat track (flight plan tracking) ◊

8 Coast (Beacon target lost) #

9 Present Position Hold ⧗

Data Block Information

10 *Aircraft Identification

11 *Assigned Altitude FL280, mode C altitude same or within ±200′ of asgnd altitude

12 *Computer ID #191, Handoff is to Sector 33 (0-33 would mean handoff accepted) (*Nr's 10, 11, 12 constitute a "full data block")

13 Assigned altitude 17,000′, aircraft is climbing, mode C readout was 14,300 when last beacon interrogation was received

14 Leader line connecting target symbol and data block

15 Track velocity and direction vector line (Projected ahead of target)

16 Assigned altitude 7000, aircraft is descending, last mode C readout (or last reported altitude was 100′ above FL230

17 Transponder code shows in full data block only when different than assigned code

18 Aircraft is 300′ above assigned altitude

19 Reported altitude (No mode C readout) same as assigned. An "N" would indicate no reported altitude)

20 Transponder set on emergency code 7700 (EMRG flashes to attract attention)

21 Transponder code 1200 (VFR) with no mode C

22 Code 1200 (VFR) with mode C and last altitude readout

23 Transponder set on Radio Failure code 7600, (RDOF flashes)

24 Computer ID #228, CST indicates target is in Coast status

25 Assigned altitude FL290, transponder code (These two items constitute a "limited data block")

Other symbols

26 Navigational Aid

27 Airway or jet route

28 Outline of weather returns based on primary radar. H's represent areas of high density precipitation which might be thunderstorms. Radial lines indicate lower density precipitation.

29 Obstruction

30 Airports Major: □ , Small: ⌜

Fig. 11-10 *These are the alphanumeric data blocks and symbols produced by the NAS Stage A computer system and are quite unlike the ARTS III symbols.*

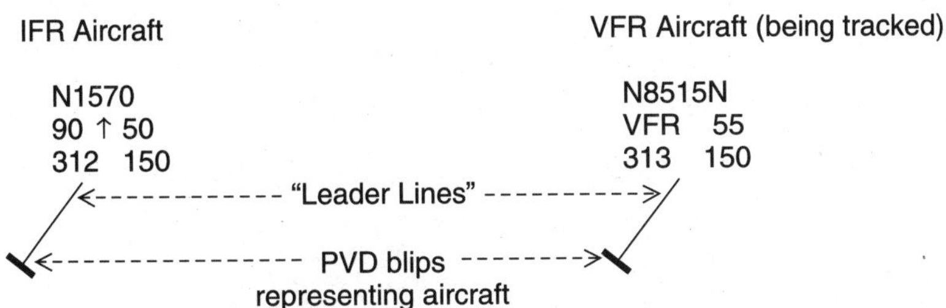

Fig. 11-11 *The design of IFR and VFR data blocks on a Center's scope with Stage A radar.*

Table 11-3 The table explains the meanings of the IFR data box in Fig. 11-11.

N1570	:	Aircraft ID
90	:	Desired altitude—9000 feet
↑	:	Climbing
50	:	Present Mode C altitude—5000 feet
312	:	Computer ID number, for computer storing or recall purposes
150	:	Ground speed in knots

The handoff process

Let's first take the case of a VFR handoff. You're coming to the limits of a controller's sector—say, Sector 40—and the next sector on your route is Sector 48. To begin the handoff, Sector 40 rolls the trackball (just as in Approach Control) to the blip by your data block and punches the console Handoff button, with Sector 48.

Your data block appears on 48's scope with an intermittent timesharing flashing of "H-48," meaning "Handoff to Sector 48." The flashing appears over the ground speed segment of the data block, showing first the ground speed and then the H-48. This continues until 48 accepts the handoff. To do this, the receiving controller rolls his or her trackball over to your blip and enters your call sign or computer identification into the computer. The computer accepts the handoff, the flashing stops on both scopes, and the 40 controller can now erase the data block from the screen. The A side then walks your flight strip to the Sector 48 scope and puts it on the slanted rack, and the handoff is complete.

At this point, or perhaps a moment or two before, Sector 40 will call you and tell you to change to one of Sector 48's frequencies, say, 125.3. The call sequences would then go like this:

Ctr: Cherokee One Five November, contact Kansas City Center on one two five point three.

You: Roger, one two five point three. Cherokee One Five November.

Make the frequency change and then reestablish contact:

You: Kansas City Center, Cherokee Eight Five One Five November is with you, level at seven thousand five hundred.
Ctr: Cherokee One Five November, Roger. Altimeter three zero one five.
You: Three zero one five. Cherokee One Five November.

That's all there is to it. From here on, keep the radio tuned to that frequency, listen for your call sign, and acknowledge all advisories.

There can be some variations in all this. For example, you're cruising along in the 3000- to 4000-foot range. As you move away from its remote outlet, that altitude could be too low for Center's radar to pick you up. You'd then be told that radar service was terminated but that you might try to establish contact again a few miles down the road.

Another variation: With a VFR flight strip in the computer, the handoff from Center to Center is now computer-generated, much as an IFR strip. If Center A is handing a VFR off to Center B and B is too busy to provide advisories, the sector controller in B will call A on interphone and reject the handoff. The sector controller in A will then advise the pilot that "Radar service is terminated. Squawk 1200 (or VFR)."

An IFR handoff is somewhat similar, inasmuch as it, too, is computerized. Using Sectors 40 and 48 again, this is what happens: As the aircraft nears the limits of 40's sector, the 40 controller puts the trackball on the aircraft's blip, hits "48" and the Enter button. The blip and data block now appear on 48's scope, along with an intermittently flashing "H-48" (H again means handoff). Sector 48 slews up to the blip and keys the Enter button, indicating that the handoff is accepted. The flashing on both scopes stops, and the 40 controller sees an "O-48" (O means OK or accepted). Then when the aircraft crosses the limits of 40's sector, that controller advises the pilot to "Contact Kansas Center on (such and such) frequency." Once the aircraft is well clear of his boundary, the controller erases the blip and data block from the scope, and the handoff is complete.

Unlike in a VFR operation, no IFR aircraft can enter one controller's sector or area until that controller has bought the handoff. Nor can an IFR aircraft reenter a sector or area that it has left without the first controller's approval. The separation of IFR flights is too critical to allow unapproved deviations. But, as I implied, this restriction doesn't apply to VFR aircraft—whether on a filed flight plan or not.

ADVANTAGES OF USING CENTER FOR THE VFR PILOT

Yes, the ARTCCs do exist to monitor and separate IFR traffic. At the same time, though, knowing what their services are, plus being able to take advantage of them, can be of tremendous benefit to the VFR pilot. Let's consider just a few of the things Center can do.

Routine advisories

It should be comforting to realize that someone down there is aware of your existence, has you on radar, and is monitoring your progress in a specific parcel of airspace. It's also comforting, but should never be relaxing, to know that you're *likely* to be advised of some of the traffic that could impinge on your line of flight, or that questionable weather might lie ahead. And it's nice to know, if you are venturing into an active MOA, that you could be informed of the F-14s involved in aerobatic maneuvers, or a formation of B-52s is barreling along the military training route you happen to be paralleling.

Those are only samples of what a Center can do to enhance safety. That should not, however, nurture complacency. Lots of VFR aircraft are out there, with and without transponders, with and without Mode C, in contact or not in contact with Center. These targets might appear as only small blips on the radarscope, their altitudes unknown to all but their drivers. Whether you are VFR or IFR in clear skies, safety begins in the cockpit. Regardless of help from the ground, it's up to us to see and avoid.

Weather problems

A situation one controller cited is a good example of how a Center can be of considerable help when weather causes in-flight problems. It seems that a VFR pilot got a weather briefing early one morning for a flight from City A to City C. Conditions were reported favorable, so the pilot departed but did not file a flight plan. En route to City C, the pilot stopped at City B for about 3 hours and then headed out again.

Midway between B and C, snow showers, poor visibility, and the potential of icing were encountered. Becoming more than concerned, the pilot contacted a nearby FSS and explained the predicament. The FSS, in turn, called Center to see if it could help get the aircraft to safety. By this time, the pilot was flying at approximately 3100 feet, which was below Center's radar coverage. With instructions to the pilot, Center was able to determine the aircraft's position by establishing a fix off two VORs.

Meanwhile, the weather at City C had deteriorated, making continued flight in that direction even more hazardous. Getting the pilot to an alternative airport (we'll call that City D) near the aircraft's present location was the only option. The pilot could have retraced the flight back to clearer weather, but the potential of icing made it critical to get on the ground as soon as possible.

Another problem arose, however: The pilot was in the immediate vicinity of a restricted area, where the military was shooting off cannons. Now there were two threats. Center called the military, however, and had them shut down the range, and then successfully guided the pilot to the lighted runway threshold of City D's no-tower airport.

Center filed an *aircraft assist* report on the incident, and, in checking back, found that the only weather briefing the pilot had had was at the point of origin, some 7 or 8 hours earlier. None had been recorded at City B, where the aircraft was on the ground for 3 hours or more.

There are two obvious lessons here: First, get current weather briefings. Conditions can, and do, change rapidly, and forecasts do not always become reality. Second, if you get in trouble, don't wait until things become critical before contacting a Center. A crisis might well be avoided if Center is brought into the picture early enough.

As a Center area manager put it, "Give us a chance to help you before you really need help. Even if things look great right now, a short call is all that's necessary: 'Kansas City Center, Mooney One Two Three Four Alpha, over Emporia at six thousand five hundred to Dallas. What's the weather a hundred miles ahead?' We might be able to tell you that there are severe storms south of Wichita, or whatever. Don't be afraid to call us, but do it before an emergency develops."

What the manager said doesn't mean you should rely on Center as your primary source for weather information. The FSS is the first and best source, but Center can and will help, when help is needed.

Emergencies—mechanical and otherwise

As some cases back in Chap. 3 illustrated, here's another reason to use Center, or at least monitor its frequencies. As dramatized by an experienced controller:

> Ginny up front suddenly breaks loose and spurts oil all over the windshield. You're frantically trying to read charts to find the nearest airport, keep the airplane level, see where you're going, and scour the terrain below for a place to put down the dying bird. And, if you still have time, squawk 7700.
>
> If you were in contact with me, I'd know exactly where you were, and I would know the closest airport to your position. I know my sector. That's my job. I could lead you to the airport and perhaps save your hide. At the very worst, had you been talking to me and couldn't reach the airport, I'd know where you had gone down and could start the rescue operations immediately.

The benefits of at least tuning to a Center frequency are apparent. Even if you haven't been getting advisories, you can get on the air in a hurry with the Mayday call when the situation gets tight. That universal distress code gets immediate attention.

The same controller told about a student who was on his first solo cross-country, hopelessly lost, with fuel dwindling. The student knew a certain VOR had been crossed 30 or 40 minutes previously, but disorientation, coupled with growing panic, had set in.

The student had the presence of mind to call Center. The controller, who was also a pilot, in a reassuring tone vectored the student toward the nearest airport, flying along a four-lane highway that led to the town where the airport was located. As the controller said, "It was a narrow runway, but it was 20 miles long." The student landed with less than 15 minutes of fuel in the tank.

Before signing off, the controller told the student to call him on the phone as soon as possible. (You can picture the student's emotions when that edict was issued.) When the call came through, though, the controller told the student that he had done exactly the right thing: He had remained calm and asked Center for help in an emergency. The controller's only request was that the student tell the instructor what had happened.

The controller concluded the story by saying that handling the student took about 20 minutes, basically tying up the frequency during that time. Meanwhile, the controller had a bunch of air carrier operations to watch, contacting the airliners only when necessary. The air carrier pilots, however, were listening to the dialogue. As the controller put it, 25 pilots would have been howling if almost all attention had not been devoted to one lost neophyte in a Cessna 152.

Perhaps these incidents at least partly illustrate the potential value of Center to those of us who fly VFR. Perhaps they also hint at the sensitivity so common to the vast majority of those wearing the headsets in the Center complex. They want to help; they're there to help; and they will help, be it a routine flight or an emergency. The routine help is on a workload-permitting basis; the emergency help receives instant attention.

Position reporting and Center

You've filed a VFR flight plan and are using Center for en route advisories. At some point, Center becomes too busy to handle you, you lose contact, or you voluntarily terminate contact yourself. Whatever the case, you subsequently have an emergency and go down. Ninety minutes after your flight plan has expired, the FSS alert notice (ALNOT) goes out, and Center receives a copy of it. In this situation, how much help will Center be?

Frankly, it's questionable. For one, as mentioned in Chap. 10, Center keeps no written record of radio contacts with VFR aircraft. It has only the flight strip for those aircraft that had requested advisories. When it receives the ALNOT, one of Center's first actions is to go through the VFR flight strips to see if yours shows up, as it would in the case at hand. Another action is to ask the controller who last handled you if he or she remembers you and any communications that would shed light on your possible whereabouts or what might have happened. Finally, if necessary, a specialist in the quality assurance office will review the tape recording of all radio communications during the period you were in contact with Center to determine the time of your last transmission. This might take a lot of time, though, and meanwhile, you could be down and injured for hours before anyone finds you. Hopefully, your emergency locator transmitter (ELT) is working.

Relying solely on Center for position reports is better than contacting no one inflight, but it's not the best way to keep ATC advised of your whereabouts. Some pilots have even tried to make these reports when they haven't been in contact with Center at all—which is an almost totally futile gesture because the only record of the call would be just a brief moment on the tape, not even a flight strip.

No, for position reporting purposes, the facility is Flight Service, not Center. At the FSS, every position or flight progress report not only is tape recorded but also is written down. With the data almost immediately available, any FSS is far better equipped to initiate a rapid search-and-rescue mission—and over a smaller geographic area.

RECOMMENDATIONS FOR VFR PILOTS

I asked several Center controllers and managers what VFR pilots do, or don't do, that bugs them or causes them problems. The following are a few of their comments and recommendations.

Radio skills

We've discussed this enough, but knowledgeable use of the radio kept cropping up. The basic points, almost direct quotes, were as follows:

- Monitor the frequency and listen before you start talking. Don't pick up the mike and jump in until you're sure that the frequency is clear. Otherwise, only squeals and squawks will drift through the headset. Two people can't talk on the same frequency at the same time.
- Depending on the nature of the call, know what you should say, plan how you're going to say it, say it, and get off the air. Disconnected messages, rambling, and inconsequential trivia drive us nuts. (This, as you've probably gathered, was one of the most frequently voiced criticisms of VFR pilots, but even the IFRs were not immune.)
- Don't leave a frequency without telling us. You want to call an FSS for some purpose? Fine, but first advise us that "Cherokee One Five November is leaving you temporarily to go to Flight Service." (This assumes, of course, that you've been getting advisories from a Center.) When the call to the FSS is completed, reestablish contact with, "Center, Cherokee One Five November is back with you."
- In the same vein, a lot of pilots who receive advisories get near their destination and start dial-twisting to reach the tower or a unicom frequency, but they never tell us what they're doing. Meanwhile, we can't raise them and don't know whether they've gone down, have radio trouble, or what. If you're leaving our frequency for any reason, please tell us first, and then tell us when you're back with us.
- Call us before you get into trouble. We can probably help you. Otherwise, it might be too late.
- Don't be afraid to ask us for advisories (which means the same as *flight following*). We're here to help, if our workload will let us.

Stay VFR

One situation was cited: A VFR pilot who had been getting advisories called the controller at a certain point, saying, "Center, I won't need advisories any more. I'm out of the clouds now."

"Gulp," said the controller.

Remember that Center's radar won't pick up cloud layers or formations unless there is thunderstorm activity in them. In this instance, the controller couldn't know that the VFR character was, or had been, in the soup. VFR means *always* adhering to the visibility and cloud separation regulations, even when receiving advisories.

Report altitude changes

With or without Mode C, if you're getting advisories, Center has you pegged at your reported altitude. Being VFR, you have the freedom to climb or descend at your discretion, but don't do either until you have notified the controller. "Center, Cherokee One Five November is leaving six thousand five hundred for eight thousand five hundred due to turbulence." When you reach the new altitude, although it's not mandatory, it's a good practice to confirm the fact with another short call: "Center, Cherokee One Five November level at eight thousand five hundred."

The reason for the first call, particularly, is that Center has you at a certain altitude and is giving you and other aircraft advisories based on that altitude. If you move up or down at will (which is still your right), you could be venturing into the flight paths of other traffic. With Mode C, your variations will be spotted, but even then, the controller might have a question. Are you really changing altitudes, or is the Mode C malfunctioning? Things do go haywire, which is one reason controllers ask pilots to verify that they actually are at such and such an altitude. As one said, "I've seen Mode C report a Cessna 182 at 19,000 feet ... a little unlikely for a 182."

En route flight plan filing

Don't use Center for filing VFR or IFR flight plans. It's not designed to provide such a service, although I have heard it offered when an IFR-rated pilot has encountered, or was about to encounter, non-VFR weather conditions. It was a voluntary offer on the part of the controller, however, to help the pilot out of a potential predicament. Flight Service is the place to file, and even then, filing while in the air should be a last resort. It takes up a lot of the specialist's time.

Visits to a Center

The FAA and controllers alike highly recommend visits to a Center. Go as a group, or on your own, or attend one of the FAA's Operation Raincheck sessions. Whatever the case, just be sure to make arrangements in advance.

Nothing can replace a personal tour to get the real feel of what goes on. Even one trip through the facility will answer a lot of questions and alleviate some of the concerns bugging too many pilots about requesting the services a Center offers.

IN LIEU OF A VISIT

While a personal visit might not be feasible for pilots who live hundreds of miles from the nearest Center, there are just as many pilots who are within an hour's drive of one but have never set foot on the property. Recognizing both realities, and the fact that a goodly number of pilots consider Center a somewhat mysterious institution, I've tried here to outline the organization of a typical facility, to explain how it functions, and to provide a few glimpses of what goes on behind the scenes. I hope, if you were previously uncertain, that you'll now have a little more confidence in your ability to use and profit from the services of a Center. There's an old adage: "What we're not up on, we're down on." What we don't understand, we avoid. But, the adage works in reverse: "What we're up on, we're not down on."

There's nothing mysterious about a Center, and the folks there aren't ogres. Many are pilots who know very well what goes on in the skies above them. Pilots or not, they're more than willing to help guide you, maybe even save you. But it's you who must make the first contact. No one in that darkened room can.

12
When an emergency occurs

UNDERSTANDING THE ROLES THAT GROUND FACILITIES PLAY DURING an emergency is important, but it's equally critical to be well versed in our own pilot responsibilities when things are tight and help is needed. Radio failure is a good place to start, followed by an examination of other in-flight emergencies.

RADIO FAILURE

A potential radio failure is pretty hard to predict, although a thorough preflight check could give some clues. A loose or broken antenna is an obvious signal; as is a popped circuit breaker; or a loose, worn, or frayed alternator belt, if you can see or test the belt. Another clue is a radio that tends to slip in and out of its rack. And still another is garbled reception on the ground or controller comments that your transmission is weak or scratchy.

If any of these symptoms exist on the ground, either the radio's sick right now or it could die on you at an inappropriate time. The only solution: Get it fixed or the potential cause corrected before you venture forth.

A failure is suspected

Let's assume, though, that everything checks out on the ground, so off you go. After a while, you become conscious of the fact that there hasn't been much chatter over the air for several minutes, which causes you to wonder if…. These are some things you can do when a problem is suspected:

- Adjust the squelch or turn up the volume. If you hear the typical static, the set's probably OK; there's just been a period of unusual radio silence.
- Push the radio in a little. Vibration or turbulence might have caused it to slip slightly from its rack.
- Wiggle and push all microphone and headset plugs to verify that they are firmly in place. (A spare microphone is inexpensive insurance.)
- Check the circuit breakers. If one has popped, let it cool for a couple of minutes and then reset it. You might get your radio back, but a popped breaker is symptomatic of a problem, so have a mechanic investigate the cause when you're back on the ground. If the breaker pops out again, leave it alone; never try to force a breaker to remain reset.
- Check the ammeter. If it shows no charge, test it by turning on the landing light. If the needle doesn't move, you can be sure the alternator has died or its belt has broken, in which case the only electric power will come from the battery. The engine won't quit, because the ignition system is independent of the alternator-battery system; but without an alternator, the life of the battery is only about 2 hours. After that, you'll have no electric power at all. Consequently, turn off all nonessential electrical equipment, except one radio, and head for home or the nearest airport. Enough battery power might be left to make whatever radio contacts are necessary before you land.

The failure is real

It's no longer a matter of suspicion: The radio is dead or rapidly dying. Now, what are your options? Five of the most likely answers depend largely on the situation.

1. You're flying locally or on a short cross-country trip away from Class B, C, or D airspaces and intend to terminate the flight back at your own uncontrolled airport. Once you realize the radio is gone, the best thing to do is head for home or some other uncontrolled field where you can get the radio repaired. There is no need to squawk the 7600 RF (radio failure) code in this environment, but do use extra caution when landing. You're coming in unannounced with presumably no knowledge of who or where anyone else is in the pattern.

2. You're going into a Class B or Class C primary airport. To make it simple, let's say that you had enough battery juice left to monitor the ATIS and to be cleared into the Class B or to establish contact with the Class C Approach Control. Once you are inside the Class B or C, though, the radio dies completely, and you've lost all transmitting and receiving contact with Approach.

At this point, squawk the 7600 code and continue through B or C airspace to the airport. Approach knows your intentions and, seeing the RF code on the radarscope, will protect you as well as advise the tower of your predicament.

When you're within the tower's 5-mile area of control, watch the tower for light signals, as summarized in Fig. 12-1, that will clear you to land or tell you to keep circling. Once on the ground, pull off on a taxiway, and continue to watch the tower for the green light that authorizes you to taxi to the ramp.

This same scenario applies if you're transiting a Class B or Class C airspace or if you're already in one of the airspaces but intend to land at a satellite airport. The main point is to keep right on going in accordance with your announced intentions. Don't wander around in those high-density areas. If you deviate from what you've told the controller, the controller won't know what to expect, which could cause confusion in his or her efforts to maintain an orderly flow of traffic.

3. You want to land at a Class D airport that has no Approach Control and is miles from a Class B or C. Some distance out, the radio dies, so you squawk the RF transponder code. The nearest Center or Approach, seeing the code on its radar, will track your flight route and if it appears that you're headed for the controlled airport, will notify the tower of your probable landing intentions.

As you near the field, keep a sharp eye out for the light gun signal, especially a red signal that tells you, in essence, not to land. If you see no signal, cross over the field about 500 feet above traffic pattern altitude, note the flow of traffic, fly upwind over the active runway, and watch for the green "cleared to land" signal. Keep an eye on the tower, though, even after the clearance signal. For a variety of possible reasons, you might get a red light on the final approach. Do a go-around then for another approach, as long as you get the green light again.

	Meaning		
Color and Type of Signal	**Movement of Vehicles Equipment and Personnel**	**Aircraft on the Ground**	**Aircraft in Flight**
Steady green	Cleared to cross, proceed or go	Cleared for takeoff	Cleared to land
Flashing green	Not applicable	Cleared for taxi	Return for landing (to be followed by steady green at the proper time)
Steady red	STOP	STOP	Give way to other aircraft and continue circling
Flashing red	Clear the taxiway/runway	Taxi clear of the runway in use	Airport unsafe, do not land
Flashing white	Return to starting point on airport	Return to starting point on airport	Not applicable
Alternating red and green	Exercise extreme caution	Exercise extreme caution	Exercise extreme caution

Fig. 12-1 *The various colors and meanings of the tower light gun signals.*

4. As opposed to the second situation cited above, this time you have not been using Center or been in contact with Approach, but you want to land at the primary airport in a B or C airspace, and the radio has failed. Your alternative? Only one: Land outside the area and request entry approval from Approach by telephone. You probably won't get it, though, unless the traffic is very light and you're close to the B or C airspace. Even then, the odds are against approval of any aircraft without an operating two-way radio.

5. You're on the ground at an uncontrolled field. The radio is dead, but you want to fly to a nearby Class D airport to have it repaired. Your only option is to telephone the airport tower, explain the situation, and ask for approval to enter the area.

Depending on the probable traffic at your estimated arrival time, approval might or might not be forthcoming. You're on the ground and there is no emergency, so airport conditions will largely determine what the Class D tower says. In most cases, though, tower supervisors want to help and, traffic permitting, will attempt to accommodate your request.

Know what to do—and have alternatives

A VFR radio failure, when viewed objectively, is really more of a nuisance than a true emergency and should not be the cause of cockpit panic. The best advice, unless you're actually in a Class B, C, or D airspace when the failure occurs, is to land at the most convenient uncontrolled airport.

On the other hand, if the set dies while you're in one of those controlled airspaces, stay with your already announced intentions and proceed directly to the field. With the RF code on the radar screen, the controller will protect you from other aircraft until you're in the tower's traffic area. From that point on, the tower controller will clear you for landing with the help of the light gun.

Quite apparently, you and I have to know what those on the ground expect of us when we're faced with a radio failure. Otherwise, we could be guilty of causing a lot of confusion and perhaps creating hazardous conditions for others and ourselves. The only answer is to be prepared for the problem and have a clear set of alternative actions in mind if the problem should ever become a reality.

IN-FLIGHT EMERGENCIES

The FAA makes it very clear that when an emergency develops in flight, only one person has the final responsibility for the operation of the aircraft. That person is the pilot. The FAA further makes it clear that rules and regulations are pretty much tossed aside when action is required to meet the emergency. In the process, however, the FAA stresses that the pilot should request immediate help through radio contact with a tower, a Center, or a Flight Service Station.

Emergency classifications

Emergencies are classified as *distress* or *urgency.* A distress condition is one of fire, engine failure, or structural failure. In other words, the situation is dire, immediate, and life-threatening. An urgency is not necessarily immediately perilous but could be potentially catastrophic, such as being lost, a low fuel supply, a seriously malfunctioning engine, pilot illness, weather, or any other condition that could affect flight safety. When any of these conditions arise, the pilot should ask for help now. Don't wait until the urgency becomes a distress.

While *AIM* outlines the appropriate emergency procedures in some detail, the following summarizes the essential elements for the VFR land pilot.

Transponder operation

This I've touched on before, but when either an urgency or a distress situation develops, immediately enter the 7700 emergency squawk in the transponder. That code then appears on the screens of all radar-equipped facilities within radar range and, by sound as well as the flashing blip, attracts the controllers' attention. As controllers put it, "Lights light and bells ring." Ground help is, of course, hard to offer if you haven't been in contact with a Center or any other facility, but at least they know that there's an aircraft in trouble out there and know its location.

Radio communications

If you have been in routine contact with a ground facility, such as a Center, and a distress situation suddenly arises, the first thing to do is to dial the 7700 transponder emergency code and communicate as quickly as possible with the Center controller. Once you are in contact with him or her, and assuming you have initially volunteered little information, the controller is likely to ask as many questions about you as the situation permits, such as the number of people aboard, color of your aircraft, and the like.

How much actual help the controller can offer at this juncture depends on how long you can remain airborne. Given time, he or she might be able to guide you to another airport, if one is near your present position, or alert you to ground obstructions that could pose a problem, or perhaps lead you to a major highway that could serve as a landing strip. At the worst, in distress situations, the controller may be limited to just making sure that rescue forces and equipment have been alerted and kept advised of where you finally put down.

Let's say, though, that you haven't been in contact with any ground facility and the emergency—distress or urgency—develops rapidly. What do you do in this case? For one, you probably wouldn't have time to search for the frequency of a tower, a Center, or whatever; so you quickly dial the 7700 emergency transponder code, tune to 121.5, the universal emergency-only frequency that is guarded by direction-finding stations, civil aircraft, Centers, military towers, Approach Control facilities, and FSSs, and make your call. If the emergency is of the distress nature, start the call with "Mayday," repeated three times. This is the universal term asking for assistance and, to refresh your memory, comes from the French word "*M'aidez,*" pronounced "Mayday," meaning "Help me." Distress messages have priority over all others, and the word *Mayday* commands silence on the frequency in use.

If the situation is of an urgent nature, begin the call with "Pan-pan," also repeated three times. Urgency messages have priority over all others except distress and warn others not to interfere with the various transmissions.

Then, recognizing the problem of time, particularly in distress situations, the FAA suggests that you communicate in your initial message as much of the following as possible, preferably in this sequence:

1. "Mayday, Mayday, Mayday" or "Pan-pan, Pan-pan, Pan-pan"
2. Name of facility addressed
3. Aircraft identification and type
4. The nature of the distress or urgency
5. Weather
6. Pilot's intentions and request
7. Present position and heading, or if lost, last known position, time, and heading since that position
8. Altitude or flight level
9. Hours and minutes of fuel remaining
10. Any other useful information, such as visible landmarks, aircraft color, emergency equipment on board, number of people on board
11. Activate the emergency locator transmitter (ELT) if possible

Pilot responsibilities after radio contact

Once in contact with a ground facility, you have certain responsibilities:

- Maintain control of the aircraft.
- Comply with advice and instructions, if at all possible.
- Cooperate.
- Ask questions or clarify instructions not understood or with which you cannot comply.
- Assist the ground facility in controlling communications on the frequency. Silence interfering stations.
- Don't change frequencies or change to another ground facility unless absolutely necessary.
- If you do change frequencies, always advise the ground facility of the new frequency and station before making the change.
- If two-way communication with the new frequency can't be established, return immediately to the frequency where communication last existed.
- Remember the four Cs:
  Confess the predicament to any ground station.
  Communicate as much of the distress or urgency message as possible.
  Comply with instructions and advice.
  Climb, if possible, for better radar detection and radio contact.

THE EMERGENCY LOCATOR TRANSMITTER

Emergency locator transmitters, designed to assist in locating downed aircraft, are required by FAR 91 for most general aviation aircraft, although certain exceptions are allowed. An ELT is a battery-operated transmitter that when subjected to crash-generated forces, transmits a distinctive and continuous audio signal on 121.5 and 243.0. The life of a transmitter is supposed to be 48 hours over a wide range of temperatures.

Depending on its location in the aircraft, some ELTs can be activated by the pilot while airborne. In other installations, the ELT is secured elsewhere in the fuselage and cannot be accessed in flight. These are activated only upon impact or by the pilot when on the ground and out of the airplane.

Because of their importance in search-and-rescue (SAR) operations, ELT batteries are legal for 50 percent of their manufacturer-established shelf life, after which they must be replaced. Periodic ground checks of an ELT should be made, but only in accordance with the procedures outlined in *AIM*.

ANTICIPATION AND ALTERNATIVES

In any discussion of emergencies, one pilot responsibility hopefully stands out: the responsibility to be prepared mentally and physically for the unexpected, the nonroutine. If you fly long enough, sooner or later you're going to encounter an emergency situation of some nature. Perhaps it will be very minor and easily correctable; perhaps it will require every bit of knowledge and expertise you have amassed. Whatever the case, the odds of something going sour sometime are close to 100 percent.

If that's a reasonable bet, preparation (and all that preparation implies) is absolutely essential. Beginning with every pilot's very first flight, he or she should be asking two questions: What could go wrong? Then, if what could go wrong did go wrong, what would I do? This is only the logical process of potential problem analysis (PPA).

A fire in flight; the engine bucks and coughs for no apparent reason; the engine quits entirely; a bird strike smashes the windscreen; a passenger has an apparent heart attack; you're lost; the fuel gauges are showing close to empty; electric power is interrupted: What would you do? It's a matter of anticipating these as well as other potential problems and then having alternative plans of action firmly in mind in case a potential problem ever became a reality. (As always, though, and above all else, fly the aircraft first, then follow through with your planned and alternative actions.)

While transponder and radio procedures are perhaps only small elements in handling a distress or urgency situation, they could be major factors in helping you get that airplane down safely and in one piece. Our entire ATC system is designed to maximize safety, and the folks on the ground have had drilled into them what to do when a pilot calls Mayday or Pan-pan or squawks the emergency or RF code. But controllers can only help pilots to the extent that pilots can help controllers. That's where personal preparation and the skill with which pilots handle the emergency come into play.

When was the last time you asked, "What could go wrong?"

13
ATC specialists

You have to be able to think abstractly, especially at the Center.
You have to do first things first, establish priorities.
You have to have automatic recall.
You have to look at errors objectively and reconstruct situations.
You have to accept the responsibilities of the job.

FAA'S AIR TRAFFIC CONTROL SPECIALISt (ATCS) BROCHURE, WHICH IS DESIGNED TO acquaint potential applicants with what the job of an ATCS is all about, opens with this summary of what is required of an air traffic control specialist. The summary doesn't exaggerate, but the brochure could easily have added other traits or characteristics, such as the ability to learn rapidly, self-control under tension, communication skills, patience, flexibility, dependability, and planning skills, to mention a few.

I have listened to, observed, and talked with many ATCSs, and all the above are realistic portrayals of what it takes to be a successful controller. The job demands quality in both its hardware and its human resources.

No one questions the need for the most sophisticated equipment available, but regardless of the technical advances, it's the human resource that brings to life whatever benefits the hardware offers. Perhaps someday automation will be so perfected that pilots will no longer need people, other than technicians, in the Centers, towers, and Flight Service Stations. Perhaps someday the only resources in the system will be the three Ms—machines, materials, and money—with the fourth M, manpower, becoming obsolete. That's 21st-century dreaming, though. Today, and in the foreseeable future, people will be the primary link between aircraft and the various groundbound facilities.

So what about these people who play such a critical role in maintaining the finest air traffic control system in the world? What weds them to the job? How do they handle the stress the job is purported to produce? What screening and training do they undergo to prepare them for the tasks at hand? What sort of people are they? Recognizing the dangers of generalities and, indeed, of exaggeration, let's try to find some answers.

WHAT SORT OF PEOPLE ARE THEY?

To start with the last question first, the traits and characteristics listed earlier give a pretty good idea of the sort of person we're talking about. The picture, however, is not complete.

Through the work of psychologists and behavioral scientists, quite a bit is known about what motivates people and some of their needs. As one example, Dr. David McClellan of Harvard developed a concept called the *need for achievement.* Among the several traits of a person with a high need for achievement, at least two seem particularly characteristic of the air traffic control specialist (ATCS): the need to solve problems, make decisions, and act on their own; and the need for concrete feedback on how they are doing.

Whether consciously aware of these "needs" or not, it's unlikely that a prospective ATCS would have even applied for the job if the need for achievement were not part of the personal makeup. Certainly, were it lacking, it is very unlikely that the student could have completed even the initial phases of the training program. If ever a job demanded the ability to solve problems now, to make decisions now, and to act independently of others, this is it. Similarly, it's a job that provides almost immediate, concrete feedback on how well the individual is performing. Working as an ATCS is not for those who want to be told what to do and are satisfied with a vague, once-a-year "You're doing OK" performance appraisal. No, the possession of a high need for achievement seems most compatible with the psyche of the typical specialist or controller.

Taken to the extreme, of course, no matter who the person or in what profession, the need can be destructive—destructive in the sense that the individual wants to do everything by himself; jumps to solutions; makes hasty, not-thought-through decisions; and resists outside counsel or advice. Or wanting feedback, someone else constantly brings to the attention of others, particularly supervisors, the things he or she has done well, the problems solved—and, in the process, drives everybody nuts. This type of person is, in effect, the perfect example of an insecure attention seeker.

Conversely, and in proper balance with the other traits listed, the need is not just a desirable characteristic; it is almost essential for anyone now in or seeking a career in air traffic control. The industry is fortunate that it has such people watching the scopes and operating the radios.

THEIR TRAINING

Much could be said about the training these folks go through, but three words seem to sum it up: lengthy, tough, and thorough. Not only is it long, taking $2^1/_2$ to 3 years to reach the full-performance level (FPL), but the pressure to succeed is almost constant. And the training is thorough, which accounts for its length.

Before even being accepted as a trainee, though, the job applicant must meet the education and/or experience requirements; pass a written aptitude test (not requiring aviation knowledge); be interviewed to evaluate personal characteristics, such as motivation, practical intelligence, and ability to speak clearly and distinctly; undergo a security investigation; and pass a medical examination. Then comes a wait of perhaps up to 6 months before an FAA regional personnel office advises the applicant about acceptance for training.

The actual training begins at the FAA's academy in Oklahoma City. There, for 11 to 16 weeks, the would-be specialist goes through a strenuous regimen of further testing, classroom work, and laboratory (meaning simulated exercises and problems) training. If the academy program is successfully completed, the trainee is classified as a *developmental* and is assigned to a tower or a Center. The assignment and its location are determined by personal preference, academy grades, previous (if any) aviation experience, and where staffing needs exist.

At the developmental's new facility, the training continues. Although the on-site curriculum is of course different for Center, tower, and Approach Control, it is consistent in that it involves further classroom and laboratory training (Fig. 13-1), plus extensive on-the-job experience under close supervision. Additionally, tower cab personnel who either bid or are assigned to Approach Control return to the academy for further radar training at the *radar training facility* (RTF). Similarly, a FSS developmental, interested in becoming a flight watch specialist, goes back to the academy for 3 weeks of concentrated meteorological training.

Thus, with some variations, it takes about $2^1/_2$ to 3 years from the time the trainee starts at the academy until becoming certificated as a full-performance-level controller or specialist. Only when attaining that level is the person considered capable of performing under routine general supervision. In the interim, the controller has been tested, graded, watched, monitored, and critiqued throughout each phase of the training. It is indeed a tough, thorough, and stressful process.

As mentioned in the preceding chapter, one commonality at all radar facilities, besides the initial academy training, is that no developmental trainee controls any traffic or communicates with any pilot, on the ground or in the air, at any stage of training without an instructor, supervisor, or otherwise qualified FPL plugged in, listening to every word and observing every action. The nature of the job simply won't tolerate anything less than certificated professionalism at the scope or on the mike.

Under that policy, the developmental is, in effect, riding on the FPL's ticket. If the developmental makes a mistake, the FPL is responsible—a fact that puts even greater pressure on the developmental, what with that FPL perpetually looking over one shoulder and monitoring every word or action. But, by the time the developmental has been

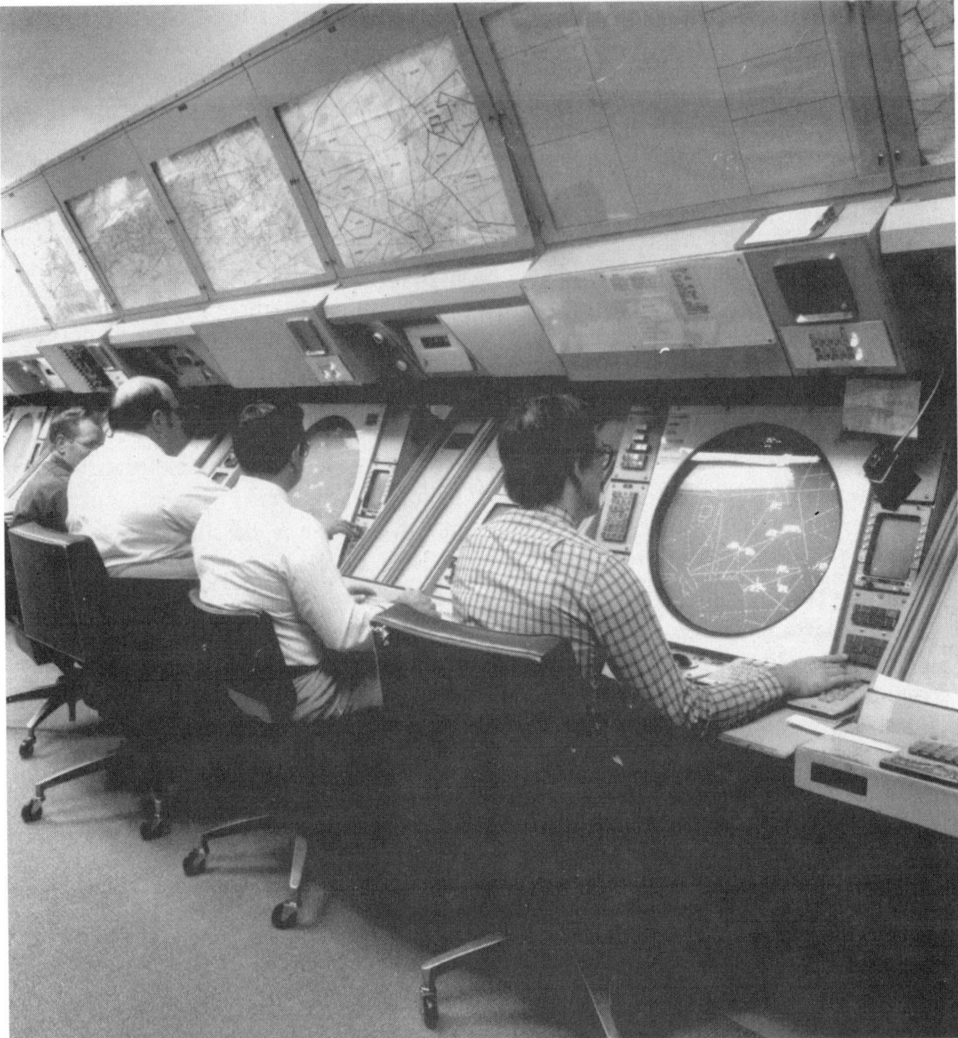

Fig. 13-1 *The Center's laboratory, or simulator training facility, is a replica of the real thing.*

through the wringer and is certificated as an FPL, the level of professionalism required is as ensured as human effort can make it.

HOW DO THEY FEEL ABOUT THEIR JOB?

When a number of ATCSs were asked how they felt about being a controller or a specialist, the responses were refreshingly constant. One said, without hesitation, "I love it, I'd do it for nothing." This from a veteran FPL. In explaining his feelings, he said, in part, that it was the sense of exhilaration, of satisfaction, of knowing that he had done a good job or a not-so-good job when the day was done.

Another equated it with playing a video game and getting paid to play the game. Others voiced the sense of contributing to pilot, plane, and passenger well-being, whether through radar and radio, or giving preflight briefings over the phone.

The elements of satisfaction and contribution emerged time after time. Perhaps I talked to the wrong people, but everyone I encountered (and there were many) voiced only genuine enthusiasm for the job. At the same time, that enthusiasm was evident as they discussed what they do and how they do it.

Not every day on the job is perfect, of course, nor is everything idyllic. However, in answer to the question "If you could change anything about the job, what would it be?" the sole response from one group was, "I wish we could have more say in some of the decisions that management makes." In other words, they would like greater lower-level involvement in the procedure and decision-making processes. (This was hardly an unusual "wish." It's one I've heard thousands of times from employees and first-level supervisors in hundreds of private as well as public organizations.)

To paint an overly rosy picture would be false and unwise. Every shop has its malcontents; every shop has its complainers; every shop has those who find the job not what they expected. Certainly, such personalities exist among the ATCSs. In the same vein, certain aspects of the working conditions can always be improved, including the equipment the people have to use.

Those realities recognized, it still seems that the vast majority of ATCSs are finding from the job many of the intangibles that make work worthwhile: challenge, recognition, contribution, opportunity (to do something of significance by their own standards), a sense of achievement, feedback, and overall satisfaction. A paycheck is important, but it's not the only thing people work for.

STRESS

The basic question put to many ATCSs was, How stressful is the job? Have the media made more of it than is justified?

The responses, of course, varied, but a common thread became evident: There can be stress, but it's a matter of how you handle it. Starting with the basic academy screening, the ability to cope with stress is constantly tested, and only those who have demonstrated calmness and stability under fire make it to the full-performace level. Many ATCSs said that they experienced more continuing stress while in training than at any other time in their careers.

Along the same line, the article "Air Traffic Safety: Stress One Factor," which appeared in the August 1987 issue of *U.S. Medicine,* substantiated that thread. Written by Dr. William E. Collins of the FAA's Civil Aeromedical Institute (CAMI) in Oklahoma City, the article states:

> All of the CAMI studies indicated that, in general, ATCSs were psychologically highly suited to their occupation. That conclusion does not mean that controllers are emotionally immune to job (or other) crises, or that their working environments need not be improved. However, the conclusion is reassuring, since the job of the ATCS is a very responsible one with the direct, central issue being the safety of people.

As much as anything, conclusions reached on the basis of tests indicate, again quoting Collins, "that the ATCS's job was not uniquely stressful, and that it was not so much the job (i.e., handling the traffic) but the context in which the job was done that was significant"—meaning, in part, how management was interacting with its employees.

More and more, the emphasis seems to be shifting from the inherent stressfulness of the job to the work overload created by the volume of traffic the ATCSs must handle. As Collins says, "Flight delays have little to do with stress or with the current level of ATCS staffing, but have a lot to do with the need for more airports and runways (a 'concrete' problem) and the habitual scheduling by airlines of a significant number of flights at two or three choice times during the day." That was an observation voiced by many ATCSs.

None of this should imply that ATCSs are above stress. It does imply that the testing, screening, and training have, to the maximum extent possible, weeded out those who weren't able to handle the situations that accelerate the heart rate and inflate the blood pressure.

Undoubtedly, some ATCSs would scoff at CAMI's test results and verbalized conclusions. It does seem apparent, however, according to ATCSs and the aeromedical profession alike, that what stress exists is caused not by the inherent nature of the job but rather by the work overload inspired by the volume of traffic in the skies today. If that's the case, in one respect, it's like any job: Tension and stress are entirely normal when you have more to do than you feel that you can skillfully and professionally handle.

In sum, ATCSs are where they are because they thrive on the challenge and the satisfaction the job provides. And they're there because they are psychologically equipped to meet the challenges that could be extremely stressful to others.

Does every ATCS fit that mold? Probably not. People have varying levels of tolerance. The vast majority of ATCSs, however, have to possess the measure of emotional stability that allows them to thrive on what they're doing.

DRUG TESTING

Are you for it or against it? To that question, the almost unanimous response among controllers was, "I'm for it." Their only concerns were related to the accuracy of the tests. "I just don't want to have a test come back positive, when I know I haven't been on drugs." Who can argue with that stance? No such tests are yet 100 percent infallible—which hopefully the FAA recognizes.

The common comment, however, was that no one could do the job and do drugs. The job's demands simply won't tolerate clouded minds or emotional instabilities. If it takes testing to ensure against drug-induced aberrations, it's an unfortunate commentary on our times, but perhaps there's no other avenue available.

Again, there are undoubtedly a fair number of ATCSs who feel differently about the issue, and perhaps justifiably so. The claim of infringements on personal rights is a powerful counterargument. Despite that or other antitesting reasons, it does appear that the majority favor such a program, simply because of the serious nature of the occupation.

WORKING WITH VFR PILOTS

First and foremost, the biggest criticism of VFR pilots is radio technique. We've already beaten that subject to death, so enough said. A group of Center controllers, however, did have a couple of other points or suggestions:

- Attend a FAA Operation Raincheck session, which is a tour of an ARTCC. This, said one, should be mandatory for every VFR pilot.
- Practice with controllers when they're not busy. You can tell whether they are or not by just monitoring their frequency and by the current weather conditions. If you hear them turn down an en route VFR advisory request, or if they're continually on the air with a bunch of IFR operations, you'll know what's going on. Even then, stay tuned and listen to the dialogues. That, in itself, is a learning and skill-sharpening experience.
- Helping the VFR pilot is part of their responsibility. They want to help, but the pilot must do his part by knowing what to do, what to say, and keeping in communication with them when they are giving advisories.
- Finally, and to underscore these and similar comments, one FPL told me, "Don't put anything in the book that would discourage VFRs from using any Center services."

If you fly VFR around Class D, Class C, or Class B airspaces, you have no choice. You must maintain radio contact with the tower or Approach Control. Center is the only traffic-controlling facility you're not required to use. If you have not had much experience operating in a controlled environment, just keep in mind that confidence will come with experience. Hopefully, the ARTCC chapter relaxed some of the apprehensions you might have had. The Center controllers emphasized their desire and their responsibility to help those of us who fly VFR; and a visit to a facility, or a discussion with a controller, would confirm the sincerity of their words.

THE ATC SPECIALIST—A LITERAL PROFESSIONAL

The FAA has several thousand controllers and FSS specialists in the ATC system. As in any amalgam of people, there are wide varieties of attitudes, personalities, abilities, character, and competence. Not all controllers are paragons of virtue, and not all are models of excellence. That said, it's fair to conclude that those who have reached the full-performance level have proved their merit and their mettle. Whether hired before or after the 1981 air traffic controllers' strike, they have been tested, probed, questioned, examined, and pressured to degrees not common in most professions. Those who stood up to the constant scrutiny made it and are on the job today. They are the ones you have been, or will be, talking to. The rest dropped by the wayside, voluntarily or otherwise.

The Mikes, Marys, Jacks, and Jills in the towers and Centers and the specialists in the FSSs are not superhumans; they're just well-balanced, well-trained folks who happen to possess certain uncommon traits that equip them for a most uncommon occupation.

On second thought, *occupation* seems a bit mundane; *profession* is more descriptive. A profession includes, in part, two elements: a science and an art. The science is the body of knowledge pertaining to the profession that must be learned and mastered. The art is the ability to put the knowledge to work with skill, adeptness, vision, and accuracy. Knowledge is the foundation, but it is of questionable value unless the practitioner possesses the skill to bring it to life.

In the broadest sense, the air traffic control specialist must be strong in both facets of professionalism—and it's safe to say the vast majority are. The record and the reputation of our air traffic control system are evidence enough. Yes, there are the doomsayers and the hypercritics among the media and the public who are continually waving red flags. When you consider, however, the volume of traffic these folks handle each day, in fair weather and foul, in crowded as well as uncrowded skies, the record is remarkable by any standard.

Abbreviations and acronyms

AAS	Advanced Automation System, or Airport Advisory Service
ACF	Area Control Facility
ADF	Automatic Direction Finding
ADIZ	Air Defense Identification Zone
AERA	Automated en Route Air Traffic Control
A/FD	*Airport/Facility Directory*
AFSS	Automated Flight Service Station
A/G	Air-ground communications
AGL	Above ground level
AIM	*Aeronautical Information Manual*
AIRMET	Airman's Meteorological Information
ALNOT	Alert Notice
AOPA	Aircraft Owners and Pilots Association
App	Approach Control
ARF	Airport Reservation Function
ARSA	Airport Radar Service Area
ARSR	Air Route Surveillance Radar
ARTCC	Air Route Traffic Control Center
ARTS	Automated Radar Terminal System
ARU	Airborne Radar Unit
ASDE	Automated Surface Detection Equipment
ASOS	Automated Surface Observation System
ASR	Airport Surveillance Radar

ABBREVIATIONS AND ACRONYMS

AT	Air Traffic
ATA	Airport Traffic Area
ATC	Air Traffic Control
ATCAA	Air Traffic Control Assigned Airspace
ATCRBS	Air Traffic Control Radar Beacon System
ATCS	Air Traffic Control Specialist
ATCT	Air Traffic Control Tower
ATIS	Automatic Terminal Information Service
ATS	Air Traffic Service
AWOS	Automated Weather Observation System
AWW	Severe Weather Alert
BRITE	Bright Radar Indicator Tower Equipment
CA	Conflict Alert
CAA	Civil Aeronautics Authority
CAB	Civil Aeronautics Board
CAMI	Civil Aeromedical Institute (FAA in Oklahoma City)
CA/MSAW	Conflict Alert/Minimum Safe Altitude Warning
CARF	Central Altitude Reservation Function
CD	Clearance Delivery
Center	Air Route Traffic Control Center
CERAP	Combined Center Radar Approach Control
CIP	Capital Investment Plan
CL	Clearance (Delivery)
CONUS	Continental, Contiguous, or Conterminous United States
CRT	Cathode-Ray Tube
CT	Control Tower
CTAF	Common Traffic Advisory Frequency
CWA	Center Weather Advisory
CWSU	Center Weather Service Unit
CZ	Control Zone
D	Developmental controller or specialist
Dep	Departure Control
DF	Direction Finder
DLP	Data Link Processor
DME	Distance-Measuring Equipment
DME/P	Precision Distance-Measuring Equipment
DOD	Department of Defense
DOT	Department of Transportation
DUAT	Direct User Access Terminal
DVFR	Defense Visual Flight Rules
DVOR	Doppler Very High-Frequency Omnidirectional Range
EARTS	En Route Automated Radar Tracking System
EFAS	En Route Flight Advisory Service

ELAC	En Route Low-Altitude Chart
ELT	Emergency Locator Transmitter
EPA	Environmental Protection Agency
ESP	En Route Spacing Program
ETA	Estimated Time of Arrival
ETD	Estimated Time of Departure
ETE	Estimated Time en Route
FA	Area Forecast
FAA	Federal Aviation Administration
FARs	Federal Aviation Regulations
FBO	Fixed-Base Operator
FDC	Flight Data Center
FDEP	Flight Data Entry and Printout
FPL	Full-Performance Level controller or specialist
FSAS	Flight Service Automation System
FSP	Flight Strip Printer
FSS	Flight Service Station
GC	Ground Control
GCA	Ground Control Approach
GOES	Geostationary Operational Environmental Satellite
GPS	Global Positioning System
HIWAS	Hazardous In-Flight Weather Advisory Service
HVAC	Heating, Ventilating, and Air Conditioning
IATA	International Air Transport Association
ICAN	International Convention for Air Navigation
ICAO	International Civil Aviation Organization
IFAPA	International Federation of Airline Pilots Association
IFR	Instrument Flight Rules
ILS	Instrument Landing System
IMC	Instrument Meteorological Conditions
INREQ	Request for Information
IPAI/D	Identification-Position-Altitude-Intentions (or) Destination
IR	Military Instrument Flight Training Route
ISSS	Initial Sector Suite Subsystem
IVRS	Interim Voice Response System
LLWAS	Low Level Wind Shear Alert System
LORAN	Long Range Navigation
MARSA	Military Assumes Responsibility for Separation of Aircraft
MLS	Microwave Landing System
MOA	Military Operations Area
Mode 3/A	Standard transponder without altitude-reporting capability
Mode C	Standard transponder with altitude-reporting capability
Mode S	Selectively addressable transponder with data link

MRU	Military Radar Unit
MSAW	Minimum Safe Altitude Warning
MSL	Mean Sea Level
MTR	Military Training Route
MULTICOM	Nongovernment air-air radio communications frequency
NAR	National Airspace Review
NAS	National Airspace System
NASP	National Airspace System Plan
Navaid	Navigational Aid
NDB	Nondirectional Beacon
NEXRAD	Next Generation Weather Radar
NFCT	Nonfederal Control Tower
NM	Nautical Miles
NOAA	National Oceanic and Atmospheric Administration
NOS	National Ocean Service
NOTAM	Notice To Airmen
NPRM	Notice of Proposed Rule-Making
NTAP	Notice To Airmen Publication
NWS	National Weather Service
PAR	Precision Approach Radar
PATWAS	Pilots' Automatic Telephone Weather Answering Service
PCA	Positive Control Area
PIREP	Pilot Report
PVD	Plan Visual Display
RAPCON	Radar Approach Control (military)
RCAG	Remote Center Air-Ground Communications Facility
RCF	Remote Communications Facility
RCO	Remote Communications Outlet
RDT&E	Research, Development, Testing, and Evaluation
RF	Radio Failure
RML	Radar Microwave Link
RMM	Remote Maintenance Monitoring
RNAV	Area Navigation
RTR	Remote Transmitter-Receiver
RVR	Runway Visual Range
SAR	Search And Rescue
SFAR	Special Federal Aviation Regulation
SIGMET	Significant Meteorological Information
SM	Statute Miles
Squawk	Activate specific number code in the transponder
SR	Sunrise
SS	Sunset
SUA	Special Use Airspace

SVFR	Special Visual Flight Rules
TA	Transition Area
TAC	Terminal Area Chart
TACAN	Tactical Air Navigation
TCA	Terminal Control Area
TCAS	Traffic Alert and Collision Avoidance System
TDWR	Terminal Doppler Weather Radar
TIBS	Transcribed Information Briefing Service
TML	Television Microwave Link
TMS	Traffic Management System
TMU	Traffic Management Unit
TPX	Military Beacon System
TRACAB	Terminal Radar Approach Control in the Tower Cab
TRACON	Terminal Radar Approach Control
TRSA	Terminal Radar Service Area
TWEB	Transcribed Weather Broadcast
UA	Pilot Report
UHF	Ultra High Frequency
UUA	Urgent Pilot Report
UNICOM	Nongovernment air/ground radio communications facility
UTC	Coordinated Universal Time
VFR	Visual Flight Rules
VHF	Very High Frequency
VOR	VHF Omnidirectional Range
VOR/DME	VOR also equipped with DME
VORTAC	VOR collocated with TACAN
VR	Military VFR Training Route
VRS	Voice Response System
VSCS	Voice Switching Communications System
WMSC	Weather Message Service Center
WST	Convective SIGMET
XFSS	Auxiliary Flight Service Station
ZULU	Sometimes used to mean UTC time, e.g., "1500 zulu"

Index

Note: **Boldface** numbers indicate illustrations

About the Author

Paul E. Illman holds a commercial certificate with single- and multiengine ratings. He is the author of *The Pilot's Handbook of Aeronautical Knowledge*, 3rd edition, and *The Pilot's Radio Communications Handbook,*, 5th edition. Illman is a member of the Aircraft Owners and Pilots Association, the United States Pilots Association, and the Kansas Pilots Association.